FREE TRADE, SOVEREIGNTY, DEMOCRACY

FREE TRADE, SOVEREIGNTY, DEMOCRACY

The Future of the World Trade Organization

Claude E. Barfield

The AEI Press

Publisher for the American Enterprise Institute

WASHINGTON, D.C.

2001

Available in the United States from the AEI Press, c/o Publisher Resources Inc., 1224 Heil Quaker Blvd., P.O. Box 7001, La Vergne, TN 37086-7001. To order, call toll free: 1-800-937-5557. Distributed outside the United States by arrangement with Eurospan, 3 Henrietta Street, London WC2E 8LU, England.

Library of Congress Cataloging-in-Publication Data

Barfield, Claude E.
    Free trade, sovereignty, democracy: the future of the World Trade Organization / Claude E. Barfield.
       p. cm.
    Includes index.
    ISBN 0-8447-4156-6 — ISBN 0-8447-4157-4 (pbk.)
    1. World Trade Organization. 2. Foreign trade regulation. 3. Democracy. 4. Capitalism. 5. Free trade. 6. Commercial policy. 7. Free trade—Developing countries. 8. International trade. 9. International law. 10. Sovereignty. I. Title

HF1385 .B37 2001
382'.92—dc 21

2001037309

1 3 5 7 9 10 8 6 4 2

The AEI Press
Publisher for the American Enterprise Institute
1150 17th Street, N.W.
Washington, D.C. 20036

Printed in the United States of America

For Michael and the Scotties

Contents

Acknowledgments

I would like to thank the following people who read and commented on portions or all of the manuscript: Arthur Appleton, Jagdish Bhagwati, Raj Bhala, Judith Bello, John Bolton, William Brock, Marco Bronckers, Edward Cowan, Christopher DeMuth, James Durling, Michael Finger, David Henderson, Robert Hudec, John Jackson, Robert Keohane, Simon Lester, Patrick Low, John Magnus, Mitsuo Matsushita, Patrick McCrory, Sylvia Ostry, Jeremy Rabkin, John Ragosta, Kal Raustiala, David Robertson, Gary Sampson, Jeffrey Schott, James McCall Smith, Cordula Thum, Alan Wolff, and Clayton Yeutter. I would also like to thank Juyne Linger for her careful and painstaking editing of the manuscript. Needless to say, any remaining errors are mine.

1

Introduction: Issues, Themes, and Recommendations

The World Trade Organization faces two formidable challenges—one external and one internal—that threaten to undermine its efforts to liberalize trade and open markets around the world. First, it must mobilize support to confront escalating attacks by outside groups and individuals proclaiming that the WTO lacks democratic accountability and merely serves as a front for multinational corporations and dehumanizing capitalist values. Second, even while it attempts to meet these external onslaughts, the WTO must ensure its own institutional viability, which is jeopardized by a formidable constitutional flaw. That internal flaw is the imbalance between the WTO's consensus-plagued, inefficient rule-making procedures and its highly efficient dispute settlement system—an imbalance that creates pressure to "legislate" new rules through adjudication and thereby flout the mandate that dispute settlement judgments must neither add to nor diminish the rights and obligations of WTO members.

At the same time, the United States faces a different, but related, set of challenges. In a world of increasing technological and economic integration, the United States must continue to balance and rebalance a defense of national sovereignty against grants of authority over its economic and social policy to international organizations such as the WTO. The United States must also devise domestic

1

political mechanisms that provide greater democratic accountability for decisions affecting U.S. international obligations.

These challenges to the WTO, to the United States, and to the future of trade liberalization are the issues this book explores.

The first draft of the book was completed during the week of the United Nations Millennium Summit in September 2000. On the opening day of the summit, the *New York Times* interviewed anti-globalization activists who were in New York *not* to protest as they did the previous year in Seattle, but rather to support the United Nations. As one leader of the anti-globalization movement explained, "We've lately begun to worry that the mandate [of the UN] was weakening and that the same ideologies that drive the WTO will appear in the United Nations." Another activist asserted, "It is our role to still insist that the United Nations is not a body that should be siding with the interests of capitalists. . . ."[1] I had to chuckle because the book I had just completed stemmed, in part, from the fear that the ideological flow was in the opposite direction—that the free market principles embodied in the rules of the WTO would be suborned by protectionism in the name of other social, economic, or political interests.

The following day, in another article directly relevant to this study, the *New York Times* reported that the European Union (EU) had rejected as still inadequate a U.S. effort to comply with a WTO panel ruling that the United States had granted an illegal export subsidy to American companies.

The EU's rejection of U.S. compliance efforts had ominous implications. Just two months earlier, then-Deputy Secretary of the Treasury Stuart Eizenstat had warned of a "major trade war" if the two sides could not come to some agreement. Sanctions in the WTO are based upon the amount of harm suffered in the international marketplace by the complaining country. Using that metric, the EU calculated that it could seek 100 percent tariffs on $4 billion of U.S. exports.[2]

Should this occur (a second WTO panel ruled against the United States in June 2001), it would be far and away the largest retaliation taken under the new WTO dispute settlement system.[3] It would come on top of two other corrosive quarrels between the two trading partners. In one, the United States levied nearly $200 million in tariffs on European goods after the EU refused to comply with a WTO ruling to alter its restrictions on banana imports from Latin America; and in the second, the United States levied more than $100 million in tariffs on European goods because the EU banned hormone-treated beef.[4]

Taken together, these snapshots of the current travails of the WTO frame the boundaries of this study: a WTO facing enormous pressures from powerful anti-globalist sentiment and determined new transnational interest groups that are effectively exploiting that sentiment; and a WTO saddled with a constitutional structure that may cripple its ability not only to deal with these antagonists, but also to settle disputes between member states in a manner that upholds the rules while satisfying the contending parties.

The large number of anti-globalization activists who came to New York City to support the UN—and explicitly link that support to their opposition to the WTO's free trade mandate—underscores an important assumption of this study: It is no longer possible to analyze the WTO and the international trading system in isolation from other multinational organizations and regimes, particularly the UN and the growing number of international environmental treaties, agreements, and declarations. Virtually unheralded, the ambition and reach of UN leaders and programs have grown mightily since the end of the Cold War. Similarly, over the past three decades, the number of environmental agreements—some with trade sanctions as the compliance weapon of choice—has multiplied, resulting in a plethora of international rules on matters such as hazardous wastes, the ozone layer, biological diversity, endangered species, wildlife preservation, wetlands, migratory species, marine pollution, transboundary air pollution, and tropical timber. This trend has already led to clashes between trade and environmental rules, as the WTO shrimp/turtle and tuna/dolphin cases described in this study demonstrate.

Another major phenomenon of the past decade is the emergence across a wide policy landscape of groups of politically and rhetorically powerful "citizen activists" who vigorously lobby governments at all levels on a broad range of issues, from trade and the environment to consumer rights, human rights, women's rights, children's rights, and animal rights.[5] Although the term nongovernmental organization (NGO) can refer to both nonprofit and profit-making organizations alike, in this study it applies only to citizen organizations. Many of these citizen activist groups directly challenge the predominant capitalist beliefs of wealth creation and hold that other social, environmental, and spiritual values are being sacrificed on the altars of free trade and footloose capital movements.

Although many NGOs are local and small, the environmental and consumer groups that have taken the lead in challenging the WTO and the doctrine of free trade have substantial budgets and payrolls and operate in many countries. Greenpeace, for example, has an annual income of more than $100 million and operates in twenty countries; the World Wildlife Fund operates in twenty-eight countries and has an estimated annual income of $320 million to support its endeavors; and Friends of the Earth International, with an annual income of $30 million, operates in fifty countries. With these formidable resources, the largest and most powerful NGOs can readily outmatch the resources that many members of the WTO can bring to bear—a reality that this study will emphasize in addressing NGO demands for more transparency and public participation in the dispute settlement (and legislative) systems of the WTO.

Some NGOs advocate a new "democratic" international order in which NGOs would offer an "alternate form of representation" in competition with governments, while others argue for a corporatist model based on the International Labor Organization, in which governments, corporations, and NGOs work in partnership to create new rules for an emerging international order. The short-term focus of NGOs and corporate interests is on access and more direct participation in both the dispute settlement and the rule-making activities of the WTO. This study will describe and analyze these arguments and offer a firm rebuttal to claims of "democratic" legitimacy through some form of corporatist division of power or through treatment of NGOs as an alternate form of representation in the international arena.

The study will also suggest reforms of WTO dispute settlement procedures that will effect greater transparency and introduce more diverse viewpoints into the process—for instance, by choosing individuals with varied professional backgrounds as members of WTO dispute panels. In the past, corporate interests have predominated in the corridors of the WTO—not through any conspiracy, but largely because few, apart from exporters and importers, really cared about the level of tariffs at the border. The most effective response to these demands for access, however, is not to allow NGOs and corporations into the negotiations and the dispute settlement process, but to place them both on an equal footing *outside* the door of the negotiating room and judicial chamber.

The WTO as "World Court"

One strong basis for the recommendations made in this study is the belief that the WTO is overextended and in danger of losing authority and legitimacy as the arbiter of trade disputes among the world's major trading nations. The situation the WTO faces today flows directly from the extraordinary success of the Uruguay Round, which greatly extended the substantive mandate of the international trade regime. Rules for service industries—banks, insurance companies, telecommunications and the Internet, energy services, and transportation, for example—meant that the trade regime would be asked to deal with complex issues that go deep into the economic and social structures of its member states. In addition, the Uruguay Round established a wholly new regime for intellectual property (IP) during a time of great ferment within individual nations over the challenges to IP emerging from new technologies such as software and biotechnology.

Many of these new substantive obligations cannot be solved with straightforward protectionist versus nonprotectionist responses, as was the case with tariffs under the General Agreement on Tariffs and Trade (GATT). As Sylvia Ostry, a former Canadian trade negotiator now at the University of Toronto, has written of the new system, "The degree of intrusiveness into domestic sovereignty bears little resemblance to the shallow integration of the GATT with its focus on border barriers. . . . The WTO has shifted from the GATT model of *negative* regulation—what governments must not do—to *positive* regulations, or what governments must do."[6]

The Uruguay Round negotiators not only extended the substantive mandate of the new WTO, but they also created a much more rigid, judicialized dispute settlement system that promised legal certainty and finality in each case. Under the new system, a ruling by a WTO panel or the Appellate Body will stand unless WTO members, acting as members of the new Dispute Settlement Body, reach a consensus against the decision.

Professor J.H.H. Weiler of the Harvard Law School has contrasted the "diplomatic ethos" of the old GATT—where "empanelment was, indeed, a continuation of diplomacy by other means," where "confidentiality" was highly prized, and where disputes were handled by "trade diplomats"—with the quite different paradigm of the "Rule of Lawyers and the Culture of Law" adopted under the new WTO Dispute Settlement Understanding (DSU) in 1995.[7] Arguing that "much of the legal culture is at odds with the ethos of diplomacy," Weiler lists crucial differences, including the following:

- In contrast to the GATT's "diplomatic" solutions, which aimed for accommodation among disputants, "Legal Disputes [in the WTO] which go to adjudication are not settled: they are won and lost. The headlines speak of 'victory' and 'defeat.'"[8]
- The rule of law is supposed to be dispassionate and objective, but when two parties both believe the law is on their side and litigate, "then it becomes a profession of passion, of rhetoric, of a desire to win, . . . all inimical to compromise. . . ."[9]
- Likewise, the legal professionals directing the process should act in an objective manner regarding the merits of a case, but in reality, they are (like other professionals) "people with ambition, with a search for job satisfaction." Thus, Weiler writes, "A huge factor in the decision whether to go for legal resolution will have been the conscious and often subconscious input by lawyers driven by ambition and their particular professional deformations. 'We can win in court' becomes in the hands of all too many lawyers an almost automatic trigger to 'we should bring the case.'"[10]

- Though the WTO members did not understand the constitutional implications of the creation of the Appellate Body (AB), the new DSU in effect made it a "high court" and gave it the final word in interpreting WTO agreements: "*De jure,* the DSU leaves the final interpretation of the Agreements in the hands of the General Council and Ministerial Conference. *De facto,* unless the Organization is to break the hallowed principle of consensus, that power has shifted to the Appellate Body." In turn, what the AB has told the panels is that their main goal should no longer be compromise and getting agreement from both parties. Rather, "It is 'getting it [legally] right,' and/or 'making it appeal-proof.'"[11]

This study contends that the new "judicialized" WTO dispute settlement system is substantively and politically unsustainable. It is not sustainable substantively because there is no real consensus among WTO members on many of the complex regulatory issues that the panels and the Appellate Body will be asked to rule upon. In many instances, moreover, the underlying treaty text contains gaps, ambiguities, and contradictory language. The system is not sustainable politically because the imbalance between ineffective rule-making procedures and highly efficient judicial mechanisms will increasingly pressure the panels and the AB to "create" law, raising intractable questions of democratic legitimacy. To correct these flaws, this study recommends alternatives that will reintroduce some of the former elements of "diplomatic" flexibility that characterized the earlier GATT regime.[12] Conciliation, mediation, and voluntary arbitration need to be added as real alternatives. If a substantial minority of WTO members clearly oppose a decision, a blocking mechanism should be used to set aside that decision until further negotiations produce a consensus. In addition, the current welfare-reducing systems of sanctions should be replaced with provisions for compensation, through either fines or trade liberalization measures, to offset the economic effect of rules violations.

Sovereignty

In a March 2000 speech, John Jackson of Georgetown University School of Law, one of the two deans of GATT/WTO legal scholarship in the United States (the other is Robert Hudec of Tufts University), warned scholars of the international trading system against falling back on a series of "mantras," which Jackson defines as phrases that "are used to *avoid* thinking certain issues through." Two of the phrases that should be used more carefully in discussions of the WTO, according to Jackson, are "sovereignty" and "government-to-government."[13]

One of the tasks of this study is indeed to think through both phrases as they relate to the future of the WTO and U.S. participation in that institution. As political scientist Stephen Krasner of Stanford University has conceptualized it, sovereignty has many dimensions, two of which are central to the issues addressed in this study: Westphalian sovereignty, which refers to the exclusion of foreign actors from domestic decision-making; and interdependence, which refers to a nation's control over the cross-border movement of goods, services, capital, labor, and information.[14] Krasner's 1999 book on sovereignty is a response to those who argue that the sovereignty of the nation-state was once "exclusive and absolute," but has been eroded by transportation and communications advances, globalism in general, and the rise of NGOs. Krasner shows that sovereignty was never absolute and always "frail as a legal principle." He concludes that contemporary trends are part of the warp and woof of historical cycles. One does not have to accept Krasner's ultimate "realist" thesis—that sovereignty was always "organized hypocrisy" that disguised more fundamental divisions of power and that nations ignored it at will in pursuit of national interests—to accept his historical judgment that sovereignty in its Westphalian form has always consisted of balancing judgments about the distribution of power between the nation-state and international alliances and organizations.

Similarly, Jackson argues for thinking about sovereignty "as a decision about how to allocate power . . . [and] about how to correctly design that allocation."[15] Agreed—but it is important to note that the conclusions and recommendations in this book proceed from a belief that, even with the revolution in communications and transportation technologies, the increase in globalization, and the rise of vociferous NGOs that clamor for recognition and shared power, fun-

damental democratic legitimacy still is a monopoly of constitutionally constructed democratic states. This is not to argue that these
states should not grant authority to multilateral organizations such
as the WTO, but rather that states should be more careful and precise in determining the "correct design," in Jackson's phrase, of the
terms of that allocation and in devising procedures to ensure that all
domestic stakeholders and institutions are involved in that design.

In a book published by the American Enterprise Institute in
1998, *Why Sovereignty Matters,* Jeremy Rabkin of Cornell University
argued that, as then constituted, "the trading system is quite compatible with traditional notions of sovereignty." He noted, for
instance, that the trading system focused only on goods and services
that cross international borders and *not* on how they were produced
inside the borders; that it operated with ad hoc panels that did not
build "ambitious case law'" that would go beyond negotiated rules;
that neither firms nor individuals had direct recourse to the dispute
settlement system; and that, unlike the North American Free Trade
Agreement (NAFTA), the WTO had no linkages to broader nontrade issues such as labor and the environment. This study finds
growing pressures that would reverse most of the virtuous characteristics that Rabkin cited.[16]

In addition, Rabkin to some degree misdiagnosed a potential ill.
He worried about the procedures for amending new rules. While
admitting that the hurdles for such amendments were quite high, he
expressed concern that the United States might be outvoted and that
the WTO could move in directions more intrusive to the U.S. constitutional system. What he did not foresee was a very different problem: the great inefficiency of the WTO rule-making (legislative)
procedures has greatly increased pressure on the dispute settlement
system (the judicial branch) to create new rules or reinterpret old
rules. Further, WTO panels and the Appellate Body are already being
pressed to include "soft" and customary law as precedents for their
decisions—a practice that Rabkin strongly condemned in his book.

International Relations and International Legal Theory

For many years, analysis of the GATT system was dominated by
economists, international trade lawyers, and law professors inter-

ested in the narrow legal aspects of the organization. Today, a growing body of literature provides analysis of the history and status of
the international trading system in light of evolving international
relations (IR) theory. In addition, collaboration between international relations theorists and international legal scholars has
increased significantly since 1990. Further, some legal scholars have
grafted economic theories onto their analyses—particularly
"rational choice" theories that hold that individuals, politicians,
bureaucrats, and academics act in their own self-interest to maximize economic or political power and influence. In footnotes and
occasionally in the text, this study will cite elements of this rich new
theoretical base for explaining the trade regime in comparison with
other international regimes. Appendix 1 describes the evolution of
IR theory during the past several decades.

International relations scholars are quite candid in admitting that
current IR theory is characterized by "nondogmatic heterogeneity"
and its insights "can be seen as partial theories or theoretical modules of pretended validity." In a 1998 article comparing the economics discipline with international relations theory, economist
Barry Eichengreen of the University of California at Berkeley stated:

> The most telling difference between international relations and economics
> . . . lies in the connection between theory and empirical work. . . . In inter-
> national relations . . . the connections between theory and empirical work
> are relatively loose. Theory-based propositions do not lend themselves
> comfortably to empirical verification and refutation. . . . As a consequence,
> research in international relations has not converged on a core of common
> theoretical assumptions and an arsenal of commonly accepted empirical
> techniques.[17]

There is, then, as in physics, no "unified field theory" that can
explain all phenomena in international relations. Nevertheless,
three strands of international relations theory help to explain the
events and trends chronicled in this study: (1) liberal (intergovernmental) theory; (2) public choice theory; and (3) knowledge-based
theory.

Liberal Theory. Liberal theories of IR view the workings of international organizations such as the WTO through dual lenses known
as "a two-level game." National positions on trade negotiations or
dispute settlement cases are first formed "liberally" through the

competition of interests groups and their interaction with governments. Then, national officials defend these positions in negotiations or in dispute settlement cases. While defending their
positions, government officials are under continual pressure from a
number of groups: domestic lobbies that may or may not have been
successful at an earlier stage; foreign and transnational interest
groups whose operations cross state boundaries; and other governments that have their own agendas. These pressures might appear
to put government officials in an impossible position. On closer
inspection, however, their strategic position between domestic and
international negotiating sites affords them considerable power.
Trade officials can manipulate the process by making side payments
to interest groups and other governments; by targeting threats and
rallying domestic and foreign constituencies; and by managing
information and manipulating ratification procedures. Later in this
study, empirical academic analysis using liberal theory will be introduced to explain the interaction between governments, corporations, and NGOs.[18]

Public Choice Theory. Public choice theory from economics com-
plements liberal IR theory in important ways: both consider domestic (and, by extension, international) interest groups as the key
focus—the fundamental actors—in international politics. Both,
therefore, eschew the assumption that states are "rational actors,"
independent of underlying political, economic, or social interests.
As Gregory Shaffer of the University of Wisconsin Law School
explains, "National positions are not abstract or static, but contingent, shaped by internal pressures from competing stakeholder
groups."[19] Public choice theory, however, focuses much more on
the drive of private interests groups and public officials to maximize
wealth or power. This study provides several examples of the potential for public choice coalitions to aggrandize power, including (1)
future alliances between NGOs, corporations, and the judicial bodies of the WTO against domestic courts and other private interests
if NGOs and corporations are granted private rights of action in
WTO cases; and (2) the symbiotic relationship between NGOs and
government regulatory officials in international environmental regulation, where the rise of NGO influence does not occur at the

expense of the state but instead signals a growing alliance with the state. According to Kal Raustiala of the UCLA Law School, "That NGOs appear more important is a direct result of the expansion of concerted state power through the promulgation of new international law."[20]

Knowledge-Based Theory. In contradistinction to the interest-based theories described above, a third group of IR theories are knowledge- or norm-based. These theories, variously called constructivist or cognitivist theories, focus on the power of ideas and view state activity as "socially constructed" through the deepening influence of particular ideas. International legal scholars are especially attracted to norm-driven theories; indeed, many argue that compliance with treaties and trade agreements is secured in large part by the perception that the rules have been legitimized by the rule-creation process itself. Legitimacy, in turn, becomes a norm that influences nations toward treaty compliance. State interaction is another means by which norms seep into the domestic political and legal processes of individual nations, "creating not only compliance but obedience." In the body of this study, research drawing on constructivist accounts is invoked in support of dispute settlement alternatives to judicial fiats that are followed by sanctions and retaliation. As one international legal scholar states, under certain circumstances "use of a flexible, less judicialized approach . . . may be more effective in resolving conflicts than an approach based purely on the enforcement of compliance through the [WTO Dispute Settlement Understanding]."[21]

Major Recommendations

The recommendations made in this study admittedly cannot be put into place in the current climate of deep division within the WTO and given the high hurdles that face any attempt to create new rules or amend old rules under the current system. Change on the order recommended here will be possible only as part of an overall negotiating package in a future trade round. And it will come about only after a significant number of WTO members—including developing as well as developed countries—recognize that, while the new WTO is and should remain an important force for more open markets and enhanced competition among countries, its current constitution is actually an obstacle to achieving those goals.

The recommendations advanced in this book also come in the midst of major reevaluations of the Bretton Woods institutions established at the end of the Second World War. In 2000, the Meltzer Commission issued a scathing report on the International Monetary Fund (IMF) and World Bank, arguing that these institutions had greatly exceeded their original mandates, were overextended, and could not deliver on the goals they had set for themselves.[22] The WTO is in somewhat better shape; the Uruguay Round of multilateral trade negotiations took an important first step toward reforming and reshaping the institution to meet new challenges during the coming decades.

John Jackson has noted the "folly" of the desire of "some people in the United States [to] reverse course and take the WTO back to the time when it was only responsible for border measures. . . ."[23] This study does not agree with "some people," but it does argue that (1) to deal with the complex new issues presented by national regulations inside the border, the WTO will have to adopt a less rigid, more flexible dispute settlement system, one that does not promise a "correct" legal answer to every problem; and (2) the best means of achieving continued democratic legitimacy is for the WTO to remain a government-to-government organization, one in which governments take decisions to the WTO after having sorted through and resolved the conflicting claims and demands of competing interests in the domestic political process.

The principal recommendations of this study, presented in detail in chapter 7, concern five key areas of reform: constitutional reform; transparency; participation; congressional oversight; and the creation of an Eminent Persons Group.

Constitutional Reform

A Safety Valve: Conciliation, Mediation, and Voluntary Arbitration. The goal of this recommendation is to move the WTO dispute settlement system partially back in the direction of the original "diplomatic" model for dispute settlement, and away from the judicial model introduced by the new Dispute Settlement Understanding of the Uruguay Round. With that aim in mind, the first recommendation is that the Director-General (DG) or a special standing committee of the Dispute Settlement Body (DSB) be empowered to step in and direct the contending WTO member states to settle their differences through bilateral negotiations, mediation, or arbitration by an outside party. The DG or DSB committee would take such action in situations where the highly divisive political nature of the contest could permanently damage the WTO; or in situations where, in the judgment of the DG or DSB committee, there is no established legislative rule or the existing language masks deep substantive divisions between WTO members.

Repairing a Constitutional Flaw: A Blocking Minority. The goal of the second recommendation is to redress the imbalance between the highly efficient dispute settlement system and the ineffective, consensus-plagued, rule-making procedures. This would be accomplished through a minority blocking mechanism: thus, at any time that at least one-third of the members of the Dispute Settlement Body, representing at least one-quarter of the total trade among WTO members, register opposition to a panel or Appellate Body decision, that decision should be set aside—blocked—and the DSB should affirm that the decision will not become binding WTO law. Subsequently, the normal legislative process of the WTO should be invoked through action by the General Council to either amend existing rules or establish new rules. If the General Council cannot reach consensus and agreement, then the issue would be set aside and settled, as part of a larger package of compromises, at the next major round of WTO trade negotiations. Even if these "diplomatic" escape clauses (mediation and a blocking minority) are established, the vast majority of disputes would likely be handled through the Dispute Settlement Understanding negotiated during the Uruguay Round.

Compliance: Substitute Compensation for Retaliation. Under this proposal, the existing option of compensation would become the sole remedy for noncompliance with a panel or Appellate Body ruling. Two alternative methods of compensation should be considered. First, compensation could be exacted through a monetary fine on the offending nation, with the sum of the fine calculated by a neutral third party or subcommittee of the DSB. Second, the offending WTO member could agree to institute trade liberalization equivalent in commercial value to the cost of the trade barrier(s) to the complaining country. Again, a neutral third party would determine the commercial cost of the trade barrier.

Direct Effect. Under the doctrine of direct effect, a nation agrees that its domestic laws will be bound by rules negotiated under a treaty. Direct effect gives a private citizen the power to demand relief from, or make a claim against, another private citizen or the state itself pursuant to the terms of an international agreement. Clearly, adherence to the direct effect doctrine alters the relationship between the state, private actors, and domestic courts. The recommendation of this study is that the U.S. Congress continue to deny direct effect and the self-execution of a treaty, as it has done in four recent trade agreements. Recent multilateral, regional, and bilateral trade agreements have produced rules that attempt to regulate areas such as services, intellectual property, and investment, which are central to domestic governance. Consequently, national legislatures, including the U.S. Congress, must be more vigilant in retaining final determination over the content of these core elements of domestic regulation and in setting precise boundaries when shifting authority to institutional organizations.

Transparency

Publication of Documents. The WTO should establish rules that provide for the publication of all government documents submitted pursuant to a panel or AB proceeding at the time those documents are presented. Such documents should be posted on the Internet. Information that is confidential for businesses would continue to be protected.

Public Access to Dispute Settlement Proceedings. If, as recommended here, all government documents are published when presented, it would also make sense to provide for public access to the opening sessions of both the panels and the AB. This would allow interested parties and the public to observe the opening arguments of all participants, including third parties. It would also protect the process from undue pressure during subsequent questioning and dialogue, and at the same time foster widespread knowledge of the basic, underlying issues of the dispute.

Amicus *Briefs.* The Dispute Settlement Body should exert strong pressure on the Appellate Body to review and withdraw its decision to allow the panels and AB to accept *amicus* briefs. Australia has taken the lead in urging WTO members to begin drafting rules on *amicus* briefs that will ensure the "preservation of members' equity, transparency, and due process" and impose "necessary disciplines" on acceptance of such briefs. As developing country representatives have argued, the issue goes beyond questions of process and raises issues of equity, because smaller countries could be continually out-gunned by the vast legal resources of multinational corporations and NGOs. In the future, the WTO may well decide to allow out-side documents to be included in dispute settlement proceedings; but this decision, and the conditions surrounding the introduction of such documents, should be negotiated by WTO members, and not introduced through the back door by the Appellate Body.

Participation

Greater Diversity of Panelists. The language of the DSU clearly foresees that, in addition to trade experts, nontrade specialists should be recruited for cases that involve issues that extend beyond commercial rules. The WTO should take advantage of this flexibil-ity and move quickly to assemble expert panelists from such allied fields as the environment, food safety, genetics, and intellectual. property. The net should be cast widely, with scientists and social scientists added to the usual list of lawyers, legal scholars, and retired diplomats.

Public Hearing during Conciliation and Mediation Proceedings. If the proposal for a less judicialized mediation and conciliation mechanism is accepted, a corollary recommendation would be in order: Contending parties should give the Director-General the authority to convene a public hearing at which a moderator would take testimony from experts and then suggest a solution acceptable to all parties. Even if the moderator failed to satisfy the parties, the process would benefit from the expert testimony and a public exploration of the issues.

Formal Consultation. Building on the experience of the WTO Committee on Trade and the Environment, the WTO should insti-tute a much more regularized system of consultation with outside interest groups and experts, including NGOs, scientific and professional societies, and corporate associations. The WTO Secretariat should be encouraged and empowered to convene a continuing series of seminars, symposia, and larger conferences to inform WTO members and staff of the technical issues raised by WTO rules and disputes among members.

Congressional Oversight

Bipartisan Commission and Joint Committee. As a means of increasing the democratic accountability and legitimacy of the WTO, national legislatures should become much more involved in, or at least aware of, the construction of rules and regulations that international organizations promulgate. This study recommends that, as a first step, the U.S. Congress should establish a bipartisan commission that would be assigned two tasks: (1) to report on the implications of the WTO dispute settlement system for the U.S. constitutional system and for U.S. domestic laws and regulations; and (2) to report on the cumulative impact of rulings, pronouncements, and resolutions that have emerged from major UN organizations such as the Economic and Social Council, the International Labor Organization, the World Health Organization, and the Food and Agricultural Organization (thereby including the impact of actions taken by groups concerned with the environment, human rights, health policy, social development, population policy, and children's and women's rights). The goal of this commission would be to provide Congress with a greater understanding of the full implications of the growing number of international policy pronouncements and regulations on U.S. domestic policy.

Congress should also consider establishing a permanent joint committee to provide continuing oversight of international bodies and the rules they promulgate to determine the impact of those rules on U.S. domestic laws and regulations.

Eminent Persons Group

Creation of an Eminent Persons Group. The WTO should establish an Eminent Persons Group (as its predecessor did with commendable results during the 1980s) to examine the systemic problems and issues surrounding WTO governance and the relationship between the WTO and other international regimes, particularly its future relationship with multilateral environmental agreements. Regarding WTO governance, two issues would lead the agenda: (1) how to reform the executive functioning of the WTO to streamline the decision-making process and, at the same time, accommodate the complaints of exclusion by developing countries; and (2) how to reform the legislative and judicial functions to achieve a more viable balance, thereby relieving pressure on the dispute settlement system to create law and change the rights and obligations of WTO members.

Plan of the Book

Following this introductory chapter, which has set forth the major themes and recommendations of the book, chapter 2 presents a brief history of the GATT and the evolution of a system for handling disputes among member states. It highlights the two approaches to dispute settlement that were present from the outset: a diplomatic approach that stressed conciliation; and a more judicial approach that sought to build a predictable set of rules.

Chapter 3 describes the major provisions of the new Dispute Settlement Understanding established during the Uruguay Round and provides a statistical overview of the results to date.

Chapter 4 analyzes the structural flaws of the new system, focusing on the implications of the imbalance between the highly efficient judicial arm of the WTO and its inefficient and unwieldy legislative or rule-making capacity. The chapter describes specific examples of the WTO Appellate Body's "judicial creativity" and then details the challenges emerging from disputes over national regulatory systems, as well as issues related to food safety, genetically modified organisms, and the "precautionary principle." It concludes with an analysis of the pressures to introduce "soft" law and customary law as guiding principles in WTO dispute settlement decisions.

Chapter 5 presents critiques, from both the right and the left, of the new dispute settlement system, as well as the operation and mandate of the WTO. It briefly examines the reasons why some corporate lawyers and law professors are calling for even further "judicialization" of the DSU, including an independent right of standing for nongovernment plaintiffs. In describing criticism from the left, the study traces the "quiet revolution" at the United Nations, including its shift in focus toward social and economic issues, along with the growing role and influence of NGOs within various UN organizations. Another section of this chapter is devoted to the emergence since 1990 of a parallel international environmental regime composed of new environmental treaties, agreements, and declarations from international conferences.

Chapter 6 evaluates the assertions of NGOs and some corporate legal representatives that a new "democratic" legitimacy should be established at the international level through direct participation of nongovernment actors in the rule-making and dispute settlement institutions and proceedings of the WTO. The study presents a rebuttal to the more extravagant claims for this new definition of legitimacy.

Chapter 7 makes recommendations in two areas. First, regarding the WTO DSU specifically, it presents arguments for returning to a less formally judicial and rigid system through two means: forcing mediation and conciliation on issues that clearly divide WTO member states and are likely to have politically explosive consequences that would damage the system; and creating a blocking mechanism at the end of the DSU process that would set aside Appellate Body decisions when a substantial minority of WTO members registered disagreement with the decision in the Dispute Settlement Body. Finally, the study makes a series of recommendations for greater transparency and limited increased participation in the deliberations and dispute settlement system of the WTO.

Appendix 1 examines various schools of international relations theories and their implications for the international trading system. It also describes and offers critical comments on several normative models that international legal scholars have advanced for the WTO. Appendix 2 reviews and recommends a number of technical changes to the DSU, including eliminating the Interim Report; creating a permanent, professional panel body; abolishing panels; and empowering the Appellate Body to remand cases.

2

The General Agreement on Tariffs and Trade

The General Agreement on Tariffs and Trade (GATT) was the residue of a failed effort to include an international trade organization among the institutions created to reconstruct the world economy after World War II. At a historic 1944 conference at Bretton Woods, New Hampshire, the finance ministers of the wartime allied nations agreed to establish charters for the International Monetary Fund to facilitate financial transactions and the World Bank to provide assistance to war-torn nations and developing countries. They also recommended that a similar institution, the International Trade Organization (ITO), be created to forge a more liberal international trading system.

Two impelling ideas spurred the drive to create a multilateral trading regime. First, postwar political leaders believed that economic mistakes—particularly the 1930 Smoot-Hawley Tariff Act and the high duties that other nations enacted at the outset of the Great Depression—were a major cause of the events leading to World War II. Second, U.S. leaders were eager to expand the successful system of bilateral reciprocal trade that the United States had initiated in 1934 and which had already begun to erode high-tariff walls.[1]

As originally planned, the ITO would have joined the IMF and World Bank in a triad of institutions emerging from the Bretton Woods consensus that a new international architecture was needed

20

to regulate international economic relations. The ITO, however, was not to be. Changed political circumstances in the United States—the election of a Republican Congress in 1946 combined with the yearning of Americans for "a return to normalcy" and a retreat from world affairs—persuaded President Truman to hold back the draft ITO charter and then to withdraw it from congressional consideration in 1950.

All that was left was the GATT, an interim arrangement negotiated in 1947 as a means of jump-starting the process of tariff reduction, pending the establishment of the ITO. The President already had authority to approve U.S. membership in the GATT under the Reciprocal Trade Agreements Act of 1934. In later years, creation of the GATT through executive agreement would have far-reaching consequences. Trade agreements achieved the *de facto* status of formal treaties, even though they were not subject to the two-thirds Senate majority provisions that governed other U.S. international agreements. Majority support in both houses of Congress became the operative rule.[2]

Initially, the GATT consisted of a number of general clauses, along with the schedules of thousands of tariff commitments negotiated during bilateral agreements between GATT signatories. The general clauses were drawn largely from draft ITO articles and included principles such as "most favored nation," "national treatment," and a series of understandings regarding quotas, subsidies, customs procedures, and antidumping rules.

The "birth defects" of the GATT left strange anomalies in organization and procedures. As Congress often reminded U.S. trade officials in those early years, because of the fiction that GATT was not an organization, GATT signatories were reluctant to delegate authority to committees or even to create a secretariat to handle business between formal sessions. During the 1950s, however, protocols were established for amending the original provisions and for creating a small institutional framework for the GATT. For its entire fifty-year existence, however, the GATT survived—and even thrived—without a formal constitution or basic document.[3]

Theories of Dispute Resolution:
Lawyers versus Diplomats

Two distinct theories regarding the fundamental premises of dispute resolution have competed for dominance throughout much of GATT/WTO history. On one side are the "legalists" or "rules-oriented" proponents, who hold that a more adjudicatory and legal approach to dispute resolution will produce more certainty, predictability, and—ultimately—fairer treatment for all GATT signatories, particularly smaller countries. The United States has been a leading proponent of this "rules-oriented" view, in part because of its legalistically oriented society. In addition, because its laws were often more consistent with GATT's free-market principles, enforceable rules and sanctions were in its interest. A number of smaller and developing countries have also espoused GATT legalism because it increased their chances of prevailing over larger, more powerful economies in trade disputes.

John Jackson, a leading U.S. legal authority on the GATT, has summarized the case for a legalist approach to the GATT system as follows:

> A particularly strong argument exists for pursuing gradually and consistently the progress of international economic affairs toward a rule-oriented approach. Apart from the advantages which accrue generally to international affairs through a rule-oriented approach—less reliance on raw power, and the temptation to exercise it or flex one's muscles, which can get out of hand; a fairer break for smaller countries, or at least a perception of greater fairness; the development of agreed procedures to achieve the necessary compromises—in economic affairs there are additional reasons.
>
> Economic affairs tend (at least in peacetime) to affect more citizens directly than many political and military affairs. . . . However, if citizens are going to make their demands heard and influential, a "power-oriented" negotiating process (often requiring secrecy and executive discretion so as to be able to formulate and implement the necessary compromises) becomes more difficult, if not impossible. Consequently, the only appropriate way to turn seems to be toward a rule-oriented system . . . which . . . when established, will enable business and other decentralized decision-makers to rely upon the stability and predictability of governmental activity in relation to the rules.[4]

Ranged against this legalist, rules-oriented approach are the so-called "pragmatists" or "diplomats," who argue that a "power-oriented" regime more accurately reflects the underlying realities of international politics. Until quite recently, European countries have tended to espouse this view of the GATT. One commentator has described the position of countries arguing for pragmatism in dispute settlement as follows:

> These countries highlighting the ambiguity of GATT rules, the political sensitivity of trade disputes, and the complex trade-offs of competing interests that go into the formulation of any trade rules have argued that GATT dispute resolution should not be particularly formal, legal, or adjudicatory. Rather, it should be characterized by consultations, negotiations, and diplomatic compromises. The goal of dispute resolution in the GATT context should not be clear-cut, binding rules or rigorous applications of the law. Instead, the process should be designed to end the dispute by ending the violation as soon as possible.[5]

A European Community ambassador to the GATT, R. Phan Van Phi, supported this view in the late 1980s: "The EEC emphasizes the need for conciliation and consensus in seeking a satisfactory solution to trade problems. It is based on the view that the rights and obligations of contracting parties under the General Agreement . . . are the result of a delicate balance of economic interests reached after a process, often lengthy and difficult, of negotiation. This delicate balance between sovereign states cannot appropriately be dealt with in a formalized legal framework."[6]

At about the same time, Oliver Long, a Swiss Director-General of the GATT, stated bluntly, "GATT cannot be a world trade court. Conciliation is our priority; it is not our job to determine who is right and wrong."[7]

Two observations should be made about these competing philosophies and the evolution of the GATT/WTO dispute settlement process. First, since the creation of a new dispute settlement system at the end of the Uruguay Round in 1994, a distinct shift toward a more rules-oriented, sanctions-based approach has occurred. Second, the WTO dispute settlement mechanisms still represent a blend of the two philosophies. Furthermore, given the complexity of the issues facing WTO panels and the deep disagreements among WTO members regarding dispute resolution, the very strong legal system recently established may be forced to rely in the future on more diplomatic, less rule-bound compromises.

History of Dispute Settlement under the GATT

The original adjudication process evolved largely through custom during the 1950s and was based upon slender reeds in Articles XXII and XXIII of the GATT. Both emphasized the "diplomatic" and "conciliation" approaches to dispute settlement. Article XXII mandated that member states give "sympathetic consideration" and "opportunity for consultation" when alleged infractions of GATT rules arose. Of greater importance, Article XXIII provided that if a member state alleged that the benefits of the GATT had been "nullified or impaired" by the actions of another member and consultations failed to produce a satisfactory solution, then the unhappy complainant could bring the matter to the attention of other GATT members, who were obliged to "promptly investigate" and "make appropriate recommendations." If the matter proved serious enough, the complainant could seek authority to retaliate by suspending concessions or obligations to the offending state.[8]

During the first few years, disputes were usually treated as diplomatic negotiations during regular meetings of the GATT signatories. In 1952, however, the GATT began to move toward a more judicial approach when it decided to handle complaints using "panels" composed of three to five experts from neutral countries rather than "working parties," which had included diplomats who, in effect, represented their national governments. As time went on, the GATT Secretariat began playing a larger role, particularly in helping to choose truly neutral panel members. Throughout the 1950s, as trade barriers fell and international trade expanded, the system was deemed to be working quite well.

The GATT's success in the 1950s could be traced to its membership, which consisted of a group of like-minded nations and diplomats who had put together the Bretton Woods and other postwar international organizations.[9] This changed dramatically in the 1960s, as the influence of the postwar generation waned and, even more important, a large number of developing countries joined the GATT. The Group of 77, established in 1964 to represent developing nations, made clear that it looked askance at elements of the 1950s consensus. Further, European countries needed breathing space to accommodate the centralizing force of the decisions accompanying the move toward a European Union. As a result, the GATT dispute settlement system fell into disuse during the 1960s.

Change came only gradually during the 1970s, spurred by an increasing awareness that nontariff barriers to trade were proliferating, that more "judicial" regulatory rules would have to be crafted to deal with these barriers, and that the GATT panels were proving inadequate to the tasks assigned to them. After several poorly articulated decisions, the GATT Secretariat requested and received new legal resources to begin instructing panels on the fundamentals of international law and custom.

The Tokyo Round of GATT negotiations during the 1970s increased the pressure for a more legalistic system of dispute resolution. For the first time, the GATT member states took up a number of issues relating to nontariff trade practices, including subsidies and countervailing duties, government procurement, civilian aircraft, and technical barriers to trade such as environmental standards. One important result of the Tokyo Round was a series of plurilateral, voluntary codes that governed these trade practices. At the end of the round, the member states also concluded the "Understanding of 1979," which simultaneously codified the central procedures of the dispute settlement system and Balkanized the procedures by recognizing different modes of dispute resolution for different elements of the GATT. In terms of diplomats versus legalists, the understanding was a standoff.

For most disputes, the understanding appeared to move slightly in the direction of legalism. It reaffirmed the right of a complainant to refer the complaint to a panel; it mandated time limits on the formation of a panel and formalized procedures for determining the composition of the panel; it specified that a report must be issued within a "reasonable time"; and finally, it maintained adoption by consensus but made the report binding, once adopted. The diplomatic approach remained strongly entrenched, however. The wording of the understanding stressed the mediating role of the panels, not the judgmental role. While giving lip service to expeditious decisions, moreover, the document set no time limits on panel decision-making. Finally, the understanding did not create any new power for enforcing panel decisions or providing for surveillance and monitoring.[10]

International Relations Theory and the Global Trading System

Political theorists Robert Keohane of Duke University and Joseph Nye of Harvard University have offered an alternative model and description of the international trading system in the years following World War II.[11] They explain the history of the system in the context of other postwar international organizations and in light of current international relations theories.

Specifically, Keohane and Nye argue that multilateral cooperation after 1945 operated under a "club" system of international governance. Each club or program area was dominated by national cabinet ministers or their equivalents with responsibility for the relevant cluster of issues: trade ministers controlled the GATT; finance ministers ran the IMF; defense and foreign ministers dictated NATO policy; and central bankers ran the Bank for International Settlements (BIS). In effect, these postwar regimes represented "decomposable hierarchies," in that membership and issues could be decomposed from other issue regimes and operated with independently constructed rules and norms.[12]

For officials negotiating agreements, the system had two major advantages. First, government officials in other issue areas generally were excluded from the negotiations; treasury and labor officials did not participate in trade talks, for example. Second, because negotiations were conducted in secret, the public and elected officials were presented with *faits accomplis*, making domestic politics relatively easy to manage. In many respects, the system was a great success: after seven trade rounds, average tariffs declined from about 40 percent in the 1940s to less than 4 percent at the end of the Uruguay Round in the 1990s. Trade ministers, representing a few rich developed countries for much of the period, developed close relationships with their counterparts in other countries. By negotiating behind closed doors, they were able to bargain effectively, while ignoring most of the parochial concerns stemming from domestic politics. Keohane and Nye conclude, "Under the club model, a *lack of transparency to functional outsiders* was a key to political efficacy. Protected by lack of transparency, ministers could package deals that were difficult to disaggregate and even sometimes to understand. . . . From the perspective of multilateral cooperation, this club model can be judged a great success."[13]

During the past decade, however, a number of important developments have combined to undermine the club system, producing the potential for renewed trade stalemate or conflict. Keohane and Nye identify four factors that have challenged the old order. The first source of stress comes from the accelerating pace of globalization, which has made it increasingly difficult for nations to retain the social buffers against outside competitive forces. The second is the change in the international trading system itself: The GATT began with 23 signatories in 1947; by mid-2001, the WTO had more than 140 members, and many more of them were demanding real participation in the organization's decision-making process. Third is the proliferation of nonstate agents, including corporations, business associations, labor unions, and NGOs pushing a myriad of causes such as new commercial rights, the environment, consumer issues, and human rights. The fourth and final new factor is "if anything, more fundamental than the other three."[14] It is the increasing demand for democratic norms and legitimacy at the international level, as a complement to the spread of democratic ideals at the domestic level.

As Keohane and Nye point out, "All of these pressures on international institutions are, ironically, reflections of their success. If international institutions were unimportant, as so-called 'realists' claimed until recently, no one would care about their legitimacy. But it is now recognized that the policies of the IMF, the World Bank, and the WTO make a difference. Hence they are judged not only on the quality of the results that these policies yield, but on the procedures through which the policies are developed."[15]

3

The Uruguay Round:
A New Dispute Settlement System

The outlook for trade negotiations appeared bleak in the early 1980s. The 1982 GATT Ministerial meeting failed to produce agreement on a new trade round or to adopt a forward-looking agenda on agriculture, services, and investment, as pressed by the United States. At the same time, however, an important consensus for doing much more in the area of dispute settlement was beginning to emerge. Developing countries, which had great reservations about assuming obligations on services and investment issues, foresaw real and immediate benefits from a strengthened dispute settlement system. Although there was no formal alliance, the developing countries and the United States shared the goal of strengthening the dispute settlement process.

By 1986, the pessimism of the early 1980s had waned, and GATT ministers meeting at Punta del Este, Uruguay, decided to launch a new round of trade negotiations.[1] Although the Punta del Este declaration was vague about dispute settlement reform, support for change was growing. First, despite flaws in the system, the 1980s witnessed a surge of cases brought to the GATT and, to the surprise of many, a series of quite sophisticated and sensible panel rulings. By the end of the 1980s, the GATT legal system was much stronger than it had been a decade before: the system dealt with 115 disputes during the decade, and by 1989 the annual rate of cases was double that of 1980.[2] This trend of leveling the playing field reinforced the belief of developing countries that a tighter, stronger dispute settlement system would work in their favor.

Despite the system's new vigor, however, the formal procedures of dispute settlement remained clumsy and jerrybuilt. The United States remained adamant that the process be made more efficient and—ultimately—binding. As Robert Hudec of Tufts University and formerly of the University of Minnesota Law School has noted, "The procedure was still voluntary. Every decision from beginning to end had to be made by consensus, which meant that the defendant had a virtual right to veto every step of the process, from the appointment of a panel to the adoption of the panel's legal ruling and the authorization of trade sanctions for noncompliance."[3]

Formal Uruguay Round negotiations began in 1986 with no suggestion of wholesale institutional reform of the GATT or major breakthroughs in the adjudicatory process. The European Community (EC) remained opposed to further "judicializing" of the system. The reasons behind the EC's traditional stance in favor of the diplomatic approach to handling GATT complaints—and the reasons it dramatically changed its position during the Uruguay Round—are highly relevant to this study.

Historically, the EC came into being a decade after the GATT was formed. Even after the 1957 Rome Treaties created the institutional basis for the European Community, power between the EC and individual member states was divided and the jurisdiction over key trade issues was unclear. (The EC itself never formally became a member of the GATT.) Because decision-making in the EC Council of Ministers at that time required unanimity, acceptance of legally binding GATT panel mandates was problematic. Another important factor in the traditional reluctance of the Europeans to tighten GATT legal rules was their fear that such panel rulings would undermine the EC's highly protectionist and subsidized Common Agricultural Policy (CAP).

By the early 1990s, when detailed negotiations on a new dispute settlement system got underway, two key developments were reshaping the outlook of the Europeans. First, their success in utilizing the GATT complaint system for redress against violations of GATT rules in the late 1980s had begun to color their attitude toward the arguments of the legalists. Second, while no major changes in the EC's CAP would occur during the Uruguay Round itself, many EC political leaders recognized that the CAP was retrograde and an enormous drain on public treasuries.

The real impetus for widespread change in the GATT dispute settlement system, however, came from actions, or threatened actions, by the United States. In the late 1980s, the United States initiated what many of its trading partners considered a major, potentially GATT-destroying change in its trade policy. This change was embodied in Section 301 of the 1988 Omnibus Trade and Competitiveness Act, which mandated that the U.S. Trade Representative designate and impose unilateral trade sanctions against GATT members found to be violating their GATT obligations or acting in an "unreasonable" manner against U.S. exporters. While the new Section 301 amendments immediately drew the ire of other GATT members, they also paved the way for a deal that produced fundamental changes in the dispute settlement process.[4]

Robert Hudec has described the political factors that produced the deal, along with the deal's potential risks and limitations:

> The change . . . seems to have been a choice between two evils: between an almost certain legal meltdown if the United States were to carry out its new Section 301 instructions, and a very serious risk of legal failure, in the somewhat distant future, if GATT adopted a dispute settlement procedure that was more demanding than governments could obey. In these circumstances, the fact that GATT governments chose the latter option does not mean that they were confident it would work.[5]

When the EU belatedly acknowledged this stark choice, Uruguay Round negotiators proposed and pushed through sweeping changes in the dispute settlement process. The most important change was removal of the veto power that individual nations held in the process. In a reversal of the previous rule, panel recommendations would henceforth be implemented unless there was a consensus *against* those recommendations. The deal also streamlined the system by establishing tight deadlines within the dispute settlement process.[6]

Major Provisions of the New System

John Jackson has called the new dispute settlement system "one of the great achievements of the Uruguay Round—an achievement that may be the 'linchpin' of the whole trading system."[7]

Most scholars point to four significant features of the new system:[8]

1. The Dispute Settlement Understanding established an integrated dispute settlement system for all parts of the GATT/WTO, including the new subjects of services and intellectual property. With some minor exceptions, the fragmented dispute system that emerged from the Tokyo Round has largely been unified. In addition, it should be noted that in crafting sanctions, cross-retaliation is possible—that is, sanctions can be exacted in any sector and are not limited to the area where a violation allegedly occurred.

2. In what one commentator has called the most radical innovation in the new system, the DSU established an Appellate Body to review the findings of the initial panels. Appeals from the panel decisions are limited to issues of law. The Appellate Body is composed of representatives from seven members "with demonstrated expertise in law." Individual appeals are heard by a rotating group of three Appellate Body members.

3. "Automaticity" has been broadly introduced throughout the dispute settlement process. In requests for the formation of a panel, in the adoption of panel and Appellate Body decisions, and in implementation of the verdicts, therefore, a policy of reverse consensus has been adopted—that is, the request will be granted and decisions will stand unless there is a consensus among WTO members *against* the request or decision.

4. In direct response to U.S. unhappiness over endless delays, deadlines have been established for each stage of the dispute settlement process. Although not airtight, as the EU demonstrated in the bananas case, the deadlines have produced stricter procedures and more timely resolution of disputes.

Deadlines: The System Streamlined

The dispute settlement process can be divided into four phases: consultation; panel deliberations; Appellate Body review; and implementation of compliance measures, compensation, or sanctions.

Consultation—a carryover from the days when diplomacy and conciliation were the predominant features of the system—remains an important element in the process; almost one-third of complaints are settled at this stage.[9] After a request for a panel, the two parties are given up to sixty days to settle their differences through consultation. If differences remain after this time, the complaining party may request a panel. If there is no agreement on the panelists suggested by the Secretariat within twenty days, the Director-General may be asked to appoint the panelists. The entire panel phase, from panel creation to submission of a report, is usually slotted for no more than six months and a maximum of nine months. If an appeal is made, the Appellate Body must complete its report within sixty days, unless an exception is granted for an additional thirty days. When a decision goes against a WTO member state, a remedy must be agreed to within a "reasonable time." The "reasonable time" provision is negotiable, but if delays ensue the complaining party can request compensation, by arbitration if necessary.[10] If the compensation is not agreed upon within twenty days, the complaining party may request authority to retaliate, with the level fixed by arbitration if necessary. Overall, there is a strong bias and pressure within the system to complete all deliberations within a year, although the implementation period may extend well beyond that.

Results to Date: What the Numbers Tell Us

As of July 2001, according to the WTO Secretariat, since the new dispute settlement system took effect on January 1, 1995, 234 requests for consultation relating to 180 distinct issues had been submitted. Fifty cases had been decided by panels and the Appellate Body, and sixteen cases were still active. The remaining cases were settled through consultation, withdrawn, or were still in the consultation process.[11]

The United States has been the world's most active user of the new system—and the most successful. As of January 2001, the United States had brought fifty-seven complaints to the WTO. Thirty-one of these have been concluded: thirteen were settled in U.S. favor through consultation, and fifteen were successful through panel or Appellate Body decisions. The United States lost only three cases.

During the same period, forty-seven complaints were brought against the United States, of which twenty-three have been concluded: eleven were settled by consultation, with the United States giving way, and eleven were lost through panel decisions. The United States prevailed in one case.[12]

Robert Hudec, who pioneered studies of the political economy of GATT/WTO dispute settlement, was the first to compile an authoritative database of GATT disputes that would serve as the foundation of subsequent empirical research on the system. He has continued to update both the database and his own hypotheses regarding evolution of the GATT and the WTO DSU. In a study published in 1999, Hudec compiled a group of illuminating statistics based upon the records of the WTO Secretariat from January 1, 1995, to May 8, 1998.[13] Hudec's study shows that the volume of dispute settlement proceedings increased greatly after creation of the new WTO system. The WTO records indicate that 98 cases were initiated during that 3.3-year period for an average of 29.7 cases per year. Contrast this rate with earlier GATT years: from 1980–1984, the rate was 9.2 cases per year; from 1985–1989, 12.8 cases per year; and 1990–1993, 15.8 cases per year. Projecting the rate of increase over these years, one might have predicted about nineteen cases per year during the 1995–1998 period. Thus, the volume of cases during the first three years of the WTO was 60 percent higher than projections would have indicated—and 90 percent higher than any comparable period under GATT procedures.

Hudec found two main causes for the additional cases brought after 1995: new legal obligations from the Uruguay Round and more cases against developing countries. Using the 1995–1998 period as a base, he estimated that 46 new cases could be attributed to some facet of the new WTO procedures. Twenty of these additional cases could be traced to new obligations (intellectual property, services, new agricultural responsibilities), representing just over 40 percent of the increased load. He also discovered that almost all of these cases were brought by the United States, not surprising given the U.S. effort to include these categories among WTO obligations.

In addition, after comparing the background of defendants in the 1980–1984 period with that of 1995–1998, Hudec found a threefold increase in the number of cases brought against developing countries (from 13 percent of total cases to 39 percent). He argued, finally, that the two causes are closely linked in that the new obligations pushed by the United States (and the EU) were aimed at perceived deficiencies in the trade laws and practices of these countries. Developing countries were also disproportionately affected by the change from voluntary codes and rules to obligations that were mandatory for all WTO signatories; in past negotiations, developing countries often opted out of these obligations.

In recent years, Hudec's pioneering work has inspired a cottage industry of empirical and statistical assessments of the GATT/WTO dispute settlement system, which has produced deeper insights into its operation and consequences. At a 2000 conference honoring Hudec's contributions to GATT/WTO scholarship, political scientists Marc Busch of the Queen's School of Business and Eric Reinhardt of Emory University noted the strong presence of the United States and the European Union throughout the entire history of GATT/WTO dispute settlement.[14] They identified 654 bilateral disputes under the GATT and WTO regimes between 1948 and 2000. Fifty-two percent of them involved the United States as either complainant or defendant, and 36 percent involved the EU (not including cases where EU nations acted alone).[15]

Other research has shown that the institutional changes to the DSU established during the Uruguay Round were not a large factor in determining the frequency of disputes; variables such as the expansion of GATT/WTO membership, the amount of a nation's total trade, and the degree of dependence on trade for national income are more strongly correlated with dispute frequency. Not surprisingly, nations with large absolute trade numbers and with trade as a significant percentage of total GNP display a heightened interest in utilizing dispute settlement procedures.[16]

Some observers have pointed to the rise in the number of WTO cases as evidence of growing confidence in the ability of the system to achieve just solutions. Recent research, however, has cast doubt on that upbeat interpretation. Many disputes arise from the failure of previous cases to achieve real change and compliance. Further, dispute resolution has been shown to spawn countersuits in retaliation for the initial complaint—and the phenomenon of a band-wagon effect as additional parties target a defendant in an effort to foreclose discriminatory liberalization in favor of the first complainant.[17] Busch and Reinhardt thus conclude that recent statistical work demonstrates that "the intuition about complaints being the result of 'growing confidence' in the dispute settlement system is misleading. Instead, the ballooning caseload is mostly a function of the expansion of the organization [WTO] and of world trade more generally; and disputes are just as likely to be responses to the failure rather than to the success of the adjudication system."[18]

For developing countries, the impact of the new dispute settlement system has been decidedly mixed. In theory, a more judicialized system levels the playing field for smaller, developing economies. There is some evidence of "strategic" behavior by panels and the Appellate Body in bending to the political demands of the largest and most influential WTO members. Overall, however, the WTO judicial bodies have attempted to interpret the law impartially between large and small nations.[19]

Yet if the new system promises more even-handed results, it has also raised the barriers to developing country participation. During the first five years of WTO operations, research clearly shows that developing countries used the new DSU less than the previous GATT dispute resolution system. For the period 1995–2000, developing countries brought 29 percent of WTO complaints, despite the fact that more than 80 percent of WTO members are developing countries. Controlling for other variables such as market power and trade dependence, Reinhardt shows that WTO developing country member states are one-third less likely to file complaints against developed countries under the WTO than they were under the post–1989 (partially reformed) GATT regime.[20] Arguing that the evidence strongly supports the claim that the new system is not working effectively for developing countries, Busch and Reinhardt state,

> One need not look far for an explanation. By adding 26,000 pages of new treaty text, not to mention a rapidly burgeoning case law; by imposing several new states of legal activity per dispute, such as appeals, compliance reviews, and compensation arbitration; by judicializing proceedings and thus putting a premium on sophisticated legal argumentation as opposed

to informal negotiation; and by adding a potential two years or more to defendants' legally permissible delays in complying with adverse rulings, the WTO reforms have raised the hurdles facing the LDCs [less developed countries] contemplating litigation.[21]

In light of this study's recommendations for changes in the DSU, a word about what the numbers tell us is indicated. For many routine commercial conflicts and issues where the barriers are clear, the new system will work effectively. But two additional points should be kept in mind. First, the truly difficult issues stemming from the rules on services, competition policy in the telecommunications agreement, intellectual property, and genetically modified organisms (with the exception of the beef hormones and related cases) have yet to enter the system. Further, not until 2001 were developing countries held fully accountable for the Trade-Related Intellectual Property Rights (TRIPs) rules. Second, as will be described in chapter 4, some decisions, while politically attractive in that they conceal significant differences, are already stretching legislative intent with judicially creative solutions.

4

Emerging Constitutional Problems and Substantive Deficiencies

The new dispute settlement system is nearing the end of its "shakedown" phase. Assessments of the technical details of the system and the larger implications of the "judicialization" of the multilateral trade regime have already begun. In addition, the Uruguay Round negotiators mandated a review of the system by the end of 1998. Because of the difficulty in achieving a virtual unanimity of consensus, this review, which was suspended after the WTO Ministerial Conference in Seattle in December 1999, notably failed to produce significant results; and little progress is expected until member states agree to a new round of trade negotiations.[1]

In this chapter, we shall analyze constitutional flaws in the dispute settlement system and examine areas where substantive deficiencies are already causing major difficulties for the new system. The chapter begins with a description of the implications and effects of the asymmetry between the efficiency of the dispute settlement system and the inefficiency of the WTO legislative process. Next, the study examines three instances where, after the legislative process failed, the panels and the Appellate Body arguably went on to "create" new law. Then the chapter explores the special difficulties for the DSU presented by two complex regulatory issues: the competition policy challenges that are looming in the services sector, using telecommunications as the example; and the complex mixture of science, risk assessment, and trade policy at the core of decisions relating to food safety, genetically modified organisms, and use of the precautionary principle. The chapter concludes with an analysis of the potential for, and implications of, major substantive changes in the mandate of the WTO as a result of the use of soft and customary law.

Negotiated Rules versus Judicial Activism

Even during the brief period that the DSU has been operating, a lively debate has emerged regarding important structural or constitutional questions that are inherent in the WTO system. The most important of these constitutional questions can be traced to the asymmetry between the relative efficiency of the decision-making process of the DSU and the practical difficulties inherent in creating new substantive rules and amending or interpreting existing rules. A second, and equally important, question relates to the ability of the DSU to handle complex regulatory issues—particularly where the underlying WTO text is unclear or contradictory and where national systems of regulation diverge markedly in their methods for achieving market-oriented deregulation.

In describing the consequences of this legislative-judicial asymmetry, trade scholar John Jackson has warned of the "constitutional dangers of a tendency for the WTO diplomacy to rely too heavily on the dispute settlement system to correct the many ambiguities and gaps in the . . . Uruguay Round texts."[2] Marco Bronckers, a noted European trade lawyer and scholar, echoed these same concerns when he expressed the fear that "governments may too easily think that progress can be made in the WTO *through* enforcement; that litigation in the WTO is a faster, more convenient way to resolve difficult issues than an open exchange at the negotiating table. That is troubling because it undermines democratic control over international cooperation and rule-making, and it prevents a more broad-based participation of all stakeholders in the formulation of international rules. Litigation is not subject to parliamentary approval."[3]

The Problematic Legislative Function. The most productive and fruitful legislative advances in the WTO are undoubtedly a result of the package deals put together at the end of periodic trade rounds.

Certainly, the Uruguay Round demonstrated this reality: it established sweeping new rules for services, intellectual property, investment and subsidies, agriculture, and textiles; and it created the new WTO and the dispute settlement system that is the subject of this study.

Relying on major trade round negotiations to create new rules or clarify and amend existing rules is fraught with problems. First, trade rounds occur infrequently, and thus are inefficient vehicles for creating new disciplines in additional program areas. Seven years elapsed between the end of the Tokyo Round and the beginning of the Uruguay Round. Indeed, the more realistic time frame for the creation of new rules would be from the end of Tokyo Round until the *end* of the Uruguay Round, a period of thirteen years. More than six years have passed since the completion of the Uruguay Round in 1994, and the failure during the 1999 Seattle Ministerial Conference to reach agreement on launching a new round means that it will be at least 2002 before the so-called Millennium Round begins. Assuming a three-year time frame for the next round, as many WTO members desire, the total lapsed time for the creation of new rules or the amendment of old rules will be at least nine years. Given the magnitude of the problems and the speed with which technology and global integration are raising major new substantive issues, rule-making by trade rounds is not a viable solution.

The time factor is not the only problem. The nature and characteristics of the rules that emerge from the negotiating process are even more important. Because the WTO is a large and diverse organization, the big package deals negotiated at the end of trade rounds necessarily contain numerous gaps, ambiguities, and even contradictions. This problem was first identified after the 1973–1979 Tokyo Round, which ventured in significant ways into nontariff barriers and behind-the-border domestic rules that impeded trade. But it was the sweeping results of the Uruguay Round—combined with the highly judicialized DSU created at the end of that round—that really brought these issues to the forefront.

A number of commentators have argued retrospectively that the reform of the dispute settlement system took aim at the wrong target. The real problems that emerged with dispute settlement in the

1980s stemmed largely from flaws in the underlying substantive GATT rules. In several prescient analyses just after the new DSU became operational, leading U.S. trade lawyers took note of the dangers and contradictions embodied in the new DSU and the inadequacies in the substantive body of WTO law. In 1995, Judith Bello and Alan Holmer, Washington trade lawyers at the time, pointed out, "Most disputes [under the GATT] . . . were resolved fairly, if not speedily. The significant breakdowns in settling disputes occurred where the substantive rules themselves were inadequate." In 1996, Alan Wolff and John Ragosta, two other prominent members of the U.S. international trade bar, warned, "A fast-track, binding international litigation procedure cannot yield a satisfactory result where there are no precise or clear substantive rules . . . [and] there are hundreds of unresolved questions in WTO agreements."[4]

Robert Hudec, who conducted the most extensive academic analysis of the new DSU, made two essential points about the old and the new systems. First, Hudec observed that the old system had received a "bad rap" and that in fact, between 1948 and 1990, more than 90 percent of decisions were resolved or partially resolved to the satisfaction of the winning party. Second, and more important, Hudec shared the doubts about the adequacy of basic WTO law:

> The [dispute settlement] crisis had nothing to do with the strength or weakness of the GATT litigation process. . . . [Arguing that the reform stemmed] from a failure in the litigation procedure is actually sort of a cover-up, an attempt to shift the blame to the GATT's litigation procedures when in fact responsibility lies in the earlier negotiating failures of the Tokyo Round. . . . The point here is not that the . . . dispute settlement reforms are wrong, but that they are not enough. . . . [A] scaled-down agreement that papers over basic differences . . . is not an evil result, but one in which . . . a strong dispute settlement reform would be an invitation to disaster."[5]

In recent papers and books, WTO legal observers have listed a plethora of major gaps, unclear definitions and articles, and contradictory elements that represent a potential source of painful disagreements among WTO members. These include elements of the subsidies codes; a substantial portion of the language in the Trade-Related Intellectual Property Rights agreement; the issue of parallel imports; competition law in the telecommunications agreement;

elements of the new antidumping rules; and a number of unanswered questions in the area of sanitary and phytosanitary regulations.

Amendment and Clarification Barriers. Short of major revisions of WTO rules pursuant to trade round negotiations, use of the WTO regular legislative procedures for creating new rules or amending or interpreting old rules is very difficult. As Bronckers has aptly stated, "Clarifying the rules is practically impossible," and "[a]dopting new rules is cumbersome." The reason, as John Jackson has noted, is that after creating sweeping new trade rules and a much more binding DSU, "In the last months of the Uruguay Round negotiations, the diplomatic representatives at the negotiation felt it was important to build in a number of checks and balances in the WTO charter, to constrain decision-making by the international institution which could be too intrusive on national sovereignty."[6]

Only the Ministerial Conference and the General Council can enact clarifications or interpretations of treaty rules. Interpretations can be adopted only with the support of three-quarters of the overall WTO membership, and such interpretations may not amend the treaty—a change that would be subject to more stringent procedures. To date, no attempt to utilize new interpretations or clarifications to resolve ambiguities in the new WTO rules has been successful.

The process of amending the rules is even more complicated. In most cases, amendments can be proposed by the Ministerial Conference and adopted with the vote of two-thirds of WTO members. If the amendment is determined to affect the rights and obligations of member states, however, then members opposed to the amendment are not bound by it unless three-quarters of the overall WTO membership votes to give them the option of either accepting the amendment or withdrawing from the WTO. Furthermore, amendments to certain rules—those involving WTO decision-making, most favored nation (MFN) status, tariff schedules, and dispute settlement, for example—must be enacted by consensus, which is defined as no individual member dissenting publicly.[7]

Implications for WTO Governance and
National Sovereignty

The bottom line, then, given the extreme difficulty of using normal legislative procedures in the WTO, is that the dispute panels and the Appellate Body will be under increasing pressure to legislate through interpretation and filling in the blanks in WTO disciplines.[8] This is occurring despite the clear injunction in the Uruguay Round text that "recommendations and rulings of the DSB cannot add to or diminish rights and obligations provided in the covered agreements" (DSU Article 3.2).

Some legal scholars applaud this trend as inevitable and regard it as a means of producing greater predictability and clarity in the rules of the international trading system. Thus, Raj Bhala of George Washington University has written, "Like it or not, the distinctions between the judges [of the Appellate Body] as bureaucrats/arbitrators, on the one hand, and as lawmakers/legislators, on the other hand, is crumbling in the WTO. A most obvious symptom of this decay is the Appellate Body's use of precedent."

In a series of three comprehensive and exhausting articles, Bhala makes the case that through the increasing use of *de facto stare decisis* (judicial precedent) by the Appellate Body, one can observe "the emergence of an international common law of procedure . . . and an emerging substantive common law." In his view, judges in the Appellate Body have also repudiated Montesquieu's theory of judges as "inanimate beings" who merely "pronounce the words of the law."[9]

Rather, the judges are "not mere passive beings. They are actively involved in construction of the international rule of law. . . . The Appellate Body members work in an arena where the imperfections of 'legislators'—the trade negotiators who produced the Uruguay Round agreements and all its progeny—are all too plain. They are compelled to resolve issues that are not addressed adequately, or at all, by the legislators in trade agreements. The adjudicators have no choice but to legislate (at least interstitially)." In the third piece of the trilogy, Bhala argues that at some point in the future, the WTO should amend its rules, establish *de jure stare decisis,* and make Appellate Body reports "a formal source of international trade law."[10]

Similarly, another prolific and distinguished legal scholar, Joel Trachtman of Tufts University, has stated, "To understand the role of dispute resolution, one must recognize that dispute resolution is not simply a mechanism for neutral application of legislated rules but is itself a mechanism of legislation and governance." Explaining the theme of an article he wrote in 1999, Trachtman stated that it is "intended to suggest the reasons why dispute resolution could be the appropriate place to determine . . . the relationship between trade and environmental values or trade and labor values. . . . [It] is [also] intended to suggest a way to predict when these issues might be better determined through more specific legislative action."[11]

Bhala and Trachtman are representative of a number of legal scholars who have written to applaud or predict increased lawmaking through the judicial process of the WTO. These analyses, however, often ignore deeper questions of legitimacy and accountability stemming from the "democratic deficit" inherent in this process.

The Democratic Process: International versus Domestic Law. Traditionally, international law—created and controlled by sovereign, independent nations—has consisted of carefully circumscribed obligations and rights with few legal remedies for redress of grievances. A leading eighteenth-century authority on international law, Swiss diplomat Emmerich de Vattel, was the first to take the principle of national sovereignty as fundamental. A distinct view of international relations and treaties then flowed from this premise. Jeremy Rabkin of Cornell University has described this view as follows: "The relevant 'law of nature' was the law that applies in a 'state of nature' where there is no common judge and each individual is free to do as he likes, if he does not violate the rights of others. Relations among nations were seen as governed, ultimately, by that law of nature because sovereign nations, acknowledging no higher authority, remained in a state of nature with respect to each other."[12]

In recent times, the boundaries between international and domestic law have blurred. Still, clear distinctions and differences grow out of the matrix of democratic institutions and practices that surround domestic laws and institutions. The old GATT dispute settlement system avoided some of the potential "democratic deficit" problems that would emerge under the new Dispute Settlement

Understanding. Although it evolved over time, the old system remained heavily dependent upon diplomacy for resolving disagreements among GATT members. Most important, decisions of the quasi-judicial panels could be blocked by any GATT member. Consequently, one could argue that the very act of achieving a "consensus" on panel decisions (particularly if it were alleged that these decisions constituted new norms or rules) produced a rough, though highly imperfect, system of representative democracy among GATT contracting parties.

Under the new system, however, the consensus process is reversed, and no individual nation or even a large group of nations can block a panel or Appellate Body decision once it is handed down. Thus, the WTO is the "supreme court of world trade disputes" and the "top court of the global economy," in the view of outside observers. And therein is the problem.

International law—and specifically the WTO DSU—lacks the fundamentals of democratic legitimacy that make judicial enforcement palatable in domestic legal systems. Individuals and organizations in the United States and other nations have recourse to democratic procedures to elect representatives, change laws, correct flawed judicial decisions, and remove judges if necessary. Dispute settlement in the WTO, however, is not embedded in such democratic surroundings; the sovereign nations that comprise its membership have only limited recourse against "unconstitutional" decisions by the panels and Appellate Body.

The challenges that international law presents for national democratic norms and practices have been set forth in a thoughtful analysis by Kal Raustiala of the UCLA Law School.[13] Raustiala suggests that, with regard to democratic theory, two problems are inherent in the workings of international law: its generativity and its insularity. By generativity, Raustiala means the ability of international law to produce new substantive rules or amend old rules through a judicial process, as in the WTO, or through nonconsensual decision-making procedures, as in some environmental agreements (majority or supra-majority rule-making). Insularity can take several forms: it can mean the degree to which the executive (as opposed to the legislature) participates in a particular international institution and its decisions, or it can mean the degree to which the public (individuals, NGOs, and corporations) participates in the international institution.[14]

Clearly, generativity and insularity are linked, and this study will argue that the two forms of insularity (executive control and public participation in international institutions) present quite different challenges and require different solutions. Chapter 7 offers recommendations on greater democratic oversight and participation in international institutions by national legislatures, as well as recommendations on participation by NGOs and corporations in the WTO (see pages 132–147).

Regarding generativity, Raustiala points out correctly that the WTO is one of the "most problematic" international institutions because its "active dispute settlement process . . . elaborates and defines WTO rules and standards *ex post*." WTO panels and the AB have done this by using an "'evolutionary' theory of interpretation" and by incorporating otherwise nonbinding international standards (e.g., food safety standards)—which themselves are evolving—into the binding WTO dispute settlement system.[15]

Raustiala notes that in domestic law, generativity by administrative agencies has been reined in through an administrative procedures act, judicial and congressional oversight, and budget control. But he observes that "[s]uch parallel controls [for international institutions] have not been provided." Further, though domestic courts are generative (and insular), Raustiala concludes that "perhaps the difference between domestic courts and WTO panels is the long acceptance of domestic courts in the larger constitutional scheme of the U.S. and the knowledge that we have transparent, political procedures for staffing them, an active practice of dissent, extensive openness to *amici curiae*, and the means to overrule judicial decisions that do not depend, as in the WTO, on achieving political consensus."[16]

Judicial Creativity

Since the new DSU took effect in 1995, there has been relatively little time for controversial "legislative" decisions to be completed and published. Nevertheless, some actions have already caused concern, even among supporters of the new system. This section will review three difficult issues where, at least in the view of some observers, the panels or the AB have indulged in "judicial creativity." The three issues of concern are (1) the right of unilateral action against non-product-related processes and production methods (PPMs) for imported goods; (2) whether panels or the AB can accept *amicus curiae* submissions; and (3) whether the AB erred in substituting its judgment for that of WTO councils on matters relating to balance-of-payments issues and regional trading agreements.[17] Clearly, the first two issues, PPMs and *amicus* briefs, are the most politically sensitive and have produced the most divisive reactions among WTO members.

Unilateral Action against PPMs. The issue of PPMs has figured in several cases, including the tuna/dolphin decision and the more recent shrimp/turtle case. The issue revolves around the scope and meaning of Article XX, the WTO rule that sets forth exceptions to WTO obligations, including those related to the protection of health or human, animal, or plant life. Article XX has been the focus of many of the controversies relating to the intersection—and potential clash—of trade and the environment. In many instances, Article XX exceptions are connected to the national treatment obligations of the GATT's Article III, which mandates that imported goods receive the same treatment as domestic goods.[18]

Traditionally, Article III has been interpreted in a manner that would treat products that have the same physical forms as "like" products even if they have been produced in different ways. Thus, no member can give special advantages to a particular product, or discriminate against a particular product, because of the process by which it was produced. Yet in recent years, particularly with the advent of the new DSU, environmental and human health exceptions under Article XX have been subjected to challenges alleging, in part, that discrimination on the basis of the production process has violated national treatment obligations.[19]

The Tuna/Dolphin Case. The best known recent case is the 1993 tuna/dolphin case brought against U.S. restrictions on the importation of tuna from Mexico (there were two so-called tuna/dolphin cases; the case discussed herein is tuna/dolphin I). In this instance, the United States had unilaterally stopped imports of tuna from countries that did not protect against the killing of dolphins in tuna nets. Mexico argued first, that this violated GATT's Article III because tuna was a "like" product with U.S. domestic tuna and with tuna imported from other countries and second, that the U.S. action was an attempt to ban a *process* (i.e., a method of fishing) by banning a product.

In deciding against the United States, a WTO panel pointed out that allowing import restrictions on the basis of differences in process actually amounted to allowing restrictions on the basis of "differences in environmental policies" and that this course would force the WTO to *legislate* comprehensive criteria for judging such policies. The panel stated that "if the contracting parties were to permit import restrictions in response to differences in environmental policies under the General Agreement, they would need to impose limits on the range of policy differences justifying such responses and to develop criteria so as to prevent abuse." The panel then stated a central point of relevance for this study: "If the contracting parties were to decide to permit trade measures of this type in particular circumstances, it would therefore be preferable for them to do so not by interpreting Article XX but *by amending or supplementing the provisions of the General Agreement or waiving obligations thereunder*" [italics added]—and not by judicial interpretation through the DSU."[20]

While the substantive details of the product/process doctrine are not the main concern of this study, it should be noted that the issues raised in these cases are profound and have implications far beyond the environmental protection of tuna, dolphin, or shrimp. As John Jackson of Georgetown University Law School has warned, allowing nations to coerce other nations into replicating the importing country's production process "is the start of a slippery slope." And Jackson asks, "What other conditions could be addressed (such as minimum wage standards or gender discrimination) and what other process possibilities should we consider? One could think of thousands of them, and they could become serious obstacles for the trade policies we are trying to promote."[21]

The Shrimp/Turtle Case. The tuna/dolphin panel's strong argument against judicial rule-making in this area was challenged—at least implicitly—by a 1998 Appellate Body decision in the shrimp/turtle case.[22] In that case, four nations complained about a U.S. ban on the importation of shrimp caught by trawlers that do not employ a special device in their nets to protect sea turtles from being trapped and killed. Once again the issue of the extraterritorial applications of U.S. standards (and processes) was the central question.

The importance of the decision stemmed more from what the AB did not state than from what it actually stated. The Appellate Body judges ruled against the United States on the grounds that its particular solution amounted to "a means not just of unjustifiable discrimination, but also of 'arbitrary' discrimination between countries where the same conditions prevail."[23] The key point was essentially a procedural one—that the United States had erred in giving different deadlines to different nations for compliance with its unilateral action.

The question left open, however, was what would have happened if the United States had applied the standards extraterritorially but in a *nondiscriminatory* manner. The AB did not answer this question directly, but other elements of the decision have led some commentators—including U.S. trade officials—to argue that the Appellate Body, at least in this case, had implicitly endorsed the use of unilateral, extraterritorial sanctions based on PPMs.[24]

The ruling recognized the validity of "unilateralism" in seeking to implement the rights of some nations under Article XX. Further, it adopted what some observers labeled an "evolutionary interpretation" of Article XX, stating that it had to be "read in light of contemporary concerns of the community of nations about the protection and conservation of the environment."[25]

When the full Dispute Settlement Body convened to review the judgment, U.S. trade officials trumpeted their "victory" and asserted that PPMs could be the basis for restrictive trade measures in the future. This provoked outrage from developing country representatives. Thailand responded, "This [decision] was a fundamental and impermissible alteration of the present balance of rights and obligations of Members under the WTO agreement." And India argued that if the decision established a precedent, "the door would be open to unilateral measures aimed at discrimination based on non-product PPMs."[26]

Outside observers worried about the implications for the long-term viability of the DSU have echoed the concerns of the developing countries. Thus, Arthur Appleton, a European trade lawyer who writes frequently on WTO legal issues, argued in 1999 that, while the AB's decision presented valid substantive arguments, the opinion also bowed in the direction of political expediency and "demonstrated the Appellate Body's determination to maintain a degree of public support for the WTO among what is frequently termed 'civil society.'" Appleton went on to state,

> The Appellate Body's decision is sound from a political and policy perspective. . . . That being said, by transgressing certain limits, however impractical, established by the DSU, the Appellate Body risks losing the confidence of certain WTO members. . . . The WTO dispute settlement system depends on member confidence. It will only remain successful if the members believe that the Appellate Body is interpreting the covered agreements as negotiated, as opposed to modifying them. . . . While the [AB] can be expected to make temporary patches for the holes that are discovered in the covered agreements on a case-by-case basis, such ad hoc repair work is no substitute for the consensual modification of these agreements, in particular the DSU, by the members.[27]

In a study of the WTO and the environment published in 2000, Gary Sampson, a former director of the GATT/WTO, explained,

> Perhaps rulings such as this have some short-term merit in finding immediate "solutions" to politically sensitive matters, but in the long term, policy choices as important as the legitimacy of unilateral applications of trade measures to enforce domestic societal preferences extraterritorially should not be left to litigation of this nature, with confusing and uncertain outcomes. These should be the subject of policy debates with the participation of representatives from all WTO members.[28]

Finally—and ironically—an important environmental group, which disagreed with the shrimp/turtle decision for very different substantive reasons, fully supported the argument that the panel had gone beyond its judicial mandate. In comments on the decision, the Earthjustice Legal Defense Fund stated, "The panel went beyond its legitimate dispute settlement role and authority to create new rules concerning the application of Article XX. . . . Such a task is inappropriate for a dispute resolution panel. Rather the creation of new rules is a legislative function legitimate only to governments directly responsible to the people affected."[29]

***Amicus* Briefs.** The second major issue that has raised questions about judicial rule-making is whether panels and the AB are obliged to accept *amicus* briefs from NGOs or other outside sources.[30] Once again, the shrimp/turtle case is at the center of the debate. The United States attached three NGO briefs to its submission and argued that nothing in the DSU prohibits panels from considering information from any source in the pursuit of information concerning the dispute. The panel, however, agreed with the complaining countries that accepting such briefs would be incompatible with DSU rules and pointed out that only parties to the dispute and agreed-upon third parties could submit information directly to the panels. Subsequently, the AB overruled the panel, stating that it "erred in its legal interpretation" because the right of a panel to "seek" information logically must include the right to consider unsolicited briefs and documents. The AB ruling states that "the thrust of Articles 12 and 13 taken together is that the DSU accords to a panel . . . ample authority to undertake and to control the process by which it informs itself . . . of the relevant facts of the dispute. . . ."[31]

Proponents of the AB ruling have argued that there is a simple logic in granting wide authority for panels to use whatever information is available under their mandate to "seek" out all relevant facts in reaching an "objective assessment."[32] But as critics of this decision have pointed out, the issue is actually more complicated than it first appears. The United States, by including the briefs, purposely left unclear (and refused to specify) which arguments it agreed with, stating only that these were not separate issues to which the AB had to respond. The complaining countries argued that this could lead to internal substantive contradictions within the briefs and to major procedural flaws in the process. Complainants, for example, could not be certain which arguments they should respond to, a potentially crucial omission in persuading the panel or AB to rule in their favor.[33]

The issue has become ever more complicated—and controversial—as a result of Appellate Body actions in two cases: a recent case concerning subsidies, countervailing duties, and the privatization of British Steel; and a Canadian appeal against a panel ruling that upheld a French ban on chrysotile asbestos.[34] In the British Steel case, a panel ruled against the U.S. contention that the benefits from subsidies provided to state-owned British Steel by the U.K. government were passed on to its successor firms when the company was privatized in 1988. The Appellate Body concurred with the results but based its decision on much narrower grounds related to the facts of this particular case alone, leaving unsettled the larger issues regarding the ability to countervail against privatized state-owned companies.

Two aspects of the Appellate Body's decision were particularly controversial: the Appellate Body's rejection of the EU's contention that the AB lacked authority to accept *amicus* briefs submitted independently by U.S. steel producers; and the AB's acceptance of the U.S. government's argument that the AB had authority to accept unsolicited submissions as part of its mandate to control the process by which it informs itself of the relevant facts and applicable legal norms and principles. The AB stated that individuals and countries that were not WTO members had no legal right to make submissions, but that nonetheless the AB on its own could accept or refuse such submissions. Specifically, the AB judges asserted the right to accept briefs when "we find it pertinent and useful to do so." But they added, "In this appeal, we have not found it necessary to take the two *amicus* briefs into account in rendering our decision."[35]

That portion of the British Steel decision produced a strong negative reaction, as more than a dozen WTO members lashed out at the AB. Countries as diverse as Japan, Canada, India, and Mexico made their objections known. Japan and Canada pointed out that this was a legislative matter for the WTO members, not the AB, to decide. Japan found the Appellate Body's reasoning "not at all convincing." And India noted that the finding would result "in a situation where not only nongovernment voluntary organizations, but also powerful business associations . . . are able to intervene in the dispute settlement process. We do not consider this to be a good development from the point of view of the long-term health of the dispute settlement system, which is meant to be a mechanism for resolution of disputes *between members* [italics added]."[36]

Despite these strong warnings, the AB once again blundered on the issue of *amicus* briefs at the end of 2000. The result was an "unprecedented reprimand" from the chairman of the WTO General Council. The criticism was triggered by a November 8, 2000, document setting forth procedures for *amicus* briefs in a Canadian appeal against a WTO panel ruling upholding a French ban on chrysotile asbestos. In an attempt to preempt critics, the AB announced that these were procedures for this case alone, and not new working procedures; the critics were not mollified. Thirteen briefs were submitted, including five from environmental NGOs. Just before the deadline for final documents, however, the AB announced without explanation that it was rejecting all of the briefs—a move that infuriated outside parties but did not assuage the anger of most WTO members.[37]

On November 23, at a meeting of the DSB, more than forty delegations registered their strong opposition to the AB's action. Only the United States, Switzerland, and New Zealand came to the AB's defense. India's WTO ambassador echoed the anger of many members that, despite their clearly expressed opposition to such moves, the AB had pressed ahead to include outside briefs in the appellate proceedings: "[The AB] has obviously ignored the overwhelming sentiment of members against acceptance of unsolicited *amicus curiae* briefs. . . . [It] wants to introduce procedures which amount to soliciting *amicus curiae* briefs from NGOs."[38]

As with the shrimp/turtle and British Steel decisions, two themes dominated these comments: first, that the AB was usurping the legislative function of the WTO councils; and second, that it was changing the balance of rights and obligations of WTO members. On the question of legislative prerogatives, the Canadian WTO ambassador, Sergio Marchi, stated that in Canada's view, "the members, not the dispute settlement system, should decide how the issue of *amicus* participation should be dealt with in the future. . . . Members must ensure that the government-to-government nature of the dispute settlement process is not weakened or compromised by the procedural initiatives of panels or the Appellate Body."[39] India, Mexico, and other developing countries also feared that the deep pockets of U.S. and EU multinational companies *and* of developed country NGOs would overwhelm the dispute system with highly sophisticated and novel arguments that the developing countries would be hard pressed to answer and rebut.

Most important, however, was the argument by complaining nations, particularly developing countries, that the AB had on its own altered the balance of rights and obligations of certain WTO members. The point was that WTO members who were not either direct parties to the dispute or agreed-upon third parties could not present written submissions.[40] In effect, the AB had granted rights to NGOs that WTO members themselves did not enjoy.[41] As Gary Sampson has stated, in the view of a number of countries, "The Appellate Body had diminished the rights of members and intruded upon members' prerogatives as negotiators to establish the bounds of participation in the WTO. Such issues should be decided by members."[42]

Balance-of-Payments Restrictions and Regional Trade Agreements. The final example of alleged judicial creativity and usurpation relates to the powers and authority of two political (executive) organs of the WTO—the Committee on Balance-of-Payments Restrictions and the Committee on Regional Trade Agreements.[43] Before the WTO was established, GATT panels had examined certain aspects of the relationship between the executive committees and the dispute settlement system. The most extensive discussion of this relationship concerned a case relating to tariff preferences given by the EC to Mediterranean countries as part of certain regional trading agreements. After long consultations and then a formal complaint, a GATT panel concluded that "examination . . . and reexamination of Article XXIV [regional trading agreements] was the responsibility of the contracting parties" and not an appropriate topic for GATT dispute settlement panels. It reasoned that "this should be done clearly in the context of Article XXIV [regional trading agreements] and not Article XXIII [dispute settlement], as an assessment of all the duties, regulations of commerce and trade coverage, as well as the interests and rights of all contracting parties were at stake in such an examination and not just the interests and rights of the contracting party raising a complaint."[44]

In the Uruguay Round negotiations, the United States requested language that would have changed the rule to allow for a broader review of unresolved issues relating to balance-of-payments questions. The U.S. position was not adopted; instead, the WTO rules allowed limited review of the application of specific restrictive measures taken for balance-of-payments purposes. Similar language was constructed for review of regional trade agreements.

The issue has recently come up again in several cases, with the result that the AB has reversed the earlier decisions and injected the dispute settlement system deeply into the determination of the legality of balance-of-payments and regional trading agreements. In 1999, two panels (Turkey–Textile Products and India–Quantitative Restrictions) reached diametrically opposing conclusions regarding the new WTO rules in these areas. The Turkey–Textiles panel, dealing with provisions of an EU–Turkey customs union, followed earlier GATT precedent and found that jurisdiction over the legality of regional trading agreements generally was the responsibility of the Committee on Regional Trade Agreements. The India–Quantitative Restrictions panel adopted a more expansive view of the DSU's jurisdiction in relation to both regional trading agreements and balance-of-payments restrictions, in effect taking a position against earlier GATT panel rulings.[45] The issues were appealed in two proceedings before the Appellate Body.

In both decisions, the AB boldly upheld the expansive views of the India–Quantitative Restrictions panel. In the Turkey–Textiles appeal, it ruled that "the competence of the panel to review all aspects of balance-of-payments restrictions should be determined in the light of Article XXIII of the GATT, as elaborated and applied by the DSU." The AB added, "If panels refrained from reviewing the justification of the balance-of-payments restrictions, they would diminish the explicit procedural rights of members under Article XXIII. . . ." In a separate ruling on India–Quantitative Restrictions, the AB made clear that the logic of this decision also applied to a panel's competence and authority to rule on the overall consistency of regional trading agreements with Article XXIV.[46]

In a review and critique of the AB ruling in these cases, Frieder Roessler, head of the GATT Legal Affairs Division from 1989 to 1995, argued that in both instances—balance-of-payments and regional trading arrangements—it was inappropriate to settle the issues through judgments for or against individual members. As Roessler explained, "Since each regional trade agreement affects the overall trade policy of members, the consistency of that policy cannot be appropriately addressed in disputes between individual members." Further, he argued,

> A panel that determines the overall consistency of balance-of-payments or regional trade agreements thus passes a judgment on an entire trade regime. . . . Since there are no agreed standards for determining the adequacy of monetary reserves and the scope of trade integration required by Article XXIV has deliberately been left undetermined, the panel must pass its judgment without having received any prior normative guidance from the WTO membership and therefore engage essentially in a legislative or political task.[47]

Roessler concluded, "Just as modern states, the WTO must ensure that its judicial organs exercise their powers with due regard to the jurisdiction assigned to the other parts of its institutional structure. . . . This ruling has shifted decision-making authority from the political to the judicial organs of the WTO, and consequently changed the negotiated institutional balance in the WTO."[48] He went on to argue that, despite the ruling, in the future, "WTO panels should respect the competence and discretionary powers of the political bodies established under the WTO." According to Roessler, "If the legal status of a regional trade agreement or a balance-of-payments restriction has been determined by the competent WTO body, panels should not reverse that determination; if the competent WTO body has not yet made its determination, panels should not step in and preempt that determination."[49] It remains to be seen whether panels and the Appellate Body will take this advice.

Each of these examples presents complex issues over which legal experts and trade negotiators can legitimately disagree. In these and other areas, however, the WTO dispute settlement system is operating at the frontier between policymaking and mere judicial interpretation. A pattern of stepping across that boundary in creating "new" law will almost certainly threaten the legitimacy of the WTO.

Regulatory Issues

At a June 2000 forum on the WTO in the new millennium, Gary Horlick, a leading U.S. trade lawyer, opined, "The big cases, the truly interesting cases in services, intellectual property, food safety . . . [i.e., major regulatory areas] have not yet surfaced."[50] Horlick's statement points to an important concern—that is, whether in plunging deeply into the economic and social complexities inherent in national regulatory systems, the WTO has overreached. Given the widely divergent philosophies of these systems and the lack of clarity in the underlying WTO rules, the DSU may not be able to deliver credible analyses and decisions. For this study, some of the difficult questions relating to telecommunications and food safety will serve as illustrations.

Telecommunications. The Agreement on Basic Telecommunications Services took effect in February 1998, with the signatures of seventy WTO members. By virtue of the agreement, these WTO members have agreed to abolish existing public monopolies over time and to create rules for competition not only between foreign firms and monopolies, but also between foreign firms and large incumbent private firms. In effect, with the telecommunications agreement and accompanying "Reference Paper," the WTO has created a competition policy regime, at least for telecommunications.[51]

In the Reference Paper, three examples of anticompetitive behavior that will invoke government intervention are listed: anticompetitive cross-subsidization, anticompetitive use of information, and anticompetitive withholding of (technical) information. These seem rather straightforward at first, but with at least one prohibition—anticompetitive cross-subsidization—the situation is quite complicated and potentially harmful to the DSU.

Commenting on "anticompetitive cross-subsidization," European trade lawyer Marco Bronckers observed, "This somewhat mysterious, pejorative term refers to a practice, which, in actual fact, is common to almost all companies."[52] All companies that sell multiple products or services cross-subsidize at one time or another. For instance, book and music sellers produce thousands of products each year, aware that only a few will be clear profit centers and that these large profits will cover the losses incurred by other releases.

Potential problems arise, however, when monopolies or dominant firms in a sector undertake to cross-subsidize various products or services. A monopolist could use profits from a monopoly product or service to cross-subsidize a product or service that is produced under competition, forcing competitors to charge prices that will produce a profit. This could violate competition laws if the monopolist, through intent or result, squeezes competitors out of the market to increase prices. But current economic theory holds that this behavior is rare and that government intervention itself can rapidly produce anticompetitive, welfare-reducing effects. From the standpoint of economic efficiency, the line of intervention is difficult to draw.

Furthermore, to make a credible case in WTO disputes, governments must become deeply knowledgeable about the company's costs and prices; in addition, they must rely on comparable accounting systems when judging between the allegedly offending company and its competitors. Governments must also have access to information that companies consider highly sensitive and confidential. Given the extremely short time frames in which WTO panels must work and the relative lack of discovery power to uncover the facts of a case, the WTO dispute settlement process would be hopelessly handicapped in handling such complaints.

Even for national regulatory systems, this is a difficult area. This has been amply demonstrated by the EU, which for ten years has been struggling to reach a consensus on a definition of what constitutes an anticompetitive cross-subsidy. Recently, the European Commission was sued for failure to act against the cross-subsidization practices of the Deutsche Post, Germany's communications monopoly. According to press reports, the reason the commission failed to act was that its legal staff had strenuously argued that there was no way to distinguish lawful from unlawful cross-subsidization within a company—even if the company is a monopoly.

After recounting this experience in light of the new WTO prohibitions, Bronckers stated,

> When reading the WTO norm, one remains blissfully unaware of these controversies and difficulties. Members have said no more than that they would act against "anticompetitive cross-subsidization" by powerful telecommunications companies. . . . [W]hat if a country decides to litigate in the WTO? The outcome of such a dispute by a WTO tribunal can only be a complete surprise, not least for the companies concerned. This is regrettable, in my opinion, and damaging to the credibility of the WTO.[53]

Genetically Modified Organisms, Food Safety, and the "Precautionary Principle." Sanitary and Phytosanitary (SPS) rules are measures that protect human, animal, or plant life within a WTO member's territory from diseases, pests, and disease-carrying organisms, as well as additives, contaminants, and toxins in foods and beverages. SPS measures were included in the original GATT agreement as part of more general rules regarding domestic standards (the Agreement on Technical Barriers to Trade), but only in the Uruguay Round were SPS rules elevated to a separate agreement: the WTO Agreement on the Application of Sanitary and Phytosanitary Measures. The rules and obligations promulgated as part of the new agreement became subject to the new dispute settlement system.

Broadly speaking, the most important provisions of the SPS agreement recognize the right of WTO members to adopt measures that result in any given level of health protection for their citizens, but also require that these measures be founded on scientific evidence and applied only to the extent necessary to achieve public health goals. Another SPS provision states that if scientific evidence is "insufficient," a member may adopt protective measures "on a provisional basis" while seeking additional information about potential hazards. This is a variation of the so-called "precautionary principle," which allows nations to take action even though scientific risk has not been proven. Trade-related sections of the SPS rules forbid application of measures in a discriminatory fashion or in a manner that constitutes a disguised restriction on trade. International standards, such as those developed in the Codex

Alimentarius (food code), are recognized, and nations that want to legislate higher standards than these internationally recognized standards must provide scientific evidence to back their decision.[54]

The disputes emerging from the new SPS standards and the revolutionary advances in genetics and biotechnology have involved dauntingly complex issues. One dispute, the beef hormones case, illustrates many of the points of uncertainty and disagreement. The initial clash, which pitted the United States and Canada against the EU, began in the 1980s after the Europeans instituted a ban on the sale, distribution, and importation of hormone-treated beef. An actual case was initiated in 1996—after the new dispute settlement system eliminated the possibility of blocking action by either party, and the United States renewed an earlier request for a dispute settlement panel.

The United States, later joined by Canada, argued that the EU ban violated the SPS agreement in several ways: the ban was invoked without sufficient scientific evidence; it constituted a disguised restriction on international trade; it was not based on any international standard; and it provided a higher level of protection than required by existing international standards. The central scientific case presented by the United States and Canada pointed out that numerous studies had found no danger from the levels of hormones in the animals and that the residues were within levels that complied with existing international standards.

In its response, the EU challenged the conclusiveness of the scientific reports and argued that none had established beyond reasonable doubt that the use of these hormones was safe for human health. The EU noted that all of the existing studies examined the hormones in isolation and therefore could not weigh synergistic effects; it pointed out that no studies could determine long-term effects at this time. A second line of defense dealt with the issue of "appropriate level of protection." The EU argued that a judgment about the level of protection was a societal value judgment and that this sovereign right was acknowledged in the SPS agreement.

Both the panel and the Appellate Body offered significant and precedent-setting findings. In its 1997 report, the panel generally agreed with many of the arguments advanced by the United States and Canada. It held that the EU ban was not based upon an adequate risk assessment supported by scientific evidence; that the ban was not based upon existing international standards; that the EU had failed to present scientific evidence for the higher level of protection embodied in the outright ban; and that the ban was arbitrary and unjustifiably at variance with levels of protection provided by other EU measures relating to these same hormones (e.g., allowing the hormones to be added to pork feed).

In its 1998 decision, the Appellate Body agreed with many aspects of the panel's findings but disagreed with the legal reasoning in several important respects, which in the future would favor defendants such as the EU. First, it reversed the burden of proof for demonstrating that deviation from international standards was scientifically based. Henceforth, the complaining party would have the responsibility of showing that the defendant's alternate system was not based on adequate science. While the results did not change the adverse conclusion for the EU in this instance, defendants would have an easier time with this issue in future cases. Of equal importance, the Appellate Body signaled that even a few minority opinions among scientists must be given due weight in determining risk; it also agreed with the EU that social and cultural factors could be included in risk determination. In general, the Appellate Body exhibited greater deference to a WTO member's own legal and administrative procedures when determining risk.[55]

Finally, the panel had introduced a distinction between risk assessment and risk management. Risk assessment was meant to encompass only the purely technical scientific analysis that would underpin regulatory actions. Risk management added elements of economic, social, or value judgments that would also be considered before making a final regulatory decision. The Appellate Body rejected this clear definitional division, but then reintroduced it using opaque language that seemed aimed at achieving the same result without provoking accusations that the AB was legislating analytic criteria independent of the language of the underlying text. The AB stated, "It is essential to bear in mind that the risk that is to be evaluated in a risk assessment . . . is not only risk ascertainable in the science laboratory . . . but also risk ascertainable in human societies as they actually exist; in other words, the actual potential for adverse effect on human health in the real world where people live and work and die."

This ringing political statement provides no guidance to nations or subsequent panels as to how to determine acceptable risk beyond the bounds of a scientific assessment.[56] As two critics of the AB's reasoning have written,

> While this reference helps to make this ruling politically acceptable, it constitutes an unnecessarily broad interpretation of risk assessment. . . . It will be extremely difficult to replace the "scientific" route chosen by the SPS with a new approach taking socioeconomic considerations into account without opening Pandora's box, and allowing WTO members to introduce protectionist measures.[57]

In this area, the dispute settlement system is being asked to deal with extraordinarily complex technical as well as political and social issues with little guidance from the textual results of negotiations. Even strong supporters of the system worry that these sanitary and phytosanitary disputes represent "a bridge too far." This is true not only because of such papered-over decisions as the one just described, but also because, given the deep feelings about genetically modified organisms (GMOs) in many countries, nations may well defy rulings that go against them indefinitely, as illustrated by the current stalemate over the beef hormones case.

Just before the Appellate Body was to demand a settlement of the beef hormones case, the EU announced that it had commissioned seventeen studies to review the risks related to the six hormones, separately and in combination. These studies were to be completed sometime in the year 2001. In retaliation, the United States imposed annual sanctions amounting to $117 million worth of EU imports, ranging from beef and pork to cheese and foie gras. At this writing, a standoff on this case continues.[58]

As the beef hormones case illustrates, in the area of food and biological standards, many questions remain unanswered. The WTO dispute settlement process is only beginning to confront these issues. One of the most important questions relates to the use—and abuse—of the "precautionary principle."[59]

No agreed-upon definition of this principle exists.[60] To some, it means that WTO members should be encouraged to use caution and prudence when reviewing new technologies—in this case new food compounds or additives. To others, however, it means banning all actions—the addition of GMOs to the food chain of animals or humans—until proponents can demonstrate conclusively that the action is free of all risk. Noting this state of confusion, one study concluded that the precautionary principle is a "culturally framed concept . . . muddled in policy advice and subject to the whims of international diplomacy and the unpredictable public mood over the true cost of sustainable living."[61]

At present, the SPS language adopts a portion of the precautionary principle (Article 5.7) and allows bans or restrictions "on a provisional basis" with the clear implication that such actions are to be temporary, pending a fairly quick emergence of new scientific evidence. As the actions and views of the EU in the beef hormones case make clear, however, some countries view "provisional" as a much longer-term circumstance.

A more troubling question is how the relationship between trade and the precautionary principle will be resolved. In the beef hormones case, the AB waded into the morass of conflicting international legal opinion about the status of the precautionary principle in international law, but it was faced with a deeply conflicted and divided international legal community on the subject.

Those who argue that the precautionary principle is now enshrined as a binding principle of international law adopt the increasingly popular tactic of pointing to general principles (soft law) enumerated in various environmental agreements. James Cameron, cofounder and former director of the London-based Foundation for International Environmental Law and Development, and Karen Campbell, staff counsel at West Coast Environmental Law, write that the precautionary principle is "arguably now an established principle of international environmental law. Its most universal statement is in Principle 15 of the Rio Declaration." They go on to argue that WTO panels should respect domestic laws based on the precautionary principle, such as the EU hormones ban, because "to not do so would be contrary to public international law."[62] While the AB in this case declined to accept this connection between environmental agreements, it also signaled that it was willing to consider such reasoning on a case-by-case basis.

The issue is highly contentious among WTO members, with developing countries deeply suspicious that it will be used to deny them access to the markets of the developed world. Writing in January 2000, a member of the Argentinean Foreign Service warned in the *Journal of Commerce* that "the EU may try to smuggle the so-called precautionary principle into the [Millennium Round] negotiations." He warned of a great danger that the principle would be used against developing countries:

> During the next agricultural negotiations, developing countries will seek to obtain better market access for their products. They will seek the opportunity to compete fairly in the market place, not by subsidizing exports, but by lowering prices and improving quality. If the precautionary principle is smuggled into those negotiations, it will be traded against those expectations. And this should be prevented.[63]

Clearly, WTO members are deeply divided on this issue and, as the examples presented in this chapter illustrate, questions surrounding the invocation of the precautionary principle should not be left to judicial interpretation but rather should be thrashed out in negotiations.[64] The balance of this chapter is devoted to a discussion of "soft law" and customary law, and their potential impact on WTO dispute settlement cases.

Soft Law, Customary Law, and Progressive Interpretation

This section briefly describes the issues and controversies surrounding soft and customary law and how they relate to developing trends in—and outside pressures on—case law in the DSU. Soft law originates with declarations, preambles, frameworks, and statements of principles rather than with formal treaties. Soft law often emanates from declarations in the UN General Assembly, or UN agreements in areas such as the environment or human rights, or even from international conferences. These documents are "affirmative of good intentions" rather than commitments to act in a particular way. The hope of those who propose them is that they can be "eased into practice and then hardened, either in subsequent treaties or by acceptance as customary international law."[65]

Customary international law consists of obligations that are established through the general practices of states, that is, "what is habitually done by states out of a sense of legal obligation."[66] Customary law—"the law of nations"—developed in the eighteenth century from practices established over a long period of time relating to matters such as rules of the sea, seizure of contraband, and piracy. In the last two decades, the concept has been used, amid great controversy, to attempt to establish wide-ranging international legal norms in areas such as the environment, human rights, women's rights, and racial and sexual discrimination.

In invoking the original eighteenth-century doctrine of the law of nations, courts look to the actual cases for evidence of actual practice. In contemporary practice, what nations say—that is, declarations at conferences or signatures on nonbinding agreements—is given equal weight, despite the vehement protests of some legal theorists. Jeremy Rabkin, a critic of the contemporary usage of customary law, has described the process as follows:

> [Customary law] is not the product of court rulings, but of international conferences. Abstract pronouncements are enough. At that, they need not even be authoritative pronouncements of supreme government authorities. Words spoken by diplomats at conferences are given much weight, and then the reconfiguring of those words by commentators is supposed to give more weight, and the repetition of the words by yet other commentators is thought to lend still more weight to contentions about the law. Soon there is a towering edifice of words, which is then treated as a secure marker of "customary international law."[67]

On substantive grounds, the arguments of those who oppose incorporating customary international law into U.S. law are similar to the arguments raised against alleged "lawmaking" by WTO dispute settlement bodies. Philip Trimble of the UCLA Law School, in a self-styled "revisionist" view of international customary law, states:

> The story of customary international law…does not fit the American political tradition. . . . The American eighteenth-century tradition exalting limited and responsive representative government lives on in today's rhetoric and political philosophy. . . . It is one thing to delegate authority to Congress and the President, checked and balanced by each other, and elected by different groups within the political constituency. But if custom-

ary international law can be made by practice wholly outside the United States, it has no basis in popular sovereignty at all. Many foreign governments are not responsive to their own people, let alone to the American people.[68]

In a recent analysis, Paul Stephan of the University of Virginia Law School has also discussed the implications of the penetration of customary international law into the U.S. legal system. He first distinguishes customary international law from the "new" international law that originates in the negotiation and interpretation of international agreements and treaties. The new international law poses questions for national democracies: it strengthens the hand of the executive and the power of bureaucracies, while increasing the ability of concentrated interest groups to get their way. But enactment requires democratic procedures and mechanisms; Congress must pass the agreements and can force amendments.

With customary international law, however, the encroachment on national democratic practices and institutions is potentially much greater. As Stephan explains,

> The uncritical incorporation of customary international law in U.S. law encroaches on democracy by taking off the table choices that democratic institutions, whether federal, state or local, wish to make. To be sure, common law adjudication generally poses issues for a democracy, because the power to make law vests in the judiciary. . . . But customary international law exacerbates this problem to the extent it involves a displacement of the common law process. It is one thing for courts, surveying precedent and relying on a variety of substantive and process preferences, to choose a rule that governs our conduct. It is another for courts to take over a prefabricated system of rules and norms, constructed by a loose alliance of like-minded academics and international law specialists through a form of advocacy that involves no democratic checks.[69]

The new theories of customary law were endorsed in 1987 by the *Restatement of the Law (Third): Foreign Relations Law of the United States,* which is the most highly regarded nonofficial statement and survey of U.S. law on foreign relations. Still, vigorous dissent within the U.S. legal community over these issues continues. This led John Jackson, in his authoritative treatment of the world trading system, to conclude, "Unfortunately, customary international law norms are quite often ambiguous and controversial. On many propositions of customary international law, scholars and practitioners disagree not only about their meaning but even about their existence. The traditional doctrines of establishing a norm of customary international law leave a great deal of room for such controversy."[70]

How does the controversy over customary international law affect the DSU and rulings by the panels and Appellate Body of the WTO? Recent rulings appear to bow in the direction of accepting expansive and "dynamic" interpretations of WTO law, along with the consequences of placing WTO law within the overall context of regular norms of international law, including customary international law.

In its very first ruling, the AB placed the WTO dispute settlement system firmly within the confines of general international public law. This meant that it incorporated into the DSU the canons of treaty interpretation as set forth in the *Vienna Convention on the Law on Treaties*, the standard guide and set of rules for interpreting international treaties—including, the ruling stated, "the customary rules of interpretation of public international law."[71] It left for future case determination the complexities of meshing WTO rules with other international legal regimes—particularly the growing body of environmental agreements, declarations, and preambles to agreements.

In the shrimp/turtle case, the AB began serious work toward melding WTO law with more general international legal norms and treaties. In deciding how to deal with the exceptions allowed in Article XX, the AB adopted a dynamic interpretation of the article, arguing that it must look at the text in light of "contemporary concerns of the community of nations about the protection and conservation of the environment."[72] Among the sources it cited as a guide in its decision (in addition to several multilateral environmental treaties) was the soft law embodied in Principle 12 of the Rio Declaration.[73]

In addition, the AB expanded the traditional interpretation of "renewable resources" in Article XX to include biological as well as mineral resources. It did so by elevating the importance of the objective of "sustainable development" in the preamble to the agreement that established the WTO. The AB stated that the preamble would be used to give "color, texture and shading to the rights and obligations of members under the WTO Agreements," and further defended its new definition of renewable resources as a response to the "recent acknowledgement by the international community of the importance of concerted bilateral and multilateral action to protect living natural resources."[74]

Critics argued that, whatever the high-mindedness of the goals, the high-handedness of the judicial interpretation in this case was disturbing. As one close observer of the history of the dispute stated,

> Principles expressed in preambles are general legal commitments rather than specific legal obligations of states. . . . This objective [sustainable development] is certainly recognized and supported by WTO members. The manner in which it is translated into rights and obligations [however] can fundamentally change the character of the exceptions provision [Article XX on exceptions to free trade] of the WTO. Indeed, a number of WTO members believe that it rendered inoperable one of the principal paragraphs of the exceptions provisions.[75]

Environmental groups have been quick to pick up on the potential expansion of environmental exceptions in the WTO through public international law—and the potential that the AB in the future will, through judicial interpretation, endorse that expansion. Thus, briefs and papers submitted by the World Wildlife Fund, the Center for International Environmental Law (CIEL), and the Sierra Club press the argument of the increasingly binding force of customary law. The World Wildlife Fund's *amicus* brief in the shrimp/turtle case argued,

> A general obligation arises from customary international law, and can be derived from treaty law, that requires states to supervise and control activities within their jurisdiction that undermine the conservation status of endangered species. These obligations are derived from, among others, the 1972 Stockholm Declaration on the Human Environment, the Convention on Biological Diversity, the Bonn Convention on Highly Migratory Species, the Convention on International Trade in Endangered Species of Wild Fauna and Flora (CITES), and UN General Assembly resolutions.[76]

The brief went on to provide more detail about the ties between declarations, nonbinding commitments, and the shrimp/turtle case:

> Several instruments dealing with the conservation of sea turtles are not in themselves binding but engage good faith obligations to act consistently with the clearly expressed political commitment or lend content to the more general rules established above or evidence a pattern of state prac-

tice. . . . The World Conservation Union lists all seven species of turtles. . . . [T]he listing of species does not create obligations directly, there being no Treaty, but its expertise and wide membership provide strong evidence of custom when a clear decision is taken by the Union.[77]

What is interesting about this list is the intermixing treaty obligations (some have potential trade sanctions and some do not) with hortatory declarations and resolutions, giving them equal status as binding upon WTO member states. A number of legal scholars strongly support the legal theories of interest groups such as the World Wildlife Fund. These scholars espouse a vision of using the WTO dispute settlement process, in combination with soft and customary law and "progressive" interpretations of the basic underlying WTO legal texts, to expand the WTO substantive mandate to encompass many of the goals of civil society.[78]

Differences among these scholars exist, of course. Nevertheless, Robert Howse of the University of Michigan has effectively illustrated the major common elements of their "advanced" vision. In a discussion of the shrimp/turtle decision, Howse strongly applauds the AB "decision to provide [an] interpretation of the treaty language [in this case, the term 'exhaustible natural resources'] based on *evolving* international law, rather than the purported original understanding of the negotiators of the 1947 GATT."[79] He defends an expansive interpretation because "retrospective, originalist interpretation almost inevitably privileges the supposed intentions and expectations of a fairly narrow 'interpretative' community, that of the treaty negotiators, over the broader community [affected] by interpretative decisions, the community implicated in the notion of democratic and social legitimacy."[80] (For further discussion of the issue of democratic legitimacy, see chapter 6 of this study.)

Howse forthrightly defends the legitimacy of a judicial legislative function in the WTO in light of what he asserts is a "democratic defect in rule-*creation.*" As Howse explains,

> Given this democratic defect in rule-*creation,* social legitimacy in rule interpretation may exist as *democratic* social legitimacy, where the exercise of the judicial power properly handles a conflict of values held by diverse stockholders. . . . WTO interpretation . . . reflects the emerging law of the "other" agenda of globalization. . . . This may include international environmental law, international labor law, and international human rights law, as it is

developing in light of an "equity-oriented" agenda . . . focused . . . on equity and distributive questions in the context of a globally integrated economic system with immense inequalities in the profit-making capacities of firms and the earning capacities of households.[81] [*Whew!*]

With Howse, we have come a long way, but in good cognitivist terms, ideas have consequences. Although Howse's own brand of utopianism may never reach fruition, his views demonstrate the new milieu in which WTO decisions are made. This chapter stands as a warning that Jeremy Rabkin's argument—namely, that the WTO was different from other international organizations and presented fewer sovereignty issues—is under attack. The WTO may well evolve in ways that Rabkin did not foresee—and would oppose. Dispute settlement bodies do not operate in a vacuum. Despite their intentions to uphold the letter as well as the spirit of WTO law, they show signs of bending to prevailing winds, which, even before the events in Seattle, were moving toward expanding the "linkage policies" that Rabkin decries.[82]

5

Critiques from the Right and Left

Mounting pressures to reform the WTO dispute settlement process emanate from across the political spectrum. On the right, international trade lawyers and law professors argue for reforming the system by creating a private right of action and standing for corporations in DSU proceedings. Other pressures for reform arise from the growing power and influence of a "parallel universe" on the left—a universe shaped by major changes in the United Nations during the past fifteen years and the extraordinary emergence of NGOs, particularly within the environmental movement, as a force to be recognized. Until quite recently, analyses of the international trading system and the workings of GATT and then the WTO have ignored these outside phenomena. Today, the ideas and politics espoused in UN assemblies, conferences, and declarations—along with the passionately held ideology and politics of NGOs—are having a profound impact on WTO policies and proceedings.

Critique from the Right:
Trade Lawyers and Trade Professors

One significant force for changing the government-to-government nature of the WTO originates in the private sector—specifically, among lawyers with large practices dealing with trade remedies for unfair trade practices that affect corporations. Much of the pressure for a greater direct role for private corporations in the WTO is in line with a model for the WTO envisioned by Richard Shell, professor of legal studies and management at the University of Pennsylvania's Wharton School.

70

Under Shell's Efficient Market Model, corporations, operating under a neoliberal, free market banner, would ultimately succeed in achieving an independent role, separate from government, within the WTO.[1]

For purposes of this study, the recent writings of two prominent U.S. trade lawyers, Alan Wolff and John Ragosta, will illustrate the arguments for introducing more formal juridical procedures and, in the case of Ragosta, the right of standing for private commercial parties in the WTO.[2] Writing separately and together, Wolff and Ragosta have mounted a detailed attack on the alleged inadequacies of the current DSU.[3]

Their starting premise is that despite the fact that the new DSU is viewed as an "enormous success," there is serious reason to believe that "this 'judicial' system has grown too far, too fast, and that the judicial body [the Appellate Body] lacks the necessary bones, muscles, and sinews to make a binding system operate fairly and well."[4] Like other commentators, Wolff and Ragosta point at the outset to the problems that stem from the gaping democratic deficit in the WTO. This deficit flows from the inherent difference between domestic and international law: "In domestic disputes, it is common to bind parties to the court's ruling. . . . After all, the individuals are not 'sovereign' and, in any case, have no fundamental complaint about the exercise of judicial authority. They elect representatives who make the law, and they participate in the political institutions that appoint and remove the judges. Ultimately, if a court issues a decision that so offends the accepted understanding of obligations, democratic remedies exist. The same is not true in the WTO."[5]

Their first reform preference would be the institution of some form of "democratic" remedy such as a mechanism that enables a substantial minority of WTO members to block a dispute settlement decision. Absent such reforms, they argue, "*At a minimum,* it is essential that procedures be adopted permitting the semblance of due process."[6] The procedures and reforms they advocate include open hearings; publication of all relevant documents; the right to retain private attorneys and/or submit *amicus* briefs; and professional and standing membership for the panels and AB.[7]

Ultimately, however, Ragosta aligns himself with a few other practicing trade lawyers and legal scholars in favoring a private right of action and standing for "real parties in interest."[8] In a journal article published in 2000, Ragosta points out that the new DSU is widely perceived as the "supreme court" or "world court" of trade.[9] Accepting this perception of the new DSU, he argues that the WTO must live up to the implications of the new judicial system and discard the most contradictory elements of the older diplomatic system. Ragosta explains, "Some object that the system is only 'quasi-judicial'. . . . [T]his is like being 'quasi-pregnant'" and can result "in an odd, and not necessarily good, mix of judicial and non-judicial elements."[10] He concludes, "[DSU] decisions are binding in a very real sense, have precedential weight, and significantly affect U.S. industry's rights. Yet, the system lacks essential procedural protections. For the WTO to function effectively as a 'world court' for trade, it must provide an opportunity for the real party in interest to participate effectively."[11]

Supporting Ragosta's view of the DSU are legal scholars who favor the development of an "international common law" and scholars who argue that the DSU represents the triumph of a legalistic, rules-based system that will foster greater predictability and stability in the trading system. Glen Schleyer, another proponent of direct private participation, has stated, "The legalist . . . takes the view that the goal of trade dispute resolution should be to preserve the integrity of the applicable rules. The benefit seen in this approach is that it encourages predictability and stability in international trade practices."[12]

Proponents cite two reasons, one economic and one political, that granting standing to private parties will enhance the WTO dispute settlement system. As University of Vienna law professor Martin Lukas explains, the economic rationale posits that individuals and companies, rather than governments, "analyze the comparative advantages of the production of goods and services in various countries and thereby decide how to most efficiently use the comparative advantages. . . . [P]rivate parties must take into account all relevant economic variables, including trade barriers." Faced with trade barriers in their daily business, companies and individuals are better equipped to discern and attack unfair trade practices directly. According to Lukas, "If the role of individuals and companies as the major economic actors in international trade is recognized, the denial of their access to the mechanism which enforces international trade is contradictory."[13]

Advocates of a direct role for corporations argue that allowing private actors to substitute for governments will "depoliticize" the dispute settlement process. If private parties have sole responsibility for a case, governments will no longer be able to introduce extraneous "political" factors in deciding whether to bring an action, how the action will be prosecuted, and how to respond to a favorable or adverse decision. In response to critics who argue that there might be instances where a government would intervene in a case "in the nation's best interests" but against those of the commercial interest that had a grievance, Ragosta states, "[This argument] demonstrates the continued confusion between the old diplomatic model, which sought primarily to encourage settlement, and the adjudicatory model . . . which depends for its legitimacy upon a correct 'legal' ruling in each case." Such extra-legal government intervention would be "less problematic in a nonbinding, nonprecedential diplomatic model, [but] it is fundamentally inconsistent with legal notions of judicial interpretations."[14]

This study will argue that there is no confusion between the diplomatic and the legal approaches to WTO dispute settlement. Accepting the validity of the criticisms of the hybrid system that Ragosta, Wolff, and others have advanced—gaps and contradictions in underlying texts, lack of consensus on fundamental issues among WTO members, and questions of democratic legitimacy—leads ineluctably back toward the introduction of even *more* diplomatic solutions as legitimizing instruments and practical safety valves; otherwise, the WTO is likely to lose fundamental authority over international trade and investment rules.

Public-Private Partnerships: The Political Economy of U.S. WTO Litigation. Current scholarship has shed new light on the dynamics of international trade litigation, specifically on the symbiotic relationship between U.S. corporations (and trade lawyers) and the Office of the U.S. Trade Representative (USTR). Because this scholarship has important implications for the recommendations advanced in this study, a brief review of the most important analytic insights is in order.

In a recent paper, Gregory Shaffer of the University of Wisconsin Law School describes the relationship as a "public-private partnership" in which the USTR and the corporations "pursue varying, but complementary goals." Shaffer also analyzes the relationship between corporations and trade officials in the EU, but here the discussion will be limited to his analysis and conclusions regarding the United States.[15]

First, Shaffer explains, firms need to "convince the United States Trade Representatives . . . that they have a strong legal case . . . [because] the USTR does not wish to impair its political credibility by bringing and then losing a weak legal case."[16] Corporations utilize several strategies to obtain USTR support, including coordinating their activities through trade associations and lobbying Congress. As Schaffer writes, "WTO cases demand significant time, expenses, and effort. The USTR is unlikely to expend scarce resources and limited political capital . . . when a claim does not have broad industry support. Where the USTR agrees to form an ad hoc public-private partnership on a specific trade matter, it wants a strong partner. Large and well-organized commercial interests are, as a result, more successful in working the process."[17]

An elaborate and sophisticated lobbying operation is another essential element of a successful campaign to move a case forward. According to Shaffer, "Firms press their case to local congressional representatives and those on the international trade subcommittees. . . . Local congressional representatives, in turn, also engage members of these committees. Whenever a USTR official visits Congress, congressional representatives raise specific trade matters—whether about meat, steel rods, or rawhide leather—however unrelated the meeting's agenda."[18]

Once a decision is made to go forward with a case, collaboration between the USTR and the corporation or trade association intensifies because, in reality, the USTR depends heavily on the industry to construct the details of the legal case before the WTO. Shaffer points out that information exchange between the USTR and industry is one of the "central tools" in the partnership to eliminate trade barriers through WTO litigation:

> If the USTR . . . decides to file a complaint before the WTO Dispute Settlement Body, the exchange of information and general coordination between the USTR and the affected industry intensifies. . . . Given the number of complicated cases that the USTR must litigate, the tight deadlines, and the legalization of the proceedings, the USTR increasingly relies on industry for the supply of facts as well as the development of legal arguments. . . . [T]he USTR often requires industry to submit convincing factual and legal memoranda as a prerequisite to its filing of a WTO complaint.[19]

All of this has produced a bonanza for private trade lawyers. As Shaffer writes, "Because of the demands of the WTO process, industries typically hire Washington trade lawyers to assist them. . . . In many cases, private counsel entirely writes the first draft of the [government] brief's factual section. . . . Counsel provides sample briefs or memoranda from which representatives at the USTR can cut and paste, as well as mark-ups of the USTR drafts."[20]

For this study, two important conclusions flow from the process. The first relates to the consequences, intended and unintended, of the heightened "legalization" of the WTO dispute settlement process. Shaffer accurately describes the tradeoff for the United States in reining in its former unilateralism: legal power has replaced raw political power. As Shaffer explains, "Yet as the World Trade Organization has constrained U.S. power politics, it has triggered greater exploitation by the United States of its comparative advantage in lawyering. The constraints on unilateral political pressures in this category of cases are offset by the expanding scope of obligations covered by WTO rules. . . ."[21]

As this study will emphasize, the overpowering strength and sophistication of the U.S. and EU legal resources create a painful dilemma for developing countries. They benefit from the fact that the new WTO dispute settlement system curbs U.S. unilateralism and levels the playing field with developed countries. At the same time, however, developing nations face a potentially daunting challenge from the tight public-private partnerships in the United States and EU—partnerships that have the potential to exploit and dominate the highly judicialized dispute settlement system and curtail the ability of developing countries to exercise their WTO rights.

The second important reality about the system is that even though the USTR works closely with industry, "firms are not 'clients' that can dictate USTR actions, and the USTR is not a gun for hire." Shaffer shows that U.S. government officials act as an independent force and exploit their position as the final arbiters regarding WTO litigation: "There are limits to this U.S. public-private cooperation, however, leading to tensions between government officials and firm representatives and their lawyers. The core of this tension is that the USTR ultimately represents the national interest, not the firm's interest. . . . While the governmental screening of direct private claims has become more porous, it still exists, safeguarding benefits that a more open trading system offers. . . . ."[22] In subsequent sections, this study contends that these empirical results should be supplemented with normative arguments in favor of governments' retaining the final authority over WTO litigation on grounds of democratic legitimacy.

A Public Choice Explanation. Although Shaffer does not make the connection, his account of the political economy of the new WTO litigation system can be interpreted from both a liberal intergovernmental and a public choice perspective. As predicted by two-level liberal intergovernmental theories, the USTR first bargains with interest groups (corporations and NGOs such as environmental or consumer groups, for example) at the domestic level to present a unified position in the WTO; then, in conjunction with relevant interest groups, trade officials argue the case before WTO panels and the Appellate Body. If the case is lost, the USTR must reopen bargaining at the domestic level to decide whether to accept the decision or accept retaliation by another WTO member. Throughout this process, the USTR must—independent of the desires of interest groups—factor in the larger national interest. This can entail weighing other trade priorities, as well as extraneous diplomatic, political, and even security issues.[23]

Although the system is still too new to evaluate developing trends and alliances fully, public choice theory would predict that a strong potential exists for U.S. trade officials (attempting to maximize their own political fortunes and power within the U.S. government and against foreign trade officials) to collaborate with corporations (rent-seeking in traditional private actor fashion) in an alliance that advances the goals of each party. Shaffer's description of the symbiosis between the public and private actors fits such a progression:

> The separate interests of the USTR and the private sector are reciprocal and overlap. The USTR depends on private sector lobbying in order to obtain support in Congress and the administration for adopting USTR policy goals and supporting USTR practical needs, from granting fast-track negotiating authority and the ratification of trade agreements, approving the accession of China to the WTO, to the allocation of budgetary funds.... In return, [the USTR] repays industry through its aggressive stance in defending industry interests, be it in multilateral or bilateral trade negotiations, WTO accession negotiations (as with China), or litigation before WTO dispute settlement panels. USTR also provides exporting industries with a voice in interagency debates so that their views are heard when the President balances multiple U.S. interests.[24]

A Parallel Universe on the Left: NGOs and International Organizations

During the past decade, a "quiet revolution" has unfolded among international organizations, as the role and influence of NGOs have grown more powerful, and accompanying new theories of governance have emerged.[25] To a surprising degree, the GATT/WTO system has remained remarkably isolated from these trends until quite recently. At the same time, most scholars of the international trading system have adhered to traditional patterns of analysis, that is, a diplomatic versus a rules-based judicial framework, developed versus developing country priorities, and multilateral versus regional approaches to trade liberalization.

But events outside the trading system—and scholarship that diverged from traditional analyses of GATT/WTO goals and operations—have insinuated themselves into debates about the future of the system. One important reason for this heightened interest and analysis is the fact that the WTO, with the new substantive mandates flowing from the Uruguay Round and the new binding DSU, has become one of the most powerful organizations in the international arena. Interest groups and proponents of new ideologies look increasingly to the WTO to promote their particular goals and interests through the coercive power of trade sanctions. Concomitantly, NGOs and "movement" groups are demanding a greater role in decision-making and judicial determinations, ardently pushing their claims through novel theories of "participatory" democracy at the international level.[26]

The sections that follow begin with a description of recent trends in the United Nations. This is where the "quiet revolution" is proceeding apace, changing the organization's mission, as well as the role of NGOs in the UN policy process. The arguments and demands of NGOs and environmental groups, which have exerted the strongest pressure for an increased presence in the WTO, will then be analyzed in greater detail.

The UN and the "Quiet Revolution." For much of the UN's history, the Security Council and, at times, the General Assembly were its most important organizations. Since the end of the Cold War in the late 1980s, however, the UN's focus has shifted to social and economic issues, and the role of the Economic and Social Council (ECOSOC) has expanded greatly.

The ECOSOC moved to center stage after the UN General Assembly mandated a series of nine conferences during the 1990s to produce a "global consensus on the priorities for a new development agenda for the 1990s and beyond."[27] The conference topics included education (Jomtien, 1990); children (New York, 1990); environment and development (Rio, 1992); human rights (Vienna, 1993); population and development (Cairo, 1994); social development (Copenhagen, 1995); women (Beijing, 1995); human settlements (Istanbul, 1996); and food (Rome, 1996). In each case, a parallel NGO forum provided opportunities for these organizations to network and publicize their particular agendas. More than 1,500 NGOs were represented at the Cairo forum, 800 at the Vienna conference, 2,100 at Beijing, and 2,400 at Rio.[28]

Conference planners and their NGO allies viewed these conferences as a continuum and an agenda for the future. The interdependent priorities of the conferences, according to one commentator, were "to stabilize the world's population; to change patterns of production and consumption; to enforce the equity principle through sociocultural changes; to make men and women 'radically equal' socially; to construct a new global ethic; and to move toward global democracy."[29] Each conference set long-term targets, with provision for five-year implementation reviews by special commissions and the General Assembly. As this process evolved in recent years, the agenda in each program area has expanded. The process has also become integral to the overall reform of UN operations that Secretary-General Kofi Annan initiated several years ago. Thus, recommendations to strengthen relevant UN agencies accompany each set of program proposals.[30]

Along for the Ride: NGOs. As the power and influence of the ECOSOC have grown, so too has the influence of NGOs. From the outset in the 1940s, Article 71 of the UN Charter provided for ECOSOC consultation with nongovernmental organizations, although clearly in an arms-length, hierarchical fashion—an "insistence that the status is peripheral to the state," in the phrase of one commentator.[31] Despite the opposition of many developing countries (including a number of authoritarian governments) during the past two decades, the status of NGOs vis-à-vis UN agencies has been gradually elevated in a process that was formally acknowledged in a 1996 ECOSOC review and subsequent resolution. Criteria for conference participation were steadily relaxed and many nonaccredited organizations were allowed to participate.

As they became an integral part of the 1990s conference process, NGOs were transformed from arms-length consultants to full participants in the development and implementation of UN policies and programs. In some cases, NGOs served as key technical and policy advisers to government delegations; in others, they participated directly as members of national delegations.[32] In addition, the various program areas developed formal caucuses—the Women's Caucus, Health Caucus, and Environmental Caucus, for example—which negotiated changes in documents directly with governments. At several conferences, the caucuses demanded and were granted the right to speak at committee and plenary sessions.[33]

These changes have been enthusiastically endorsed and promoted by UN Secretary-General Annan, who avows that NGOs are "indispensable partners, not only in development and relief operations, but also in public information and advocacy," and even as "implementing partners." In July 1997, Secretary-General Annan stated, "I see a United Nations keenly aware that if the global agenda is to be properly addressed, a partnership with civil society is not an option; it is a necessity."[34]

For this study, three observations about the evolution of the UN agenda and the new roles for NGOs are relevant. First, there is a decided north-south split among NGOs operating in the UN system. Several thousand NGOs have formal status, but only several hundred of them are from developing countries. Further, NGOs from the United States occupy an overwhelming majority of the developed country slots.[35]

Second, the politics of most NGOs is decidedly and proudly left-of-center to radical. Legal scholar Diane Otto of the University of Melbourne, a defender and proponent of the new "paradigm," notes that the real leadership is coming from NGOs associated with "new social movements." She describes these NGOs as "organizations that aim to represent values and aspirations associated with peoples rather than with states, including the promotion of human rights; gender and race equality; environmental protection; sustainable development; indigenous rights; nonviolent conflict resolution; participatory democracy; social diversity; and social and economic justice."[36]

Critics of the goals of the new social movements view the phenomenon quite differently. Arguing that the new left has "highjacked" the economic and social programs of the UN, journalist and global governance expert Marguerite Peeters writes, "The new model defies traditional values, national sovereignty, the market economy, and representative democracy. It demands radical changes in individual and social behavior and perceives culture as the last frontier of global change. The standard denounces as unethical the principles of modern industrial civilization, individualism, profit, and competition."[37]

The third observation relates directly to global governance and the advancing claims of NGOs to a place of equality in the UN—and ultimately in the WTO. Peeters and others have described the arguments behind the "quiet shift from traditional representative democracy to participatory democracy." As Peeters explains,

Participatory democracy comes about through a growing perception of NGOs as representative of civil society at the international level and through their expanding and more formalized role. . . . The UN concept of the *sovereign equality of all its members* seems now to apply informally to all partners: governments, the global civil society, business, and international organizations. NGOs have become more than mere consultants: they have grown into full-fledged partners in global policymaking—a revolutionary development that has consequently made the UN, governments, and the business community accountable to NGOs.[38]

One important difference in the histories and current power structures of the UN and the WTO will exert a major influence on the outcome of proposals for organizational changes. According to observers such as Peeters, the growing influence of NGOs in the UN can be traced at least in part to absent-mindedness on the part of UN member states, most of which considered the nine conferences of "marginal interest" and the resulting substantive proposals "irrelevant to national policymaking."[39] The situation in the WTO is very different. Because of the direct economic impact of WTO rules and dispute settlement judgments, governments pay close attention to events and trends in Geneva. In a detailed study of the WTO Committee on Trade and Environment, Gregory Shaffer explains,

State delegates perceive that words are more likely to have "consequences" in the World Trade Organization because of the economic impact of decisions rendered by its binding dispute settlement process. . . . As a representative from an African nation to the Committee on Trade and Environment confirmed, "Delegates are wary of the WTO. GATT is a binding contract. People are not as open and freewheeling as in other international fora. In the WTO, everything you say matters and can be used against you."[40]

In addition, governments have always been jealous of their individual roles and prerogatives, a reality that has become even more important as developing countries have assumed a larger role in recent years. Further, the WTO Secretariat, unlike the relatively uninhibited UN bureaucracy, has always been held on a tight leash and shows no signs of forming alliances with NGOs.

International Relations Theory and Trends at the UN. IR scholars have analyzed current trends in the UN from the perspective of both liberal and "postliberal" theories.[41] Postliberal theorist Diane Otto notes that strands of "republican liberalism" have contributed a partial underpinning for an imagined "transnational cosmopolitan democracy" that is being adumbrated by recent trends in the UN. As noted elsewhere in this study, liberalism holds that "the individual should be the normative unit in international law, and the international legitimacy and sovereignty of states are merely derivative of the confidence of their citizens."[42] That confidence is built upon the protection of "universal human rights" and the democratic processes that ensure full representation of all people.

In emphasizing a vision of international civil society as populated by individual actors, this strand of liberalism, which goes against some important trends in the UN, is suspicious of "group autonomy" and group power: "The primary identification of people arises from their cosmopolitan citizenship and not from national, cultural, class, gender, racial, or other associations."[43] The result is a restricted role for national and international NGOs. The priorities of republican liberals include actions against government encroachments on individual freedoms and claims against states that perpetuate human rights violations.

Postliberal paradigms, on the other hand, insist upon a more activist role for social movements—and for the NGOs that advance their causes. Postliberal theorists hold that individual identities are more complex than liberals perceive and include commonalities with foci such as indigenousness, race, gender, culture, class, and sexuality. Individuals thus identify with and support social movements that espouse these elements of the human perspective in which "identity can be simultaneously local and transnational."

Furthermore, postliberal political goals emphasize participatory democracy "in contradistinction to the reliance of republican liberalism on electoral formality and the highly artificial notion of consent through the ballot box."[44] In the view of some postliberals, this "cosmopolitan democracy" would include a grant of "compulsory jurisdiction" to the UN to resolve international disputes and redress human rights violations, as well as authority for the General Assembly to create international law. This vision would entail creating regional and international democratic assemblies, as well as strengthening local participatory democratic processes. Finally, pending these reforms, Otto holds that liberals and postliberals would "generally promote an expansive and emancipatory role for NGOs in the UN."[45]

UN Millennium Events. Before dismissing the political agenda Otto describes as left-wing utopianism, it is useful to review recent reports by UN bodies, as well as recommendations from the conferences convened as part of the UN Millennium Agenda. As part of his reform agenda, Secretary-General Annan proposed a Millennium Summit for the General Assembly and world leaders during the year 2000. That meeting took place in September 2000. Annan also convened a Millennium Forum for NGOs in May 2000, which was preceded by three planning conferences during 1999.[46]

The third of these preliminary conferences, held in Montreal in December 1999, dealt with issues of global governance and the role of NGOs. One proposal discussed at the meeting was for governments to include NGOs routinely in governmental delegations and, more generally, for governments to commit themselves to share power with civil society. Some organizations advocated the creation of a world parliament and a world environmental authority or court. In general, NGOs are divided on the proper organizational status for NGOs: some prefer a permanent, regular NGO forum, in effect making the Millennium Forum a permanent fixture in the UN; others favor the creation of a permanent people's assembly or a bicameral General Assembly, with one body for governments and one for NGOs.

Although the UN Secretariat has not yet endorsed specific proposals for a change in the UN constitution, the UN Development Program (UNDP) has endorsed the NGOs' demands for more equal status with governments. An independent body linked to the ECOSOC, the UNDP is authorized to promote a range of program objectives, from eliminating poverty to empowering women, managing environmental resources, and fostering democratic institutions. With 132 offices in 170 countries, the UNDP serves as the conduit and liaison between other UN bodies and individual nations.

Each year, the UNDP issues a development report that assesses UN programs and the progress of member states in meeting common UN goals. The 1999 *UNDP Human Development Report* took a direct stand in favor of a bicameral assembly, which would give NGOs equal status with governments in the future governing of the UN.[47]

Thus, while there are huge obstacles facing those who favor institutionalizing what Secretary-General Annan calls the "global associational revolution," the "quiet revolution" can no longer be considered far-fetched—and Otto's postliberal vision of the UN is more than academic fantasy.[48]

Clearly, debates about the role and operation of the WTO can no longer be conducted wholly within the insular world of trade policy and politics. Momentous changes in the reach and interconnectedness of international organizations have occurred during the past decade. As a result, trade policymakers and theorists must integrate academic theories and political actors from outside the traditional framework of analysis into debates on the future of the trading system. And they must do so with the clear stipulation that "integration" by no means assumes acceptance of either the underlying premises or the specific recommendations for changes in the WTO advanced by some environmentalists, postliberal activists, and international legal scholars.

The WTO and the Environmentalists' Challenge

The multiplicity of vociferous attacks against the WTO in Seattle in December 1999—from more than 30,000 activists representing environmental, labor, consumer, human rights, women's rights, religious, indigenous peoples, and anticapitalist groups—illustrated the widespread discontent with the international trading system among "social movement" groups. Among these groups, the environmentalists have mounted the most powerful and sustained lobbying effort for a radically changed WTO, including opening the institution to players beyond governments. The environmentalists, NGOs, and academics associated with the environmental movement have made the most explicit demands for institutional reforms and provided the most deeply thought-out arguments in favor of those reforms. This section describes the international environmental movement, its role in the evolving international environmental regime, and the arguments in favor of new relationships with the

WTO. The section concludes with the case against many, though by no means all, of the demands of environmental leaders and their academic allies regarding the WTO.

The New International Environmental Regime and the Role of NGOs. Environmental NGOs have been on the international stage for decades, but only in the late 1980s did they move briskly and effectively to assume new relationships with national governments and international organizations. Roots of the heightened international activism of the 1980s go back to the UN Conference on the Human Environment in Stockholm in 1972. The commitments made at that conference produced three substantive agreements on environmental issues: trade in endangered species; updated rules on whaling; and rules on ocean dumping. Equally important, conference participants decided to establish a UN agency for the environment: the UN Environmental Program (UNEP).[49]

In 1982, UNEP convened a conference to review progress during the decade since Stockholm.[50] The delegates recommended, and the UN subsequently endorsed, the creation of a World Commission on Environment and Development that was to be headed by Gro Harlem Brundtland, then Prime Minister of Norway. In 1987, the commission issued a widely publicized report, *Our Common Future*—known as the Brundtland Report—which popularized the philosophy of "sustainable development," which was defined as "[meeting] the needs of the present without compromising the ability of future generations to meet their own needs."[51] The concept, according to one commentator, "is based on a model of 'market failure,'" and "argues that the free market is reaching its ecological limit." In the future, the Brundtland Report argued, governments would have to act to conserve "finite" resources through measures such as restricting population growth; imposing limits on consumption by taxing usage of the "international commons" (fisheries, seabed mining, transportation); and taxing various aspects of international trade.[52]

Although the Brundtland Commission was important symbolically, the UN Conference on Environment and Development (UNCED) in Rio in 1992 was a more galvanizing event.[53] The press and politicians hailed UNCED as a watershed event, as the nations of the UN formally committed themselves to the goal of "sustainable development" and to new policy initiatives that would advance that goal, including trade sanctions "to enhance the effectiveness of environmental regulations."[54] Although environmentalists and environmental NGOs were split over the content and significance of the final declaration, their extraordinary integration into the process that led to the conference was of far greater importance. A series of preparatory conferences and regional meetings established precedents that gave NGOs new access to the UNCED process and to government ministers and bureaucrats. Indeed, rules for accreditation were so loosened that accreditation was offered to "virtually every NGO that applied."[55]

As it turned out, many NGOs that did not have consultative status with the ECOSOC were admitted to the UNCED planning process and indeed formed a majority of the consulting organizations. These NGOs made formal statements at meetings, served as representatives on government delegations, lobbied government officials, and presented draft language for policy proposals. Several coalitions of NGOs—the International Facilitating Committee and the Environmental Liaison Committee International—were formed to facilitate and coordinate NGO access and policy goals.

Matthias Finger of Columbia University, who studied the process extensively, has noted that there was "tension" between the "desire of governments and of intergovernmental organizations to use NGOs as providers of data and expertise, as information disseminators, and as legitimating agents, on the one hand; and, on the other, the desire of many NGOs to use the UNCED to bring about fundamental change in world development."[56] One important result of the process, contends Finger, was that some NGOs came to represent a "new type of actor in international environmental politics." These NGOs could "transcend traditional politics and become independent bargaining partners with governments and international agencies."[57]

In reality, the UNCED process only accelerated an ongoing trend toward integrating NGOs into UN environmental treaties and regimes. Before 1980, treaties rarely included provisions for NGOs, although the 1973 Convention on International Trade in Endangered Species (CITES) did contain relatively strong language on NGO participation that has become a model for future agreements. But some subsequent conventions (the 1979 Bonn Convention on the Conservation of Migratory Species of Wild Animals and the 1979 Geneva Convention on Transboundary Air Pollution) were comparatively restrictive or made no provision for NGOs.[58]

A breakthrough came with the 1987 Montreal Protocol on Substances that Deplete the Ozone Layer, which stated: "Any body or agency, whether national or international, governmental or nongovernmental, qualified in fields relating to the protection of the ozone . . . may be admitted unless at least one third of the parties present object."[59] The limitations included a "qualified" criterion and the necessity for a supermajority if challenged (although the latter represented a substantial easing of a UN Charter rule that allowed individual national vetoes). All subsequent conventions and treaties—hazardous waste (1989), biological diversity (1992), and climate change (1992)—contain almost identical wording.[60]

Size, Reach, and Expertise. The largest and most politically active environmental NGOs have a substantial international presence and focus. Friends of the Earth International has about 50 national affiliates around the world. Greenpeace, based in Amsterdam, has members and national organizations in 20 countries. The World Wildlife Fund lists 28 national affiliates; and the World Conservation Union-IUCN, an umbrella organization, includes more than 450 government agencies and private groups.[61]

Further, major U.S.-based environmental groups such as the Sierra Club, the National Audubon Society, and the National Wildlife Federation have created international departments and alliances, as have specialized litigation groups such as the Environmental Defense Fund and the Natural Resources Defense Council (both founded during the first burst of environmental activity in the 1970s). Both the legal NGOs and policy research organizations such as the World Resources Institute and the Worldwatch Institute provide intellectual resources for environmental alliances bent upon influencing policy-making and adjudication.[62]

Many of these organizations can bring ample funds and resources to bear on lobbying and litigation. The power and resources of environmental and other international NGOs are abundantly apparent in media mogul Ted Turner's gift of $1 billion to the United Nations in 1997—the proceeds of which will go to UN environmental, health, and population control programs, with substantial funds funneled through NGOs.[63]

A brief rundown of the endowments and income of some of the most prominent and politically active environmental NGOs further illustrates the fact that they have the resources to be powerful actors on the national and international scene. Conservation International has assets of $9,974,000 and income of $18,371,000; the Environmental Defense Fund has assets of $18,355,000 and income of $27,141,000; Greenpeace (U.S.) has assets of $14,567,000 and income of $9,636,000 (Greenpeace's worldwide income is $101,000,000); the National Audubon Society has assets of $109,601,000 and income of $105,724,000; the National Wildlife Federation has assets of $69,224,000 and income of $101,950,000; the Natural Resources Defense Council has assets of $39,694,000 and income of $26,475,000; the Sierra Club has assets of $52,000,000 and income of $73,000,000; the World Resources Institute has assets of $46,826,000 and income of $17,565,000; and the World Wildlife Fund has assets of $89,515,000 and income of $320,000,000.[64]

For this study, it is important to emphasize that budgets and resources of this magnitude far exceed those that many—if not most—of the member states of the WTO can bring to bear on either policymaking or litigation. When analyzing the pros and cons of opening up the DSU to environmental NGOs or corporations (which certainly have comparable, if not greater, resources), this fact of life must be considered. The complaints of many developing countries that they would be "outgunned" and ultimately overwhelmed by such reforms should be taken seriously.

How the Game Is Played: Governments, NGOs, and Corporations. Legal scholar Diane Otto's "radical" vision of the future role of NGOs in the United Nations was set forth in a previous section. Before turning to the normative debate concerning stakeholder representation and the WTO, it is important to examine less normative, more empirical studies. First, Kal Raustiala of the UCLA Law School explains the role of NGOs and the reasons that governments and international organizations have turned to them on international environmental issues. Then Gregory Shaffer of the University of Wisconsin analyzes the role of governments, NGOs, corporations, and international bureaucrats in the evolution of environmental policy within the WTO, using the history of the WTO Committee on Trade and the Environment as a test case.[65] In Shaffer's formulation, "Examining *What Is*. . . provides us with the tools to better assess proposals for *What Ought.*"[66]

Raustiala. Kal Raustiala argues that the dramatic change in the activities of environmental NGOs over the past fifteen years is "not unpredictable or random. It is based on the confluence of governmental incentives and NGO comparative advantage and resources."[67] As the number and scope of international environmental agreements and regimes have multiplied, the power and influence of NGOs have grown. NGOs have assumed a variety of roles, from the provision of scientific analysis to political coercion.

First, the attempt to create wholly new disciplines in areas such as ozone depletion, air and water pollution, global warming, hazardous waste, and biodiversity, among others, has been fraught with scientific uncertainty, political controversy, and difficult monitoring and enforcement issues. The larger environmental NGOs, with substantial staff and resources, have supplemented governments in conducting scientific and policy research. As Raustiala explains, "Most transboundary environmental issues are relatively novel, and little experience exists to guide the policymaking process. New problems appear that have never been anticipated or contemplated. . . .The existence of large, expertly staffed NGOs that devote considerable effort and resources to policy and development helps alleviate these problems." Government then can "maximize policy information and research while minimizing expenditures."[68]

A similar labor- and resource-saving function is provided in the monitoring of environmental agreements: "Certain NGOs are well positioned to provide independent assessment of individual states' compliance records . . . [and] provide an alternate route for information about state behavior."[69] In some situations, NGOs provide "fire alarms" when they observe noncompliance and thus alert other governments to "free riding," i.e., governments agreeing to, but not complying with, treaties. During negotiations, they can "alleviate the problem of information overload" through the timely provision of technical (and political) details for government negotiators. In terms of IR theory, then, government can use NGOs to reduce the negotiating and transaction costs of managing regimes.[70]

As noted, international diplomacy has been described as a two-level game that requires negotiators to achieve both domestic and international political agreements. NGOs are well positioned to act as facilitators and powerful pressure groups in both the negotiating and ratification processes. They can also aid in the "hard-wiring" of international environmental policy by using their power and influence to thwart the reversal of environmental policies they support.[71]

States often find themselves at odds with important environmental organizations and their demands. But the core empirical insight that Raustiala offers is that, contrary to the view of political commentators who have argued that the rise of NGOs signals the decline of the nation state, recent history reveals an increasingly symbiotic relationship between states and NGOs. Raustiala explains, "Some observers have proposed that [the] growth of NGO activity may indicate an emerging transformation of the international legal and political system—a decline in the importance of the sovereign state and the state system. . . . [I suggest] that sovereign states remain the creators of international environmental law but do so in a manner both empowered and enabled by the expansion of participatory and procedural guarantees to private organizations. NGO participation does not undermine but rather strengthens the regulatory powers of states and the state system."[72]

Raustiala bases this judgment on an historical analogy, first suggested by international legal theorist Anne-Marie Slaughter of Harvard Law School, that views the postwar international system as a projection of the New Deal regulatory state. Raustiala notes, "The genesis of the New Deal was the crisis of the Great Depression, and the notion that government must better protect its citizens from the dislocations of unfettered capitalism. . . . Unregulated private action produced major public problems. The response was the creation of a complex domestic regulatory regime. As regulation and the role of the state increased, private party participation and procedural rights also increased. These procedural changes led in turn—or were hoped to lead—to substantive changes in the nature of the rules promulgated, which would enhance the effectiveness, efficiency, and equity of administrative rule-making."[73]

He sees the same progression occurring in international environmental (and other economic regulatory) law, though the parallels are not precise:

> International public law increasingly looks like domestic public law in that it seeks to regulate and proscribe [in the public interest] private actions of an economic and social nature. The activities international public law is regulating often occur behind the borders of states. . . . This shift in the locus of legal/political activity and this expansion into novel issue-areas raise the demand with international environmental law for the NGO resources. The result is a world in which states and NGOs interact to produce and maintain global governance. That NGOs appear more important is a direct result of the expansion of concerted state power through the promulgation of new international law.[74]

Three points about Raustiala's analysis are important for this study. First, while he describes in positive terms the professional and political resources that NGOs bring to the process, he is circumspect with regard to normative judgments regarding the role of NGOs. Thus, he concludes:

> While I characterize [the] benefits to states, not all states benefit nor in the aggregate can NGO participation be considered an unmitigated good. Lobbyists in the U.S. Congress, for instance, provide many of the same services to legislators—information, political cover, monitoring of deals, and so forth. . . . Yet few applaud the role of lobbyists in American politics. . . . Civil society is not inherently "good" and state power "bad." Enhanced participation by civil society in governance may enhance the power of self-interested groups that are already powerful—in resources, organization, political influence—and this may undermine the political processes and lead to a low level of regime effectiveness.[75]

Second, even while describing the symbiotic relationship between states and NGOs, Raustiala makes clear that ultimately, it is states that retain the legitimate coercive authority. He points out that NGOs are almost always excluded from the final bargaining sessions in treaty negotiations and that, though NGO influence is both sought and manipulated by states, in the end "environmental cooperation must rely on the legitimate coercion that only states wield."[76]

Finally, although Raustiala does not explore it, there is a strong interpretive case to be made for his narrative as a case study for public choice theory. In this formulation, national politicians and bureaucrats (environmental appointees and civil servants) combine forces with NGOs to maximize their political gains at the international level. As legal scholar Jonathan Macey of Cornell University Law School and economist Enrico Colombatto of the University of Turin write, "Recent global regulation appears to contradict the theory that the nation-state would act to maintain its autonomy."[77] Public choice theory, however, explains this apparent contradiction by positing (1) that bureaucrats, politicians, and interest groups make policy, not some abstract concept of the "state"; (2) politicians, bureaucrats, and interest groups act in their rational self-interest and attempt to maximize their personal power; and (3) technological changes, market processes, and other factors may deprive national regulators of the power to act unilaterally, and in these cases it is in their interest to engage in international coordination to survive.[78]

In this evolving international environmental arena, therefore, it is in the interest of some national politicians and NGOs to join forces and create new international laws and regulations that will increase their power and influence. As Macey and Colombatto conclude, "The behavior of politicians, interest groups, and bureaucrats in the international arena is no different than their behavior elsewhere. . . . [R]egulators are political-support-maximizing actors; they respond to political pressure and to self-interest. . . . And regulators will not agree to enter into international agreements unless it is in their [private] interest to do so."[79]

Shaffer. The goal of the WTO's Committee on Trade and Environment (CTE), which ultimately proved unachievable, was to construct a legal framework for dealing with environmental issues in the WTO. Gregory Shaffer has examined the history of the committee against three competing theoretical frameworks: a two-level (liberal) intergovernmental model, a supranational technocratic model, and a civil society/stakeholder model. Each of the models is built upon predictive assumptions concerning the behavior of major actors in the WTO and CTE process: the WTO Secretariat, chiefs of governments (COGs), trade bureaucracies, multinational corporations, national and transnational environmental NGOs, and development-oriented NGOs from southern developing countries. Shaffer concludes that the first theoretical framework—the two-level intergovernmental model—best explains the internal dynamics and ultimate policy results of the CTE, and he uses these empirical findings as the underpinning for certain normative judgments about the WTO.[80]

The second theoretical framework, the supranational technocratic model, would predict that relatively autonomous lower-level national bureaucrats would ally with international bureaucrats (in this case, the WTO Secretariat) to dominate the proceedings and results of the CTE. The results, as Shaffer explains them, would be as follows: "A supranational technocratic approach would predict that WTO outcomes reflect the bureaucratic interests and ideological . . . biases of trade elites, and thus do not reflect national interests as determined through national political processes. . . . [S]uch networks would likely have a *neoliberal* bias."[81]

The third model, the civil society/stakeholder perspective, views the CTE process as the product of steady and increasing pressure from NGOs to introduce environmental norms and practices into the world trading system. As noted above, some advocates of this model also argue that transnational NGOs (specifically environmental groups) are already shaping international policy as direct participants in what they label "world civic politics."[82] Although all three models have both normative and positivist descriptive aspects, the civil society/stakeholder model particularly stresses the normative deficiencies of the WTO as presently conceived—and the necessity of incorporating "stakeholder" (nonbusiness) interests directly into WTO negotiating and dispute settlement processes.

The two-level, intergovernmental model is essentially a variation of the liberal IR theory described in chapter 1 and appendix 1 of this study. Domestic private interests compete among themselves to achieve policy dominance, and COGs form national positions from this process. These national positions—which are themselves not static but subject to changing domestic forces—are then defended in the WTO in competition with the interests and goals of other states. COGS, though buffeted by conflicting pressures, retain great power because of their central linkage with both domestic and international politics and their ability to play off other nongovernment and government actors against each other.

Based upon his detailed examination of the history and results of the CTE, Shaffer draws a series of conclusions regarding the realities of the CTE process and the roles of the major actors. First, neither the WTO Secretariat nor mid-level national trade bureaucrats are powerful forces in WTO decision-making (as predicated by the supranational technocratic perspective). Trade bureaucrats are constrained by political officials and other agency bureaucrats, and the WTO Secretariat has "always been kept on a tighter leash" by governments because of the high economic stakes involved in WTO rules and disputes.[83]

Further, regarding the determination of national positions, he notes that while trade bureaucracies are usually biased toward neoliberal free trade, "national policy on trade and environmental matters tends to have a more nationalist, mercantilist orientation, which, on the one hand, attempts to exploit environmental arguments to limit imports and, on the other hand, is wary of environmental arguments by other countries that could prejudice exports."[84]

Commercial interests (corporations) do play a large role in most states, but the result is not necessarily the predominance of free trade policies in the WTO. The WTO is not a "bastion" of free trade ideology, because "positions of national commercial constituencies are not necessarily *neoliberal*, since many national sectors—agriculture, steel, and textiles—often have protectionist proclivities." National political leaders must therefore adopt positions in the WTO that balance free trade exporting interests with protectionist import-competing industries and pro-environmental NGOs with commercial interests hostile to increased regulation. As liberal intergovernmental theory predicts, "The positions advanced by state trade delegates on specific trade-environment issues reflected those of their own most vocal stakeholders."[85]

Responding to northern environmental NGOs that attack the WTO as undemocratic and call for greater direct stakeholder participation in WTO rule-making and dispute settlement, Shaffer makes a number of points based upon the experience of the CTE. First, northern NGOs do not represent the views of all of civil society: "While northern environmental NGOs may be 'internationalist' in orientation, . . . they do not represent a 'global civil society.' They have a specifically northern perspective, and often, even more specifically, an Anglo-Saxon one. Their representatives were raised and educated in the North. Almost all of their funding comes from contributors from the North. They obtain their financing by focusing on single issues that strike the northern public's imagination. . . ."[86] For these reasons, the civil society/stakeholder theory is flawed normatively. As Shaffer explains, "[This study] finds that implementation of a 'civil society/stakeholder' model is fraught with much greater problems of over- and under-representation than the model's advocates admit. This is particularly the case for developing-country constituencies whose stakeholders are always underrepresented internationally from the standpoint of direct participation."[87] In the end, the CTE process was stalemated not because the WTO is undemocratic but because it suffers from an excess of pluralism. Shaffer writes,

> NGOs often criticize the WTO as if it were an undemocratic force independent of states. Yet the explanation for the stalemate within the WTO Committee on Trade and Environment lies in conflicts within and between states, not independent action of the World Trade Organization. . . . [Northern NGOs] have been thwarted because their interests conflict with those of U.S. and EC export-oriented businesses domestically, and those of businesses as well as other nongovernment constituents from developing and smaller developed countries. . . . Northern environmental groups were simply unsuccessful in harnessing U.S. and EC clout to attain their aims. Internal divisions within the United States and Europe hamstrung the ability of the U.S. and EC to exercise political and economic power in furtherance of northern environmental groups' goals."[88]

Shaffer concludes, "This article's findings demonstrate that, despite critics' claims, the WTO is not an autonomous neoliberal-dominated organization that is by nature anti-environment and anti-democratic. Rather, decision-making processes within the WTO are, for the most part, properly based on an 'intergovernmental' model that . . . best ensures relatively unbiased participation of disparate interests around the globe in an international forum."[89]

Taken together, Raustiala's and Shaffer's empirical findings buttress normative judgments that will be advanced in subsequent chapters. Their contention that states retain the final authority over decisions taken by international organizations, for example, can be linked normatively to the public choice implications of an alliance of NGOs and government officials to produce new supranational regulatory systems, as posited by Raustiala. This study argues that the lack of a foundation of democratic legitimacy for such a domestic-transnational alliance remains a central argument for national governments' retaining firm control over international trade rule-making and dispute settlement—and, even more important, for a greater role for national legislatures in oversight of the substantive international commitments proposed by officials of the executive.

6

Whose WTO Is It? Democratic Governments versus Stakeholders

The calls for NGOs and private citizens to participate directly in WTO rule-making and adjudicatory processes raise profound questions about the fundamental operations and nature of the multilateral trading regime—and ultimately about the relationship between national sovereignty and international trade laws and regulations. Although this study deals primarily with the dispute settlement system, many of the arguments for NGO participation in WTO rule-making are based on the same assumptions and logic.

Theorists who favor NGO participation alongside governments in the WTO aim for new international norms and procedures based upon "participatory democracy." In building a version of liberal international relations theory, legal scholar Richard Shell has posited the "normative superiority" of a stakeholders model that "emphasizes opening dispute resolution and policymaking processes to environmental, labor, and other groups," with the result that "a wide array of interests can join businesses and nation-states in the important task of constructing the economic and social norms that will make global trade a sustainable aspect of a larger transnational society."[1] Operationally, Shell's goal is to "break the monopoly of states on international dispute machinery and to extend the power to enforce international legal norms beyond states to individuals"[2]—and to organizations as well.

Daniel Esty, director of the Yale Center for Environmental Law and Policy, goes further, arguing that NGOs offer an "alternate form of 'representation,'" and therefore should be allowed to compete on an equal footing with governments: "Our growing appreciation of the richness and diversity of 'civil society' reinforces the suggestion that it would be a mistake to think that all interactions among people can be mediated through the narrow channel of national governments. . . . Too often both the international civil servants and government officials are happy to ignore issues that fall beyond their bailiwick. . . . The logic of *horizontal* competition—between governments and NGOs—builds on the basic economic understanding that welfare gains can be achieved by having competing options available."[3]

And Claudio Grossman, dean of American University's Washington College of Law, stated at a symposium on sovereignty and private actors,

> [International law] needs to recognize and incorporate into its jurisdiction all international actors. The states, international organizations, and private actors such as transnational corporations; trade unions; consumer, environmental, development, and human rights NGOs; and private individuals are all engaged in the ongoing process of formulating and implementing international legal standards. An international legal process that fails to allow nonstate actors to participate fully in the process cannot develop legal norms that are fully responsive to the international community. . . . The deficiencies of the present international legal order based on *de jure* sovereignty of the nation-state and a relatively clear distinction between international and domestic legal issues are obvious."[4]

As these comments and the recent history of events at the UN demonstrate, NGOs and the legal theorists who support their views are determined to have these groups play much larger informal and formal roles in international organizations. For the trading system, NGOs have both long-range and short-range goals. At least some environmentalists and legal theorists foresee not only a *de facto* but also a *de jure* partnership between NGOs and the WTO. One model often mentioned is the International Labor Organization (ILO), which is organized along functional lines, with representation for governments, labor unions, and corporations. For the short term, environmental and other NGOs focus on three broad areas: greater access to WTO documents; the right of observer status, the ability to file *amicus* briefs and, ultimately, the right of standing before WTO panels and the AB; and, finally, "a seat at the table" in WTO activities such as committee meetings.

Democratic Theory at the International Level: What Is Legitimate?

The more sweeping claims of NGO leaders and the academics that support them raise important questions about democratic legitimacy and the allocation of power among international organizations, national governments, and nonstate actors. This section first examines the larger issues of democratic legitimacy and provides a rebuttal to the claims made for a new international legitimacy based upon NGOs and other stakeholders. The study then focuses on the issues that generate the most intense debate between proponents and opponents of direct participation through the expansion of standing for NGOs and private corporations.

Robert Keohane and Joseph Nye, of Duke and Harvard Universities, respectively, have written a thoughtful paper that provides a good starting point for analyzing the arguments for a participatory revolution in the WTO. The two authors admonish analysts and academics dealing with the conundrums of legitimacy and democracy at the international level to take seriously the validity of two types of democracy: the traditional "adversary" democracy and a second form known as "participatory" democracy. "Adversary democracy," they state, "assumes conflicting interests and employs established procedures to make decisions in the face of conflict." On the other hand, "Unitary or participatory democracy assumes that people have the same interests, but may not know, individually, what is best to do. Face-to-face deliberations, as in the New England town meetings, are, in this view, the democratic way to reach decisions."[5]

They note that, although participatory democracy is utopian in large democracies and certainly at the international level, the concept possesses "an inherently normative appeal" over adversary democracy. Keohane and Nye explain, "The desire to play a role in one's own fate—to govern as well as to be governed—has been a recurring theme of democracy since Aristotle." Finally, they argue, "Participatory democracy is more an impulse than an actual set of institutions. . . . However, its ideals should be kept in mind, because to some extent, they seem to lie behind the protests against international institutions, and the difficulties of legitimacy they are encountering today."[6]

While this study accepts these admonitions, it contends that they must be viewed and accommodated in light of a fundamental, underlying reality: Only at the level of the nation-state can one find the full panoply of democratic processes, and national sovereignty is therefore still the defining filter through which democratic goals can be best obtained. To their credit, Keohane and Nye acknowledge the "democratic deficit" in all international policymaking:

> International institutions lack the key feature that makes democracy possible and that, in democracies, facilitates accountability: an acknowledged public, operating within a political community in which there is a general consensus on what makes public decisions legitimate. . . . Most meaningful voting and associated democratic political activities occur within the boundaries of national states that have democratic constitutions and processes. Minorities are willing to acquiesce to a majority in which they may not participate directly because they feel they participate in some larger community. This is absent at the global level, [and] creates severe normative as well as practical problems. . . .[7]

Kal Raustiala of UCLA Law School, who sympathizes with many of the substantive goals of the environmental NGO community, has also warned of the dangers of bypassing democratic checks and balances in international agreements, particularly recent environmental agreements. Specifically, he argues that national sovereignty represents an important safeguard against "illegitimate" international environmental rule-making. He describes the increasing tendency of some environmental leaders to espouse a mechanism by which treaties can be ratified by supermajorities that ignore minority dissent and then modified by "technical annexes" without the formal consent of any nation. He notes that although technocratic decision-making commonly occurs without direct legislative control in domestic settings, most democratic nations have some kind of administrative law of due process to check the power of bureaucracies.

But there is not now, nor is there likely to be soon, a body of international administrative law. That being the case, national sovereignty performs a vital function as "a guarantor of democratic control over foreign affairs." Raustiala concludes, "Sovereignty, for all its faults, acts as a protector against increasing democratic deficit in rule-making, and perhaps as an unwitting champion of democratic values in a globalizing world. . . . Both sovereignty and democracy are based upon the notion of consent, and the empirical requirement of consent at the international level protects the consent theoretically embodied in democratic political systems."[8]

Greater Participation and Standing for NGOs: Advantages and Disadvantages

Trade lawyers and NGOs have advanced several key arguments in favor of greater NGO and corporate participation in the work of the WTO, as well as a private right of action and standing before WTO panels and the Appellate Body. In examining the most important of these arguments, this study analyzes the validity of comparisons of international institutions; evaluates the alleged flaws in the democratic process at the national level; considers the feasibility and fairness of selecting NGOs or corporations to participate in the WTO; and assesses NGO claims that their participation would infuse democratic legitimacy in international organizations.

Comparisons of International Institutions. Given the rapidly evolving practices of other international organizations regarding NGOs, it is natural that legal scholars sympathetic to NGOs, such as Washington trade lawyer Steve Charnovitz, former director of the Global Environment and Trade Study at Yale, point to the practices and experiences of the UN and other international bodies as precedent-setting, providing NGOs with "solid legal ground in seeking greater transparency and participation in the WTO." Charnovitz cites with approval the UN's Agenda 21 program, which urges all intergovernmental organizations to use NGOs for policy-making, program design, implementation, and evaluation. And he points to the UN Educational, Scientific, and Cultural Organization (UNESCO); the Organization for Economic Cooperation and Development (OECD); and the International Labor Organization as models of international organizations that have integrated NGOs into their decision-making processes.[9]

The flaw in this analogy, as Philip Nichols of the University of Pennsylvania's Legal Studies Department has noted, stems from "undisciplined comparisons of international organizations."[10] Neither UNESCO nor the OECD is a rule-making or enforcement body whose policies could have a direct effect on national laws. The ILO, although technically granted a limited amount of such authority, has been notable through much of its history for a failure to legislate or enforce rules for labor worldwide. In addition, the ILO, which dates back to the post–World War I era, is the only international body organized along corporatist lines, with a tripartite representation for governments, labor unions, and corporations. Given this highly skewed organizational framework—that is, special rights for corporations and labor unions, but none for other political or social interest groups—a move to confer upon the ILO real authority to legislate and enforce worldwide regulations for labor would undoubtedly trigger a backlash from other elements of "civil society," especially environmental groups, which have often been at odds with pro-development coalitions of business and labor.

The WTO has become a unique international organization. No other body presides over rules that extend so deeply into the life and fabric of domestic economies, and no other body possesses a strictly binding dispute settlement system, complete with legal retaliation. During eight rounds of trade negotiations, WTO members have carefully calibrated concessions they have made against those that other members have made. The fine meshing of rights and obligations represents a delicate balance, one that must be continually defended in domestic politics. Consequently, governments will not lightly grant authority to private or nonprofit competitors to change the terms of the complex compromises reached in successive trade rounds. It is for these reasons that Nichols correctly lambastes "dubious" comparisons and concludes, "Comparative analysis cannot be reduced to a simple 'me, too' argument."[11]

Democratic Flaws at the National Level. A second argument used to advance the cause of NGOs is related to alleged flaws and omissions in the democratic processes at the national level. According to this argument, governments are not truly representative, the "second bite at the apple" with international participation is a misconceived analogy, and transnational citizenship necessarily goes beyond the national polity (the same would apply to multinational corporations).

In separate articles, Steve Charnovitz and Daniel Esty point to the alleged defects of national democracies. Charnovitz writes that the proposition that "national governments do not adequately represent the interests of all of their constituencies . . . is surely true. Indeed, many national governments fail to represent the interests of even a majority of their constituencies as periodically reflected by low approval ratings."[12] And Esty argues, "States are . . . imperfect representatives of public opinion. When governments speak with one voice, they inevitably neglect minority viewpoints within their jurisdiction. NGOs can ensure that views not reflected by national governments can be heard in the course of international policy development."[13]

Several elements of these arguments can be quickly refuted. When Charnovitz equates the quality of representative government with ever-changing public approval ratings, for example, it suggests that he may be deeply afflicted by the disease of Clintonism—the day-to-day, hour-to-hour policymaking by polls. Representative government—as opposed to plebiscitary democracy—is at its finest when it takes the longer view and does not succumb to the sudden shifts of opinion that sweep electorates from time to time.

Much the same is true with Esty's argument that national governments are not representative because in individual decisions, a minority view is, inevitably, overruled.[14] As Keohane and Nye stated, the point is that the dynamics of a functioning democracy allow that minority to go out and win elections, and to appoint officials to carry out new policies and judges to enforce what had been minority views. The claims against democracy at the national level are especially ironic at a time when democratic government has been triumphing in country after country around the world. These democracies may not be perfect by U.S. or European standards, but more than any time in history, national populations are being served with the blessings and responsibilities of democratic government.[15]

In a 1994 study of the relationship between international trade policy and democracy, political scientist Daniel Verdier conducted a comprehensive analysis of several countries and concluded,

> Voters control policymaking because elections provide policymakers with incentives to reproduce within their institutional microcosms the parametric structure of the electorate. . . . Voter control is indirect, since voters do not choose the outcome; rather, they create the incentive structure that motivates politicians to legislate in accordance with voter concerns. In short, if electors do not necessarily choose policies, they *do* choose the decision rules by which lawmakers make policies.[16]

Responding to the argument that NGOs are asking for a second bite at the apple after failing to achieve their end in national politics, Esty states, "While national representatives in Geneva officially represent their governments—and thus their publics—at the WTO, individuals for a variety of reasons may not feel adequately represented by their governments. . . . [M]any people today do not have their identities determined by the geographic political jurisdiction in which they happen to live. NGOs cut across political boundaries and define 'communities of interest.'"[17] Through their national and local branches, however, international NGOs such as the World Wildlife Fund, Greenpeace, and Friends of the Earth International, as well as large multinational corporations and business groups such as the International Chamber of Commerce, do lobby and compete vigorously in the politics of individual WTO member states. And it is the failure to achieve their goals in the national arena that impels them to move up to international forums. As Martin Wolf of the *Financial Times* has written in a trenchant essay critiquing the claims of NGOs and civil society, "If the NGOs were indeed representative of the wishes and desires of the electorate, those who embrace their ideas would be in power. Self-evidently they are not."[18]

Furthermore, there is no practical means of legitimizing so-called "transnational values" internationally. One can understand the frustration of Esty and others who lament that "[a] citizen who cares very deeply about ending whaling, for instance, almost certainly will find his or her views better represented internationally by the Worldwide Fund for Nature than by his or her own government, which has many goals it must simultaneously pursue."[19]

But as Sylvia Ostry of the University of Toronto has countered in a recent article, "It's not clear what the word citizen means in this context. There are no 'world' citizens but only citizens of nation-states. Governments are accountable to their citizens, albeit some more than others."[20] And Kenneth Anderson of American University's Washington College of Law, a strong critic of NGOs' claims to special political legitimacy in international organizations, has stated bluntly, "When international NGOs assert that they are the voice of the world's citizens, the assertion makes no sense because the world is not a polity that has citizens—it has, to be sure, people, many of them with great needs—but to be a 'citizen' is to be part of a constituted polity, not just a supporter of an NGO and its agenda."[21]

Thus, it all comes back to the resolution of political and societal issues within the confines of national polities. As Wolf further states, "A civilized society is one in which the state alone has a monopoly of coercive power, exercised under law, by a government responsible to the electorate as a whole. To grant *any* private interests a direct voice in negotiations over how coercion is to be applied is fundamentally subversive to constitutional democracy. . . . Only elected government can be properly responsible for the making of law, domestically and internationally."[22]

Other critics of formal NGO participation in the WTO have pointed to additional deleterious results for the trading system itself. Nichols points to the inevitable conflict between member governments and domestic interest groups:

> Allowing private parties that were not successful when values and goals were balanced at the national level to have standing before dispute settlement parties would create an irreconcilable dissonance for countries engaged in the delicate process of trade negotiation. . . . Expansion of standing would undoubtedly lead to the spectacle of domestic constituencies opposing the positions of the governments that are supposed to represent those constituencies.[23]

Selection of NGO and Corporate Participants. What first seems merely a practical question of how NGOs and corporations would be "credentialed" to participate in WTO activities turns out to have important implications for the "rights and obligations" of WTO members. These issues are particularly significant when related to a private right of standing before, or submitting *amicus* briefs to, panels and the AB. Proponents of allowing NGOs and corporations to have standing in the DSU, or at least to submit *amicus* briefs, play down the practical questions of deciding just which—and how many—NGOs and corporations would be allowed to participate; and they point to other international organizations such as UN agencies as models. Once again, however, the problem of an "undisciplined comparison" arises.

UN agencies—the UNCED process is often cited—are poor and misleading models for the WTO, particularly for dispute settlement. Although the meetings often produce "soft law" proposals that could evolve into binding laws and regulations in the future, these conferences have served primarily as forums for developing wish lists. NGOs and private sector consultative activities have therefore been of much less consequence than they would be in the "real" world of WTO rule-making and adjudication. As demonstrated in recent years, loss of an important WTO case can cost hundreds of millions of dollars in compensation or from retaliation. With real money on the table, attempts to shift the balance of power by introducing new actors or documents into the DSU as a matter of right are likely to trigger an intense battle among WTO members.

Other questions concern timing and scheduling. In the DSU, the panel process is normally limited to six months and the appeals process to two months. There are literally thousands of NGOs and many potential corporate interests, and within subject areas such as the environment, positions and views are diverse. As events in Seattle amply demonstrated, numerous other "social movement" groups, such as feminist, consumer, animal rights, and human rights groups, view the multilateral trading system as a means of levying sanctions against what they consider improper behavior.

Given the stakes involved—in money for corporations and in advancing ideological positions for many NGOs—proposals for self-selection lack credibility. On the other hand, any process of winnowing down the potentially long list of applicants to be heard would inevitably induce overt or covert normative and, in the end, arbitrary judgments.

Two other realities would add to the inequity and unfairness of allowing standing or even *amicus* briefs as a matter of right.[24] A number of northern NGOs have large endowments and sizable annual budgets that dwarf the resources many developing countries can mobilize for trade disputes. Inevitably, those groups with the greatest legal and political resources will benefit most from expansion of standing or the submission of *amicus* briefs.

Further, a large imbalance exists between northern and southern NGOs in terms of their number, size, and clout (several thousand northern NGOs and only several hundred southern NGOs are registered with the UN). Developing countries, acutely aware of this gap in resources, adamantly oppose opening the process to outsiders. India, Thailand, and Mexico opposed the AB decision to partially open the process to *amicus* briefs, citing the threat this posed from "powerful" business associations and nongovernmental voluntary associations.

Sylvia Ostry has pointed out that demands for *amicus* briefs are "strongly rejected by southern governments and their NGOs who regard the present evidentiary-intensive and increasingly legalistic system as already biased against them."[25] Gregory Shaffer's in-depth interviews with trade representatives and NGOs from developing countries confirm that they are deeply suspicious of the motives behind northern demands for greater transparency: "Southern states and southern NGOs . . . distrust [the] demands [of their northern counterparts] for greater WTO transparency. Southern interests are wary that greater WTO transparency will merely permit northern NGOs, defending northern interests, to better exploit the media to pressure state delegates, the WTO Secretariat, and WTO dispute settlement panelists to take their views into account and thereby advance northern ends."[26]

Democratic Legitimacy in International Organizations. NGO leaders argue that their participation in international organizations is necessary to give those organizations democratic legitimacy. Esty explains that NGOs "offer an alternative form of 'representation' that may, in some instances, allow for a more refined and closely tailored reflection of an individual's views...than will be obtained through his or her government."[27] The problem is that NGOs themselves often do not live up to this standard. In many cases, NGO leaders are not accountable directly to their members, and their members are not likely to be informed of, or react to, particular policy stands. As Peter Spiro of Hofstra University Law School has written, NGO operations usually "lack safeguards for accountability and trans-parency." According to Spiro, the "absence of standard public law safeguards concentrates significant power in NGO secretariats."[28]

Furthermore, Spiro writes that it is "more often money than membership that determines influence, and money more often rep-resents the support of centralized elites, such as the major founda-tions, than that of the true grass roots. . . . Armed with the leverage of large membership and knowing that those members are likely to be docile, NGO leaders have emerged as a class of modern day, non-territorial potentates, a position rather like that commanded by medieval bishops."[29] This observation led Philip Nichols to con-clude, "Far from 'democratizing' the process, expanded standing could create a forum for well-monied special interest groups. In all likelihood, those groups would be more concerned with protecting their advantaged positions than in working for the common good."[30]

The Political Dynamics and Consequences of Allowing Standing for NGOs and Corporations

Two recent research papers—one by Robert Keohane of Duke and Andrew Moravcsik and Anne-Marie Slaughter of Harvard; the other by Gregory Shaffer of the University of Wisconsin—have focused on the likely political dynamics and consequences of granting more generous rights of standing to NGOs, corporations, and individuals. Shaffer's research is particularly relevant to the question of standing for corporations. In the view of the author—although not necessar-ily the view of the researchers themselves—the analysis and con-clusions of these two papers reinforce the normative policy recommendations advanced in this study: that is, that the WTO should remain a government-to-government organization that does not allow the formal representation of either corporations or NGOs within its deliberations or judicial proceedings.

Keohane, Moravcsik, and Slaughter, in a 2000 paper, compared the history of two types of dispute settlement: "international" and "transnational." In international dispute settlement, access to the adjudicatory process is confined to states (e.g., in the International Court of Justice or ICJ); in transnational dispute settlement, non-state parties can file briefs and bring cases (e.g., in the European Court of Justice or ECJ).[31]

They found that transnational dispute resolution became much more expansive over time because governments had lost control of their power as gatekeepers. This expansion, they posit, was the result of a *de facto* alliance between the plaintiffs and their lawyers on the one hand, and the federal court (along with national courts) on the other: "When the ECJ rules, the decision is implemented not by national governments—the recalcitrant defendants—but by national courts. Any subsequent domestic opposition is rendered more difficult. In sum, transnational third-party dispute resolution has led to a *de facto* alliance between certain national courts, certain types of individual litigants, and the ECJ."[32]

Once again, although the authors do not advance this theory, their example seems to fit a classic public choice phenomenon, quite similar to Jonathan Macey's illustrations, cited previously. In this instance, compelling incentives exist for a public body, the ICJ, to form an alliance with private actors, in this case the trade bar that specializes in ICJ cases, to increase the power and influence of each party. National courts, which have allied themselves with the ICJ and which in many cases carry out the directives of that court against their own governments, also benefit. This progression fits squarely into Macey's analysis of national securities and bank regulators who join forces with international regulatory bodies to defend and increase their power at the national level.[33]

An expansion of standing to NGOs and corporations in the WTO would likely set in motion a similar dynamic and eventually change the power relationships between the WTO and national governments, as well as between NGOs and corporations and national governments. As Keohane and his colleagues concluded, "What transnational dispute resolution does is to insulate dispute resolution to some extent from the day-to-day political demands of states. . . . Legalization imposes real constraints on state behavior; the closer we are to transnational third-party dispute resolution, the greater those constraints."[34]

In a forthcoming article on the partnership between U.S. trade officials and private corporations using the WTO dispute settlement system, Gregory Shaffer evaluates several proposals to change the system, including the call for granting corporations a private right of action to participate directly in the WTO dispute settlement process. He acknowledges that under such a system a "significant number of parties could benefit" from the litigation and this "would drive the process of global economic integration forward."[35]

The downside consequences, however, outweigh these benefits in Shaffer's mind: "A system of direct private enforcement of WTO legal rights remains problematic from the standpoint of unbiased participation and, in particular, would raise even more serious issues of legitimacy and democratic accountability. . . . Under a system of direct private suits, large organized interests could . . . muster resources to strategically exploit legal procedures...without any political screen."[36]

Echoing points made earlier in this study, Shaffer states, "The deeper underlying problem is that WTO law, as compared to national or even EC law . . . requires consensus to modify, so that unintended consequences are difficult to correct." Further, "Because of the complex bargaining within the WTO, rules are often purposively drafted in a vague manner as part of a political compromise." A "democratic deficit" in the WTO flows from these circumstances and raises fundamental problems, according to Shaffer:

> Herein lies the crux of the democratic deficit within the WTO dispute settlement system. WTO judicial panels must interpret relatively vague rules without legislative or administrative guidance or the possibility of legislative or regulatory correction. Because of the WTO judicial body's remoteness and isolation from democratic legislative controls, together with the difficulty of amending WTO rules, WTO dispute settlement panels are more subject to challenges of illegitimacy and unaccountability than are national courts.[37]

Ultimately, Shaffer explains, in a normative judgment similar to that adopted in this study, "Because of the WTO's frail legitimacy, governments should retain the sole authority to determine when—and when not—to initiate WTO lawsuits. Under the current system, governments may somewhat protect the WTO system from a popular backlash unleashed by zealous exploitation of WTO rules by private interests."[38]

7

Proposals for Reform and Reasons for Retaining the Status Quo

Constitutional issues related to the operation of the WTO dispute settlement system are inextricably linked to questions of the democratic legitimacy and participation of outside parties. This chapter deals with these issues separately: first, it considers reforms in the process and rules of the WTO dispute settlement system; then it examines issues related to the role of NGOs and corporations, as well as the integration of the international trade regime with the evolving international environmental regime.

Proposals for Constitutional Reform

The proposals for changing the structure of the DSU that are recommended in this study proceed from one overarching conclusion: the WTO's highly judicialized dispute settlement system is stretched beyond its capacity to deliver decisions that WTO member states will accept as legitimate. This dangerous situation is not the result of public choice rent-seeking by the panels or Appellate Body, but rather of structural flaws in the WTO constitution itself. Specifically, the current problems stem from the imbalance between the blocked legislative function in the WTO and the highly efficient adjudicatory system whose decisions become binding "law" unless unanimously overturned. The language in the agreements, moreover, is often vague, unclear, and even contradictory, providing little or no guidance for dispute settlement participants, including WTO panel and AB members, as well as the contending parties.

Two principles undergird the specific recommendations made in this chapter: first, the WTO should remain largely a government-to-government organization; and second, a move toward a more "diplomatic" approach to dispute settlement, one that would complement the legal system and provide a safety valve, is essential for the survival of the WTO as a viable institution.[1]

This study envisions an alternate system for dispute settlement, with changes at both the front and back ends of the dispute settlement process. At the front end, the study recommends a system of mediation, conciliation, and arbitration. At the back end, it recommends that some type of blocking action be adopted if a significant number of WTO members disagree with a panel or AB decision. The proposals are separable, and it might well be that WTO members could select one without the other.

The Front End of the Dispute Settlement System: Mediation, Conciliation, and Arbitration. The front-end proposal builds upon rarely used provisions for mediation and conciliation in the Dispute Settlement Understanding. Although they have drawn scant attention, these DSU provisions afford a series of alternatives to the adjudicatory model of the panels and AB, including good offices (DSU Article 4); conciliation and mediation (DSU Article 5); the convening of an expert group to resolve factual issues (DSU Article 13.2); and binding arbitration (DSU Article 25).[2] One problem with these alternatives is that only sixty days are allowed for consultation or for the Director-General to provide his services for conciliation, mediation, or good offices.

- *Recommendation: The goal of the first recommendation is to move the WTO dispute settlement system back in the direction of the original "diplomatic" model of the GATT. With that aim in mind, this study suggests that in certain cases, either the Director-General or a committee of the DSB be granted authority to step in and direct the contending WTO members to settle their differences through bilateral negotiations, through mediation, or by agreeing to arbitration by an outside party. If, by whatever means, the parties were unable to reach an accommodation during the time frame provided by the new DSU, the case would be held over for a decision during the next round of trade negotiations (unless the relevant WTO council—e.g., GATT, Services, or TRIPs—reaches a consensus on the matter in the interim).*[3]

Two criteria for triggering intervention to head off the more judicialized dispute settlement process are proposed. First, if, in the judgment of the deciding official or body, the dispute has a highly divisive political content likely to cause permanent damage to the WTO, then the contending parties should be forced to reach an accommodation among themselves outside of the panel/Appellate Body process. Second, if, in the judgment of the deciding official or body, the dispute concerns issues that have not been resolved by negotiation (legislation) or where the language clearly papered over deep substantive divisions, then the contending parties should be forced to reach a temporary compromise until the matter can be resolved in subsequent negotiations among all WTO members. The arbitration described in DSU Article 25 would be a voluntary alternative, although once undertaken, it would become binding on both parties.[4]

One proponent of an expanded role for mediation and arbitration, Thomas Schoenbaum of the University of Georgia Law School, has suggested that in cases where the "economic and political factors involved outweigh legal considerations," WTO panels and the AB should be given authority to suspend the proceeding and direct the parties back to a negotiation process. He would also allow them to decide the case later if no compromise is reached and a decision is "necessary or appropriate." Like the proposal espoused in this study, Schoenbaum's suggestions would allow the panels and AB *not* to render a decision if that is the "appropriate" conclusion.[5] The problem with allowing the panels or the AB to decide these questions is that the judgments called for are not based on legal interpretations, but rather on political or economic issues. Panelists or members of the AB are not chosen for their political or economic skills and therefore are not likely to have strong capabilities in these matters. Thus, it would be better to lodge the authority with either a committee of the DSB (members who function in a quasi-legislative capacity) or the Director-General (who is elected and functions in a quasi-executive capacity).[6]

The Director-General would be a better choice than a DSB committee for two key reasons: one person can expedite decisions more effectively; and the DG is likely to have greater knowledge of the WTO as an institution, as well as greater sensitivity to the political and economic nuances of particular cases. This study contends that granting this authority to the DG would also fulfill the larger goal of giving more authority and political stature to the WTO Director-General. This assertion is in strong agreement with a major point that Robert Keohane and Joseph Nye emphasized in their 2000 Kennedy School of Government conference paper regarding the "most serious 'democratic deficit'" in the WTO. "What is missing?" they asked. "The legitimating activity of broadly based politicians speaking directly to domestic publics. This may have mattered less when [nontrade] issues were less linked. . . . But with the linkage of issues, there is a need for the involvement of politicians who can link specific organizations and policies with a broader range of issues through electoral accountability."[7]

For the WTO, a stronger DG would be crucial to addressing the democratic deficit, according to Keohane and Nye: "To do so in the WTO would require creating a strong office of the Director-General—a move that would surely be resisted by many governments. But having an institutionally empowered Director-General would not be sufficient. Somehow, that Director-General would have to identify the constituencies that would be relevant, and develop institutionalized ties with them."[8]

Assuming, as Keohane and Nye do, that nations would balk at this substantial grant of authority to the Director-General, then a widely representative, possibly trade-weighted committee of the DSB could be empowered to render judgments regarding the separate judicial or mediation/arbitration tracks.

Discussion. Washington trade lawyer John Ragosta has advanced one argument against establishing a diplomatic track. Attempting to refute an argument in favor of governments' asserting the national interest over the particular legal doctrine in a WTO case, Ragosta states:

The comment demonstrates continued confusion between the old diplomatic model—which sought primarily to encourage settlement—with the adjudicatory model, the decision of which will have precedential value—which depends for its legitimacy upon a correct "legal" ruling in each case. . . . Some object that the system is only "quasi-judicial." . . . [T]hat is a little like being "quasi-pregnant." Being "quasi-judicial" can result in an odd (and not necessarily good) mix of judicial and nonjudicial elements.[9]

Both Ragosta and trade lawyer Steve Charnovitz point to potential situations where for political reasons—or for other reasons unrelated to the legal aspects of a case—a government might decide to present a case that differs from that desired by a corporate entity or an NGO, or even decide not to bring a case at all. Charnovitz suggests several such scenarios: where governments may have other cases in international courts or domestic courts that conflict with a position in a WTO case; where different agencies within the executive branch may have conflicting positions or the government itself does not favor the domestic law being challenged in the WTO; or finally, where a case may have implications for future trade negotiations. Beyond Charnovitz's examples, one could even imagine that the U.S. government might not bring a case against Japan or Brazil or Korea, for example, because of competing diplomatic, security, or economic goals.

Because of such situations, Charnovitz concludes that the assumption "that governments can be depended on to synthesize and balance values is not warranted."[10] Similarly, Ragosta and trade lawyer Alan Wolff argue that the introduction of "'broader' interests . . . would compromise what Congress and the private sector believe international dispute settlement should be—an extension of the process of enforcing legal rights." This view, they contend, is "antithetical to the U.S. belief in fairness, [which holds] that individual rights should take precedence over government agencies' perception of broader interests in the disposition of specific cases and controversies."[11]

While advanced in good faith, these arguments are ultimately misguided—and unrealistic. The issue is not "individual rights" but rather the competing economic claims between corporations from different WTO members.[12] Charnovitz's contention that we cannot rely on governments to balance competing interests and values misses the point. Balancing values, competing interests, and interest groups is precisely what governments in these situations *are* doing—and must and should do. The national interest, even when it is concerned with the "low politics" of balancing the positions and claims of various interest groups, should still trump the narrow legalism of admittedly vague and imprecise WTO trade rules.

Thus, Philip Nichols of the University of Pennsylvania provides a more accurate evaluation when he affirms, "Having sorted out trade policy issues at the national level, bureaucrats are free to cooperate with other governments to maximize national and global welfare without the intrusion of special interests."[13] From the liberal IR theory perspective this study has adopted, a caveat should be added: bureaucrats are never really "free" to maximize national or world welfare. In this case, interest groups will follow the bureaucrats to Geneva. But more important, in Geneva, government bureaucrats will have the added weight of democratic legitimacy, through the democratic procedures and electoral processes in which they (or their elected leaders) have participated at home.

Support from Environmentalists. Support for greater use of mediation and nonbinding solutions in the trade and environment intersection has come from a surprising source: environmental NGOs. Two prominent international environmental organizations— the Center for International Environmental Law (CIEL) and the World Wildlife Fund International (WWF)—have published policy briefs on the WTO DSU that advance mediation, arbitration, and nonbinding solutions as the preferred means of resolving conflicts between trade and the environment.[14]

CIEL has also developed a model trade-environment framework for settling disputes in the WTO. This framework involves a three-step process: a preliminary exchange of viewpoints; informal bilateral negotiations or negotiations with other interested WTO members; and nonbinding third-party assisted dispute settlement. According to CIEL, "This process may be described as facilitated negotiations, and involves a third party to clarify the facts underlying the dispute to facilitate communications between the disputants, and to encourage them to reevaluate their positions. The third party may also offer compromise suggestions and solutions . . . ."[15]

WWF notes a precedent for such a parallel process in Article 5 of the DSU, but unfortunately, no disputant has used this alternative. CIEL suggests that members could develop guidelines to govern Article 5 procedures and take steps to promote facilitation and mediation as separate options.

Writing for CIEL, staff attorney Matthew Stillwell argues that the goal of the framework is "dispute prevention" and not judicialized dispute settlement. Reflecting on the lessons of the shrimp/turtle decisions and the conflicts over GMOs, he states that these "policy conflicts demonstrate the need for a more effective way to prevent trade-environment-development conflicts . . . from escalating into divisive international disputes that threaten the integrity of the multilateral trading system."[16] Regarding the tradeoffs of the panel-AB process, Stillwell writes: "Binding dispute settlement, at the WTO and elsewhere, represents an important contribution to the international rule of law. Nevertheless, because of their adversarial nature, binding dispute settlement procedures should only be considered after cooperative efforts have been exhausted, and as a last resort for resolving trade-environment disputes."[17]

What is striking is the preference for pragmatic solutions (in keeping with the old GATT "diplomatic" approaches) rather than a "correct" legal ruling. Stilwell explains, "The goal of any *process* of dispute settlement is to come to a *substantive outcome* that is acceptable to the parties—one that balances competing interests, maximizes synergies between trade-environment-development policies and equitably resolves conflicts."[18] Commenting on third-party mediation, he notes, "As an informal process, it can operate outside the formal WTO structure and requires no changes to WTO rules. . . . [I]t may also address environmentalists' legitimate concerns about the WTO dispute settlement system becoming an international environmental court."[19]

Support from the International Corporate Community/Trade Bar. The Trans-Atlantic Business Dialogue (TABD), an influential group of U.S. and EU-based multinationals with strong ties to their respective governments, has added its support for increased use of mediation and arbitration as alternatives to the DSU legal system. At a conference in Cincinnati, Ohio, in November 2000, the TABD made the following recommendation:

> The TABD expects both governments to use all avenues both before and throughout the dispute settlement process to solve disputes amicably. In particular, the TABD calls on both sides to try to avoid trade disputes through the use of [an] Early Warning system. Business stands ready to play a constructive role in this process. Furthermore the consultation phase of the dispute settlement process, as well as the good offices of the WTO Director-General as mediator in a dispute, could be explored and utilized more extensively than is presently the case. The TABD calls on both governments to look for alternative ways of settling disputes, where possible, including increased use of mediation and arbitration. . . .[20]

In early 2001, Alan Wolff, who has represented a number of companies and trade associations (particularly in the U.S. steel and semiconductor industries), denounced the "corrosive effects of an excessive reliance on litigation" and called for scrapping the binding dispute settlement system and substituting mediation or direct bilateral negotiations between the disputants. He stated that the main problem with the current system is

> the inappropriateness of placing on dispute settlement the burden of resolving major issues among the largest trading nations that in the final analysis cannot be resolved other than by negotiation among sovereign nations. . . . There is no substitute for commercial diplomacy in relations among sovereign states. Resolution of differences where matters of national interest are concerned cannot be fobbed off for third party resolution in the trade arena, just as they cannot in the foreign policy context.[21]

Support from Academics. Recent scholarship by international relations and legal theorists raises important questions about the viability of the new "hard law" of the WTO dispute settlement system and offers alternative means of reaching accommodation in conflicts among WTO members. In the summer of 2000, the quarterly *International Organization* devoted an entire issue to the concept of legalization and its application to international regimes and institutions. The analyses and conclusions of two sets of contributors—Kenneth Abbott and Duncan Snidal; and Judith Goldstein and Lisa Martin—provide an underpinning for the normative judgments and recommendations advanced in this study.[22] Before examining their work, this study reviews scholarship that advances alternative dispute settlement approaches, using Kal Raustiala's exploration of the issues of compliance and effectiveness in international regulatory regimes as an example.

Raustiala. Kal Raustiala holds that the debate over the causality behind treaty effectiveness (in this case WTO rules) largely entails competing visions of rationalist (realist, institutionalist) and norm-driven (constructivist, cognitivist) international relations theories.[23] Realists, in particular, are concerned with the importance of deterrence and attempt to calculate the optimal level of sanctions to compel compliance with a particular international agreement.

Norm-driven theories focus on the power of ideas and view state activity as "socially constructed" through the deepening influence of particular ideas. Norm-driven theorists known as "managerialists" have developed theories of compliance that argue, in direct contradiction to realist theory, that punitive enforcement is generally counterproductive. Although others have espoused similar ideas, managerialist theories are often associated with the work of Harvard legal scholars Abram and Antonia Handler Chayes.[24] Positing that noncompliance is usually nonvolitional—because of unclear substantive rules or the lack of means to comply—they hold that the best response to treaty violations is technical or financial assistance combined with ongoing dialogue and negotiation with recalcitrant nations. As the Chayeses explain, "This process of noncompliance should be discursive, nonconfrontational, forward-looking, and broadly cooperative. . . ." Realist critics argue, conversely, that managerialist theory can work only with "shallow" treaties where compliance is easy, never with "deeper" treaties that require costly actions. In those situations, according to realists, sanctions and punishment are required.[25]

Raustiala uses norm-driven managerialism as an empirical tool and provides academic support for lower-cost, less confrontational means of increasing the "effectiveness" of international regimes and rules. His basic argument is that under certain circumstances the "use of a flexible, less judicialized approach . . . may be more effective in resolving conflicts than an approach based purely on the enforcement of compliance through the DSU."[26] His empirical examples are drawn from environmental agreements and the WTO TRIPs agreement.

In his empirical analysis of a group of environmental treaties, Raustiala points to several alternate techniques that have been successfully employed to enhance the effectiveness of environmental agreements.[27] He is particularly interested in the use of system implementation reviews (SIRs), in which international rules are promulgated, with or without potential sanctions, and then formal or informal international reviews of domestic implementation are conducted periodically. As illustration, he describes the history of SIRs in the Montreal Protocol on Substances That Deplete the Ozone Layer, the European air pollution convention, and the nonbinding agreement to decrease marine pollution in the North Sea.[28]

Based upon these empirical accounts, Raustiala finds great explanatory power in the managerialist model. He states, "What is most significant is that these nonbinding instruments have led to observable, sometimes marked, changes in behavior, and sometimes these changes in behavior appear greater than the likely change under a regime of binding rules."[29] He admits that there are advantages to both binding and nonbinding approaches but concludes, "The central point . . . is that the paradigm of creating binding rules and then seeking to achieve compliance with them is not the only possible route to effective international cooperation. While nonbinding instruments are not a panacea, the evidence suggests that more consideration of their utility in international cooperation . . . is warranted."[30]

The Trade-Related Intellectual Property Rights agreement contains innovative, sweeping, and difficult obligations for WTO members, particularly for the many developing countries that do not have a complete intellectual property system written into law and do not have a tradition of enforcing IP rights. In addition, the TRIPs agreement, which took effect in January 1995, was necessarily broadly worded and replete with gaps and omissions. Equally important, because IP rules are a moving target even in developed countries, a number of new substantive areas were not included, specifically those dealing with electronics, software, and key areas of biotechnology and genetics. Yet all WTO members (including developing countries since the year 2000) are subject to the full, binding adjudicatory system.

Raustiala suggests that given the complexity and novelty of the issues, some method of system implementation review would be helpful, even indispensable, if TRIPs is not to create major turmoil within the WTO. And he sees the beginnings of such a review within the TRIPs Council, which is charged with reviewing the national systems of TRIPs laws and regulation. Members are increasingly using the five regularly scheduled council meetings to submit questions, explore in greater depth the meaning of particular substantive provisions of TRIPs, and debate areas where ambiguities exist. Council members are also probing for potential violations of TRIPs obligations and asking pointed questions in cases where they believe a nation has taken an action that could constitute such a violation, thereby prefiguring and potentially heading off formal adjudication.

Raustiala very much applauds this alternate approach because the combination of new, evolving rules and a strong DSU is "volatile and may work to the detriment of the TRIPs and the dispute settlement process. . . ." In the end, he argues that use of the council for implementation reviews, backed on rare occasions by the threat of formal adjudication, "may be more likely to yield an . . . effective TRIPs than is an aggressive focus on compliance achieved through contentious judicial solutions."[31]

Managerialist theory and Raustiala's empirical evidence fit comfortably with this study's recommendations for greater mediation and conciliation efforts at the front end of the dispute settlement process, as well as a blocking action mechanism at the back end of the process (see next section on the case for a limited blocking capability). As noted, the underlying political and textual conditions of WTO rules—unclear language that often papers over negotiating disagreements, and complex regulatory, health, and safety questions upon which there is no global consensus—make a powerful case for a less judicialized system.

Abbott and Snidal. In their contribution to *International Organization*, Kenneth Abbott of Northwestern University Law School and Duncan Snidal of the University of Chicago analyze the tradeoffs between "hard" and "soft" law in international agreements. By hard law, they mean that rules are binding and precise, and third parties have been granted the authority to interpret and enforce the rules. By soft law, they mean that rules are less binding and less precise, and there is less delegation of authority to third parties. Abbott and Snidal's goal is to "explain government behavior as well as the behavior of groups that evaluate their interests for or against legalization."[32] Like Raustiala, Abbott and Snidal hold that both rational self-interest and norm-driven values are explanatory variables. As the two authors explain, "Legalization has effect through normative standards and processes as well as self-interested calculations, and both interest and values are constraints on the success of law. . . . [W]e reject vigorously the insistence of many international relations specialists that one type of understanding is antithetical to the other."[33]

Certainly the new WTO DSU was a decisive move toward hard law within the multilateral trading system. According to Abbott and Snidal, the virtues of hard law include the ability to reduce transaction costs, strengthen the credibility of commitments, and resolve problems associated with incomplete contracts.

Hard law reduces transaction costs by fostering clarity and continuity through the enforcement of precise rules by independent tribunals. It thus aids in the management of agreements. Abbott and Snidal state, "Procedurally, hard law constrains the techniques of dispute settlement and negotiation. . . . Compared to alternatives like frequent negotiations, persuasion, or coercion, it materially reduces the costs of enforcement."[34]

Problems arising from incomplete contracts reflect the fact that most, if not all, international agreements are negotiated under conditions of asymmetric information and uncertainty. Abbott and Snidal write that "given . . . the pervasive uncertainty in which states operate, they can never construct agreements that anticipate every contingency." Thus, hard legal regimes give great independence to judicial bodies, and at the same time require states to follow agreed-upon principles. The authors posit that states will grant such authority "when the anticipated gains from cooperation are large and there is reasonable consensus on general principles."[35]

Soft law has distinct advantages over hard law under a number of conditions, including reducing contracting costs, reducing "sovereignty costs," allowing forward movement in the face of uncertainty, and providing an important tool for forging compromises on divisive substantive issues. It can reduce contracting costs at the front end of a negotiating process by inducing states to reach agreements that are less binding and more flexible. Further, soft law reduces so-called "sovereignty costs"—that is, the costs that states incur when they delegate authority to supranational organizations—by providing less binding commitments and less extensive delegation of power. As Abbot and Snidal explain, "Even if rules are written precisely to narrow their range, . . . states cannot anticipate or limit all of their possible effects. . . . States can limit sovereignty costs through arrangements that are nonbinding or imprecise or do not delegate extensive powers. . . . Soft legalization allows states to adapt their commitment to their particular situations. . . ."[36]

In the final analysis, soft law should not be viewed as simply a way station to hard law, according to Abbott and Snidal, and hard law should not be considered superior to soft law:

> Soft law is valuable on its own, not just as a stepping stone to hard law. Soft law provides a basis for efficient international "contracts," and it helps create normative "'covenants" and discourses that can reshape international politics. . . . [S]oft legalization helps balance competing considerations, offering techniques for compromise among states, among private actors, and between states and private actors. In addition, soft law helps actors handle the exigencies of uncertainty and accommodate power differentials.[37]

The changes recommended in this study represent a move away from the hard law provisions enacted at the end of the Uruguay Round. Both the specific suggestion for mediation and conciliation at the front end of the process and the proposal for a blocking mechanism detailed in a subsequent section aim to use soft-law escape routes that will produce settlements that take account of the reality that Abbott and Snidal describe: "Politics permeates international law and limits its autonomy."[38] In addition, soft law—and a move toward more diplomatic solutions—ameliorates some of the serious questions of democratic legitimacy that concern this study.

Goldstein and Martin. In their contribution to *International Organization,* Judith Goldstein and Lisa Martin, political scientists from Stanford and Harvard Universities, respectively, examine the impact of greater legalization and more precise rules on the domestic political forces in WTO member states; they also assess the implications of more binding GATT/WTO rules on these governments.

Goldstein and Martin point out that more detailed rules will increase the information available to domestic groups on the distributional implications of the new commercial rules. This in turn will produce unintended consequences in the mobilization of forces that support and oppose free trade. According to the authors, the balance of power will be tipped against free trade in the negotiating phase, but in favor of more open markets on subsequent issues of compliance: "Antitrade group pressures make negotiations more difficult, and to the extent that transparency encourages mobilization of antitrade groups, it will hinder liberalization negotiations. During trade disputes, politicians similarly strategize about how to reveal information so as to mobilize groups appropriately—in this instance to maximize the mobilization of exporters in the target country."[39]

More important for this study are the consequences of the more tightly binding rules and greater legalization of the WTO that the two authors foresee. Using the empirical research of political scientists George Downs and David Rocke, Goldstein and Martin argue that the dynamics of domestic politics create a necessity for "some optimal level of 'imperfection' in the applications of international rules"—and with regard to the trade regime, some imperfection in enforcement mechanisms through controlled laxity and flexibility.[40]

Goldstein and Martin acknowledge the difficulties of finding the right balance between flexibility and legally binding rules: "The enforcement structures of the GATT/WTO thus face a difficult dilemma. . . . If enforcement is too harsh, states will comply with trade rules even in the face of high economic and political costs, and general support for liberalization is likely to decline. On the other hand, if enforcement is too lax, states will cheat, leading to a different dynamic that could similarly undermine the system."[41]

In the end, however, they conclude that the old GATT dispute settlement system came closer to the right balance of "imperfection" than does the new more binding regime: "We suggest that the GATT dispute settlement structure, by being more attentive to the realities of power and uncertain economic environment, but also by providing publicity and possible sanctions when states blatantly disregarded regime rules, may have optimized the trade-off between constraint and flexibility that liberalization requires."[42]

They note that, given the short history of the new WTO DSU, empirical results must remain tentative. Nevertheless, Goldstein and Martin state:

> Here we suggested that trade regimes need to incorporate some flexibility in their enforcement procedures; too little enforcement may encourage opportunism, but too much may backfire, undermining the ability of domestic actors to find support for an open trade policy. By decreasing the ability to breach agreements, WTO negotiators may have underestimated the inherently uncertain character of the international economy and so the need to allow practical flexibility in enforcement of regime rules. . . . Similarly, our investigation of the WTO dispute settlement mechanism gives us little reason to think that legalization in the realm of settling disputes will have significant effects on trade compliance. The GATT system was relatively effective at deterring opportunism in spite of its political nature.[43]

To a striking degree, the authors of both articles agree on the necessity of flexibility in international trade law as well as the dangers that the new DSU system may "backfire" and cause a reaction against trade liberalization and the international trading system. Although these authors may not agree with the particular recommendations made in this study, the proposals herein are advanced with their research and admonitions very much in mind.

The Back End of the Dispute Settlement System: The Case for a Limited Blocking Capability. Writing in the early 1990s, after the major outlines of the new WTO dispute settlement system had become public but details had not been finalized, trade scholar Robert Hudec, then at the University of Minnesota Law School, questioned the ability of a more "judicialized" Appellate Body to function properly because underlying GATT substantive rules did not provide a "minimally coherent legal structure." As Hudec stated,

"GATT law is full of gaps, omissions, inconsistencies, and outmoded provisions."[44] As noted, the problems associated with vague and incoherent text stemming from compromises that obscured real disagreements were compounded by far-reaching new rules—particularly for services and intellectual property—created during the Uruguay Round.

A more fundamental reason for curbing the power of the panels and the AB lies in the "democratic deficit" at the core of the WTO as an institution. Wolff and Ragosta described the basic political fault lines quite accurately almost immediately after the new system was put in place:

> At first blush, the WTO system does not appear quite so revolutionary. On closer inspection, however, it is indeed radical. . . . [I]n domestic disputes, it is common to bind parties to the court's ruling, whether they believe that they had accepted the legal basis of the ruling or not. After all, the individuals are not "sovereign" and, in any case have no fundamental complaint about the exercise of judicial authority. They elect representatives who make the law; they participate in the political institutions that appoint and remove the judges. Ultimately, if a court issues a decision that so offends accepted understanding of obligations, democratic remedies exist. The same is not true in the WTO. Indeed, a change in a WTO rule to "correct" or modify a panel decision would require a "consensus" that almost certainly cannot be achieved.[45]

John Jackson has also warned of "emerging constitutional problems" with the new dispute settlement system. In a 1998 article, he wrote:

> It has to be recognized that there is a delicate interplay between the dispute settlement process on the one hand, and the possibilities or difficulties of negotiating new treaty texts or making decisions by the organization that are authorized by the Uruguay Round treaty text, on the other hand. . . . [T]he dispute settlement system cannot and should not carry much of the weight of formulating new rules either by way of filling gaps in the existing agreements, or by setting forth norms which carry the organization into totally new territory. . . .[46]

In 1992, when Robert Hudec wrote his assessment of the proposed new dispute settlement system, he argued that because of the weak substantive legal foundation, reform of the GATT dispute settlement system should retain a good deal of political flexibility:

> The various inadequacies of the GATT legal system are in a sort of balance or equilibrium. Each of the inadequacies tends to serve as a natural adjust-

ment or response to the other. A badly structured law needs the flexibility of a more political jurisprudence. So do structurally weak institutions that are not capable of generating the authority to make law, or to compel adherence to it. Lawyers cannot function like pure technicians (relatively speaking) when neither the law nor the institution applying the law is capable of working properly under that methodology.[47]

Hudec suggested several options for reform of the system, including a "strong option"—similar to the one proposed in this study—of setting aside a decision if a majority or substantial minority opposes it. Hudec explained, "A strong option would . . . [provide] that the report would automatically be adopted unless the special council meeting decides to set aside the panel report. The option need not demand consensus, or consensus-minus-two, to set aside. The standard could be one of a majority, or even substantial support as determined by the chair."[48]

- *Recommendation: The specific recommendation advanced in this study is that the WTO reintroduce political flexibility and a greater balance between its legislative and judicial processes by providing that if at least one-third of the members of the DSB, representing at least one-quarter of total trade among WTO members, express disagreement with a panel or AB decision, then that decision should be set aside—blocked—and the DSB would affirm that it is not binding WTO law. An alternative, which also should be considered, would be to allow the decision to stand for the parties at issue, but to have the DSB formally declare that members should not consider the ruling binding WTO law.[49] Subsequently, through the normal WTO legislative process, the General Council could either amend an existing rule or create a new rule to deal with the issue, depending on the circumstance. If the General Council could not reach consensus or agreement, then the issue would remain to be settled at the next round of WTO trade negotiations, as part of a larger package of compromises.*

The reasoning behind this proposal is twofold. First, whenever a substantial minority of WTO members—members that were not party to and had no particular commercial stake in a dispute—take issue with a panel or AB decision or the rationale behind it, then the WTO should take action to reorder the balance between the stalemated legislative function of the WTO and the all too efficient, fast-track DSU. Otherwise, support for the dispute settlement system will gradually erode. After the shrimp/turtle decision, according to witnesses, virtually every WTO member who spoke in the DSB, with the exception of the United States, opposed the reasoning behind the decision. More recently, strong and bitter protests were registered in the British Steel and the Canadian asbestos cases—not just from the losing party and not so much concerning the commercial aspects of the case as the constitutional implications.[50]

On both pragmatic political grounds and grounds of democratic legitimacy, the proposal stands at odds with calls by a number of legal theorists for the dispute settlement system to fill the gaps left by messy negotiating compromises. As noted on page 42 of this study, Raj Bhala of George Washington University has proclaimed that the "Appellate Body members work in an arena where the imperfections of 'legislators' (trade negotiators) . . . are all too plain. . . . [They] have no choice but to legislate. . . ."

In a 2000 draft paper, Robert Howse of the University of Michigan Law School wrote, "Given [the] democratic defect in rule-*creation,* social legitimacy in rule interpretation may exist as *demo-cratic* social legitimacy, where the exercise of the judicial power properly handles a conflict of values held by diverse stakeholders, taking into account . . . the actual understandings and expectations of those diverse stakeholders. . . ."[51]

While the WTO must take steps to integrate its rules and actions into other international regimes (e.g., environmental treaties and the ILO), it would be unwise for the trade organization to expand into the guarantor of other norms and values. And it certainly would be a disastrous mistake to attempt to achieve this already unwise goal through judicial interpretation and expansion.

This study proposes to increase the legitimacy of the WTO by a wholly different means. The new blocking mechanism would buy time for decisions to be made through the normal legislative processes. This means, first, attempting to amend old rules or add new rules where necessary during regularly scheduled meetings of the relevant WTO councils. If this fails, then the fallback would be to convene a major trade round—as contemplated for 2002. Rule-making by means of big-picture trade negotiations is not the most efficient way to write trade rules, but it does have the virtue of allowing all WTO members to participate in the legislative process.[52]

Compliance, Retaliation, and Compensation

The issue of the impact of WTO obligations on national sovereignty has been raised in two other contexts: whether the United States and other countries, under the new WTO rules, can refuse to follow a panel or Appellate Body ruling and merely accept retaliation or grant compensation; and whether WTO rules should be granted a "direct effect" on U.S. domestic law, including the attempts of U.S. citizens or other nationals to invoke WTO rules against U.S. statutes. This section deals with issues related to compliance, retaliation, and compensation; the next section considers issues related to direct effect.

In several highly publicized cases, countries have opted to accept retaliation rather than bring their laws and practices into compliance with the panel findings. In fact, the Dispute Settlement Understanding does not explicitly establish a definitive legal obligation that a WTO member must follow the determinations and recommendations of a panel or Appellate Body report; however, John Jackson has argued that a series of separate clauses in the DSU comprise an implied obligation to conform to dispute settlement rulings. One DSU article states that dispute settlement "is a central element in providing security and predictability to the multilateral trading system." Another article states that "members affirm their adherence to the principles for the management of disputes heretofore applied...and the rules and procedures as further elaborated and modified herein." And a third states that "neither compensation nor suspension of concessions or other obligations is preferred to full implementation of a recommendation."[53] Others, such as practitioner and international legal theorist Judith Hippler Bello, argue that states may elect not to comply and accept compensation because WTO law is "not 'binding' in the traditional sense."[54]

Whatever the merits of direct compliance with panel or Appellate Body rulings, there is a strong possibility that WTO members will increasingly opt for noncompliance and accepting retaliation—responses that are available under the new dispute settlement system. In two high-profile cases—the bananas case and the beef hormones case—the EU accepted retaliation measures. In these cases, the United States placed tariffs on what was judged to be the equivalent amount of goods to that lost by the quota on bananas and the ban on hormone-fed beef.

Critics of the widespread use of sanctions and retaliation have pointed out that trade sanctions fundamentally conflict with the whole purpose of WTO dispute settlement. The goal of the process is to *reduce or eliminate* trade barriers, but the invocation of trade sanctions actually results in a net *increase* in trade barriers because barriers against the guilty party are added to barriers already in place against the aggrieved party.[55]

Ironically, the trade sanctions against an offending party punish the complaining country's consumers and businessmen as much as they punish the offending country's producers. By raising prices for consumers and businessmen, the sanctions reduce available consumer income as well as the competitiveness of businessmen as consumers of intermediate imported products.

- **Recommendation:** *A potential alternative would advance the trade-liberalizing goals of the dispute settlement process, as well as the goal of punishing nations that violate WTO rules. Under this proposal, the existing option of providing compensation would be mandated as the sole remedy for noncompliance. Compensation could be exacted through a monetary fine on the offending nation; or the offending WTO member could agree to institute trade liberalization equivalent in commercial value to the cost of the trade barrier(s).[56]*

Under current DSU rules, when nations refuse to comply with panel or Appellate Body decisions, compensation is designated as a fallback option along with sanctions. Article 22.1 of the DSU states, "Compensation and suspension of concessions [sanctions] are temporary measures available in the event that the recommendations and rulings are not implemented within a reasonable period of time." The DSU, however, does not spell out mechanisms for carrying out the compensation option. Thus, compensation at present is voluntary (and no defendant has offered it), and the complaining country is under no obligation to agree to this method of redress. Further, no method for determining what constitutes "due" compensation has been developed.

Several proposals to make compensation a viable alternative to trade-reducing sanctions have been offered. First, future rules could be changed to make compensation mandatory.[57] Then, either a separate tribunal or the panel that tried the case could be designated to calculate the cost of the defendant country's trade barriers to the complaining WTO member. There are two potential methods for structuring the actual remedy.

Under one scenario, compensation to the complaining country could be derived from a monetary fine imposed on the government of the country found guilty of a WTO rules violation. These public funds could then be given to the complaining government, which could, in turn, pass on the funds to the domestic industry injured by the offending trade barriers.[58]

Alternatively, the guilty WTO member could be required to institute trade liberalization measures equivalent in commercial value to the cost of its trade barriers to the complaining country. The offending country might also be given the option of several liberalization packages and allowed to choose among them.[59] The Trans-Atlantic Business Dialogue has strongly endorsed the trade liberalization alternative. At its conference in Cincinnati, Ohio, in November 2000, the TABD stated the following:

> The TABD calls upon the EU and the U.S. to rethink the present system of sanctions. Rather than accepting sanctions, the two sides should look for compensating trade-liberalization measures. Although not an acceptable alternative to implementation [of a panel or AB decision], compensatory measures such as lowering of tariffs or some other form of trade-liberalizing measure at least has the virtue of reducing the overall level of protection and acts as a temporary offset to a continuing WTO violation.[60]

Either method is feasible and would be superior to the use of trade sanctions. The virtue of offsetting trade liberalization as compensation is that it does result in lowering additional trade barriers. An even greater virtue comes from the fact that these liberalization actions must be offered to *all* WTO members because of the most favored nation principle. On the other hand, liberalization of additional sectors may pose great difficulties for the offending country domestically and draw greater opposition from import-competing industries.[61] Further, levying a fine does focus the penalty directly on the specific trade barrier and its costs—though the downside of levying a fine may be opposition to adding to the use of public funds when the benefits of the trade barrier accrue to private parties and corporations.

International Law versus National Law: Direct Effect

Under the international legal principle of direct effect, a nation agrees that its domestic laws and regulations will be bound by obligations undertaken in international treaties and agreements. Direct effect gives a private citizen the power to demand relief from, or make a claim against, another person or the state itself on the basis of the state's obligation under a treaty. A claim may also be made against implementing legislation on grounds that the law violates international law. Clearly, adherence to the direct effect doctrine substantially alters the power relationship between the state, private actors, and domestic courts. It grants enhanced authority to private actors, who derive private rights and obligations directly from the treaty; and it reinforces the position of courts vis-à-vis governments in that they may overrule legislation or rules as inconsistent with international law.[62]

Two national traditions govern direct effect: historically, some nations, such as France, have followed the "monist" doctrine, under which treaty language is assumed to become domestic law without the necessity of legislation ("transformation," in trade terms) by the parliament. Other countries, such as England, follow a "dualist" tradition, in which domestic law prevails over international law, absent an explicit change by the legislature.

In recent years, particularly in academic trade circles in Europe, a growing body of literature has favored moving toward monist principles. Ernst-Ulrich Petersmann, a leading German legal scholar, has argued for "constitutionalizing international trade principles, elevating the rights of an individual to trade freely with foreigners to the level of a fundamental human right."[63] Petersmann and other writers in this school espouse the laudable goal of providing restraints on the protectionist behavior of national governments. And they also receive support from some smaller and medium-sized nations, such as Switzerland, which are heavily dependent on the rule of law in international economic relations.

Critics, particularly those from the United States, stress the negative impact that allowing treaty law to supersede domestic law would have on the constitutional balance of power and on federal checks and balances. Ultimately, as one observer notes, these critics believe that allowing "treaty law to be superior to federal legislation (let alone to the constitution) would be dangerous to the idea of democracy and democratic representation of individuals."[64]

Ironically, until quite recently, the United States followed an ad hoc "nonpolicy," applying direct effect to some treaties and refusing to apply it to others. Official commentaries on U.S. domestic and treaty law have suggested that, absent a request by Congress or the President for implementing legislation, a treaty signed by the United States would be self-executing and would override existing domestic law. Several earlier court decisions have suggested that the issue must be handled on a case-by-case basis.

Since the late 1980s, however, strong intervention by Congress has changed the situation substantially. In four major trade agreements—the U.S.–Israel and U.S.–Canadian Free Trade Agreements, NAFTA, and the Uruguay Round Agreement—congressional consent was granted only on the condition of an explicit denial of direct effect, or self-execution. The legislation implementing the Uruguay Round expressly prohibits direct reliance on the agreement by courts in cases brought by or against individuals or states.

These actions are part of a larger trend in which Congress has been reasserting its constitutional authority over "foreign commerce" after years of deferring to the executive branch and the courts. Congress is also responding to the changing nature of trade agreements and the growing number of trade rules that go far beyond traditional border measures relating to tariffs. With the GATT and now the WTO enacting rules relating to what had long been regarded as domestic issues—government subsidies, services regulations (banking, insurance, and telecommunications, for example), and intellectual property—Congress has signaled its determination to retain clear authority over what it considers core elements of U.S. domestic practices and regulations.

In several recent contributions, international legal scholars have noted that the issues raised by direct effect are, in reality, an extension of the debate over a private right of action by corporations or NGOs in the WTO. Joel Trachtman, professor of international law at Tufts University's Fletcher School, notes that "by invoking the domestic legal system, directly effective international law takes advantage of a 'traditional' sovereign, and its powers to make law binding, even against the domestic state itself . . . [and] shifts control to private litigants."[65] Yet, he argues, both the new DSU and proposals for direct effect must be evaluated in light of the continuing "unruly political context" of international law.

In the end, Trachtman warns of two dangers from attempts to invoke direct effect of WTO law—one stemming from issues of democratic legitimacy, and the other from the realities of power politics and the fragility of the new WTO dispute settlement process. Thus, he notes that direct effect

> is a policy question to be answered in political terms. . . . Of course, in the EC and U.S. systems, there are substantial circumstances in which judges are permitted to decide whether international legal rules have direct effect, or are self-executing. This fact can be interpreted as an implicit delegation to courts of this decision, with the possibility of legislative or perhaps constitutional reversal. Denial of direct effect and weak mechanisms of compliance may be viewed not necessarily as gaps in compliance, but as mechanisms to reinforce democratic legitimacy, to the extent that the state is the locus of democratic legitimacy. . . . Direct effect without more direct democratic participation in formulation of the directly effective law raises as many issues as it resolves.[66]

Another issue concerns the realities stemming from the "rough and imperfect" condition of international law. Trachtman contends that, given these realities, powerful states must be given more "flexibility" in meeting WTO obligations:

> This implicit discrimination may, of course, be criticized from one perspective. However, it might also be interpreted as preserving and maximizing the constraint on powerful states by avoiding circumstances in which they find themselves with no alternative but to renege formally on their

obligations. As every good fisherman knows, some give in the line is necessary to reel in the big fish, because if the line breaks you have nothing.[67]

- *Recommendation: With the decisions taken during the Uruguay Round, WTO rules have moved into areas once thought entirely the domain of domestic policy. Particularly with regard to services, these obligations have widespread implications for how nations regulate key industries such as financial services and telecommunications. In the Millennium Round, some nations are calling for additional rules on competition policy and international investment. With the multilateral trade regime now operating so deeply in the domestic economic and social affairs of WTO members, Congress would be well advised to continue its caution and vigilance regarding the overlay of trade policy on U.S. regulatory policy; it should also continue the recent practice of denying self-execution and direct effect in trade agreements. Congress may choose to enact all treaty provisions into U.S. law, but this decision should be consciously undertaken by elected representatives and not given by default to trade negotiators.*

Transparency and Participation

On both theoretical and practical grounds, proposals for a more open WTO can be divided into two categories: demands for greater transparency in the procedures of the WTO; and demands for greater public participation in the deliberations and judicial functions of the organization. The latter demands, as this study has shown, present far greater problems and challenges to the international trading system.

Transparency. Opponents of the WTO have effectively focused on the alleged "Star Chamber" proceedings in WTO dispute settlement and the power of "unelected international bureaucrats" to use the judicial process to lower environmental and safety standards. The proceedings of the panels and the AB are currently closed to the public. Participation by third parties, as well as other WTO members, is also restricted. On occasion, panels convene hearings where third parties can make their presentations separately. A number of the documents generated by this process are confidential. The United States has taken the lead in pressing to open the process, and in a May 1998 speech to the WTO, President Clinton presented a set of specific proposals for transparency.[68]

Opponents of open, public hearings and wide circulation of documents express their desire to keep a sense of collegiality and comity within the proceedings. They fear that making the process public will lead government representatives to indulge in various "grandstanding" tactics to impede the process and create legal and technical roadblocks to confuse and confound the panels.[69] Some have argued that public discussion of national submissions during the deliberations could exert undue influence on panelists.

But as Robert Hudec has noted, the days of collegiality are largely over, and the new judicialized system has already moved far along the path toward a more adversarial approach. In these circumstances, the need to deflect and counter the criticism of NGOs and private lawyers that the closed system is undemocratic more than offsets the arguments for confidentiality. As Hudec has stated, "While the proposal to allow public access to documents could well have a negative impact on party behavior, such public access would help to deflect serious attacks on the legitimacy of WTO legal rulings."[70]

- **Recommendation:** *All documents that governments present (and any* amicus *briefs that the panels or AB accept) should be made public at the time they are submitted; this would include posting these documents on the Internet. Information that was confidential for businesses would continue to be protected. The United States has agreed unilaterally to make public all of its submissions and has urged other nations to follow suit.*

   Regarding the issue of opening the panel and dispute settlement hearings to the public, a cautious step-by-step approach is recommended. It is hoped that others will follow the U.S. lead in making all submissions public; it therefore seems sensible to provide for public access to the opening sessions when the panels first address a particular dispute. This would allow outsiders to hear the opening arguments of all participants, including antagonists and third parties.

Providing public access would represent an important first step that would not subject the panels to undue pressure, as would be the case if NGOs and corporations were allowed to monitor subsequent questioning. After some experience with a partially open process, the DSB could be asked to reevaluate the issue of closed versus open hearings. Because governments have the right to appoint private persons (generally lawyers) to their litigation teams, the possibility that nongovernment persons will be part of the process already exists.[71]

Amicus Briefs. The issue of *amicus* briefs has been left in a legal no-man's land. The AB has asserted, over the strong protests of a number of WTO members, that outside organizations have no legal right to submit briefs, but that both the panels and the AB itself have the authority to accept outside material when they "find it pertinent to do so."

As noted, India, Mexico, and other countries have complained that the dispute settlement system gave greater rights to NGOs than to WTO members and cited the strict limitations on third-party submissions and member attendance at hearings. The unease of some members escalated during the summer of 2000 when the United States refused requests from Australia, Japan, and several other members to sit in on consultations between the United States and the European Union on the U.S. plan to institute "carousel" trade retaliations. Under the novel carousel approach, the United States proposed to rotate the list of items targeted for retaliation on a regular basis, thereby affecting many more industries over time. The approach was clearly important to all WTO members, but the United States argued that the requesting countries had not shown a "substantial trade interest" as required by WTO rules. Coupled with the new liberal approach toward *amicus* briefs by businesses and NGOs, even countries such as Australia, which has favored more transparency, joined a number of developing countries in protesting the contradiction and impact on the rights of WTO members.[72]

At this point, both the panels and the AB have accepted independent filings from major U.S. trade associations such as the American Iron and Steel Institute; the Specialty Steel Industry of North America; and the American Society of Composers, Authors, and Publishers. Thus far the EU has opposed the United States in its drive to allow outside briefs; in light of recent rulings, however, it will not be long before trade associations and corporations within the EU will be clamoring to be heard independently. Large environmental and other NGOs with substantial financial resources are undoubtedly scrutinizing pending cases for possible intervention.

In July 2000, Australian WTO Ambassador Geoffrey Raby suggested that members begin to draft rules for governing the submission of *amicus* briefs, arguing that such "rules will be important in ensuring the preservation of members' rights of equity, transparency, and due process in disputes and should impose necessary disciplines on the acceptance of *amicus* briefs."[73] Given the wide differences among members, however, and the need to achieve consensus, it may be some time before such rules are adopted. Meanwhile, the AB has provoked stinging dissent by promulgating at least temporary rules for friend-of-the-court briefs.

Supporters of the AB's decision to assert its authority to accept outside briefs frame the issue as a procedural one, arguing that it flows from the necessity to obtain as much information and argumentation as needed to reach an informed decision. In reality, much more than procedure and fact-finding is at stake. Depending on how the rules are finally written, allowing *amicus* briefs will change the political dynamics of the DSU. Unless fairly tight restrictions are placed on the number and scope of outside briefs, smaller, developing countries risk becoming overwhelmed by the process. The resources that U.S. or EU multinationals or NGOs can bring to bear on WTO cases will far outweigh those of many national governments.

Furthermore, unless some means is found to regulate the timing of briefs—allowing their submission at the beginning of the process, for example, so that all parties have a chance to respond—WTO members, both large and small, risk being blindsided by highly sophisticated and novel arguments to which they will have no chance to respond. Philip Nichols alluded to this prospect when he wrote, "Rather than resulting in a democratization of trade policy-making, expansion of standing might instead be a boon to select groups of well-monied interest groups."[74]

Allowing the submission of *amicus* briefs also diminishes the authority of governments over outside organizations. Almost certainly, environmental and other NGOs will be submitting briefs that contradict and dissent from their own government's position. This, Nichols has warned, will lead to "the spectacle of domestic constituencies opposing the positions of the governments that are supposed to represent those constituencies."[75]

- *Recommendation: If the EU remains opposed to independently submitted outside briefs, leading WTO developing countries— India, Brazil, and Mexico, for example—would do well to join the EU's trade negotiators in pressing the Appellate Body to reverse its initial ruling until tighter rules regarding the timing and quantity of such material can be negotiated among WTO members. Always ready to nip at U.S. heels, the EU might well take on this issue in an effort to curry favor with developing countries and receive reciprocal benefits in the future. Furthermore, a number of observers believe that the AB is sensitive to political currents and, in the case of amicus briefs, "lets itself be overawed by the campaign of NGOs of major trading entities."[76] Countries opposing the rulings should therefore continue to raise complaints loudly and clearly in the DSB and other WTO forums. Such a course may well cause the panels and the AB to exercise caution in the actual use of amicus briefs, at least until matters can be sorted out by negotiations.*

At some point, *amicus* briefs may well be allowed in dispute settlement proceedings. If this happens, it should occur only after rule-making negotiations among all WTO members. It should not evolve from panel or Appellate Body decisions, either as an adjunct to particular cases or through AB rules for appellate procedures.

Access to DSU and WTO Deliberations. In many ways, the excessive rhetoric and claims concerning a new role for NGOs has served as a deterrent to sensible compromises that would retain the government-to-government character of the WTO, and at the same time accommodate NGOs' arguments for a more formal structured role (see, for example, Daniel Esty's claim that NGOs offer horizontal competition to governments).[77] Further, the dream of duplicating the partnership with the bureaucracy that various bodies within the UN have attained will not be realized in the WTO. First, UN declarations generally consist of supposedly high-minded rhetorical pronouncements that aim, at most, for the equivocal status of soft law. WTO rules and dispute settlement cases, on the other hand, can often have major economic consequences, as the EU's potential multibillion-dollar victory over the United States in the export tax subsidy case dramatically illustrates. As one salient observer of the WTO has noted:

> State representatives contrast the tenor of the discussions in the WTO with discussion in UN bodies where states do not confront the same "consequences" when negotiating generalized principles concerning environmental norms. . . . As a representative from an African nation . . . confirms: "Delegates are wary of the WTO. GATT is a binding contract. People are not as open and freewheeling as in other international fora. In the WTO, everything you say matters and can be used against you."[78]

Even before GATT/WTO rules had the reach and bite of the current system, governments retained tight control over the negotiating and dispute processes, the Secretariat, and various working committees. The Uruguay Round established much broader substantive obligations (services and intellectual property, for example) and the negotiation of rules governing regulatory questions far from the border. As a result, governments—particularly those from developing countries—have increased their surveillance of, and participation in, WTO activities.

- **Recommendation:** *Certain reforms that would not violate the principles espoused throughout this study are worth considering. Two proposals regarding the dispute settlement system deserve scrutiny: one relates to the composition of DSU panels, and the second relates to potential NGO participation in an expanded conciliation/ mediation stage of the DSU.*

   Although the language of the DSU clearly assumes that trade experts would staff the dispute panels, it does allow for nontrade experts: "Panels shall be composed of well-qualified governmental and/or nongovernmental individuals, including. . . ." It then lists various types of trade experts, but does not specifically exclude nontrade experts. Given this freedom, the WTO should instruct the Secretariat to recruit experts in allied fields such as the environment, food safety, genetics, and competition policy to serve where disputes entail "trade and" issues. The net could be cast widely, with scholars and scientists sought, as well as the lawyers, diplomats, and economists who now staff the panels.[79]

A second potential reform would combine the proposal made in this study for greater—even mandatory, in some cases—use of mediation and conciliation with former GATT/WTO director Gary Sampson's proposal that, at least in environmental cases and in cases where the contending parties agree to it, some kind of public hearing under the good offices of the Director-General be convened. After the two parties have agreed to the mediation alternative, the DG would appoint a moderator to preside over a hearing to take testimony from experts in the area under dispute and to facilitate a resolution without formal adjudication. Under Sampson's proposal, the moderator would be empowered to suggest a solution after the hearing.

Whether combined with the proposal advanced in this study or considered separately, Sampson's suggestion has merit. The less formal mediation process he advocates poses little danger that the NGOs that might be tapped to provide experts would assert their right to participate. And as Sampson notes, "Even if there were not a positive outcome in terms of a clear decision, this process would be totally transparent—something sought by many representatives of civil society. The possibility of providing technical experts is another advantage. And the more formal dispute settlement process would be avoided if the mediation were successful. . . ."[80]

Consultation. Increasingly, deliberations by the councils and committees of the WTO are assuming greater importance. WTO observers agree that even when issues are not advanced—as with the tradeoff between trade and the environment throughout the 1990s—these forums have served to thrash out, if not settle, policy differences.

The experience of the Committee on Trade and the Environment (CTE), created in 1991, is illustrative. Because of deep divisions between and within developed and developing countries, the formal report of the committee in 1996 largely reflected a stalemate and therefore was deeply disappointing to NGOs. But the process of interaction became a model for opening up WTO internal deliberations to the public, to NGOs, and to business groups.[81]

The CTE secretariat was the first to create a website, which published in timely fashion detailed reports of the committee's deliberations and minutes of the meetings.

Over time, the secretariat persuaded an increasing number of governments to lift restrictions on their own submissions and papers prepared by the WTO staff as soon as they were formally submitted. During the course of the decade, the CTE secretariat also organized a series of six NGO symposia, at which WTO delegates met with environmental and development NGOs, corporations and business associations, and research and academic institutions. Over half of WTO members sent representatives to the symposia, while nonstate institutions sent several hundred representatives.[82]

As Raustiala has shown, the TRIPs Council is, in effect, conducting system implementation reviews of the highly complex new intellectual property rules that now bind all WTO members. It is reviewing members' laws, including amendments and updates, for conformance with the new TRIPs obligations. It has established contact with the World Intellectual Property Organization, which handles technical questions regarding intellectual property, and has organized workshops on technical issues that have emerged with the implementation of the new regime.[83]

- **Recommendation:** *Clearly, as the TRIPs Council and other councils such as those for Trade in Services and Trade in Goods, along with important committees such as the Committee on Trade and Development, move forward with their separate agendas, the CTE model should be progressively established for interacting with NGOs and the business community. This should produce real-time provision of information and documentation, as well as regular meetings, conferences, and seminars between WTO members, the WTO Secretariat, and NGOs to discuss relevant policy issues.*

While these steps will go far toward giving NGOs more access to the system and information about policy initiatives, limitations are built into this model. The most important is that, by and large, NGOs and corporations should not participate directly in the actual meetings of the councils and committees. To avoid inflexibility on this issue, one could envision special situations where public meetings would be held—possibly even formalized gatherings once or twice a year.

But there are two reasons—one substantive and one political—why meetings of the WTO subgroups should remain closed to outsiders. First, the candor and depth achieved in the deliberations of the CTE, which are likely to be duplicated in part in the TRIPs Council, would not be possible with interest groups in the room. Second, developing countries would adamantly oppose such a change, aware that it would increase the already overwhelming pressure on the process from northern corporations and NGOs.

It should be noted, finally, that northern NGOs and corporations, under the current system, effectively lobby their governments in their home capitals and in the halls of the WTO in Geneva. In addition, there is nothing to stop governments from adding representatives from both groups to their delegations if they so choose—and some do just that. NGOs no doubt can make a good case that, in the past, business interests have had a much stronger influence on WTO decision-making than other groups have. But the solution to this problem is to level the playing field outside the negotiating room—not to allow any group inside that room.

Congressional Oversight

In their 2000 paper on the WTO and democratic legitimacy, Keohane and Nye make the important point that one "means of strengthening the democratic accountability of international institutions is to strengthen the mechanism of domestic accountability." They cite the example of Denmark, whose parliament has developed a system that provides it with a great deal more information than any other EU parliament has about the actual policies that its government is pursuing within the various institutions of the EU. As a result, the two authors argue, the Danish government is held to greater accountability for its actions at the federal level than the governments of other EU member states.[84]

It is time for the U.S. Congress to consider establishing a similar mechanism—but with a broader mandate—to inform itself not only of individual actions, policies, or cases but also of the overall trends within international organizations that will have an impact on the normal workings of the U.S. political system and its constitutional boundaries.

The challenge of protecting national sovereignty while preserving the viability of the WTO requires Congress to take a more active role in determining the future course of the U.S. relationship with major international institutions such as the WTO and the UN. Congress must also examine the implications of the cumulative obligations building up through new treaties, agreements, and soft international law, as well as the judicial creativity of the WTO dispute settlement process.

In an important new study, political scientist Lisa Martin of Harvard has demonstrated the key role of national legislative bodies in establishing the credibility of state commitments to international agreements. She argues,

> Institutionalized legislative participation in processes of international cooperation enhances the credibility of commitments through a number of mechanisms. . . . [It] provides the executive and other states with better information about legislative and societal preferences, reducing the chances of reneging. It also creates institutional obstacles to changing policy, enhancing the stability of policies. Enhanced credibility in turn leads to greater levels of international cooperation. . . . In international cooperation, organized legislatures are a democratic asset.[85]

- *Recommendation: What is being proposed here is that Congress establish an ongoing, bipartisan commission, with a tenure of at least five years, to take on two tasks: (1) to report on the implications of the WTO dispute settlement system for the U.S. constitutional system and for U.S. domestic policies; and (2) to report on the cumulative impact of the rulings, pronouncements, and resolutions (particularly on the environment, and other social and economic issues such as human rights, women's rights, health policy, social development, population policies, food policy, and education policy) that emerged from major UN organizations such as the Economic and Social Council, the International Labor Organization, the World Health Organization, and the Food and Agricultural Organization.*

    Congress should also consider establishing a permanent joint committee to provide continuing oversight and analysis of the rules that international bodies enact and their impact on U.S. domestic laws and regulations.

The commission proposed here differs substantially from the WTO Dispute Settlement Review Commission that Senator Robert Dole proposed in 1995. Under Dole's plan, the review commission would have had five federal judges who would examine all WTO decisions that were adverse to the United States to determine if the panels had exceeded their authority or had acted outside the mandate of the Uruguay Round agreement. If the commission determined that the panels had violated the terms of the agreement, it would issue an "affirmative determination." If three such determinations occurred within a five-year period, any member of Congress could introduce a joint resolution for the United States to withdraw from the WTO. None of this was really binding upon Congress, which in any case could always withdraw from the WTO on six months' notice; however, the commission could have had a strong political influence if it had indeed condemned three WTO decisions—or even one or two. Despite its ultimate toothlessness, Dole's bill was clearly seen at the time as a direct attempt to influence and intimidate WTO panels.[86]

The commission proposed in this study would have none of these WTO-threatening aspects. While the commission's reports might discuss individual cases, the thrust of its mandate would be to analyze overall trends and give Congress a comprehensive view of how the new international trading system and the new UN social and economic commitments are evolving.

As envisioned here, the commission would be composed not of federal judges (always a controversial element of the Dole plan), but of experts and practitioners in the fields of trade, international relations, and politics in general, including former elected or appointed political leaders. The commission would issue a report after several years of study, and then again at the end of its tenure.

Congress may ultimately determine that, on balance, both the direction of WTO decisions and the commitments made under the new UN agreements are in the best interests of the United States, but at least Congress will have made those decisions on the basis of informed advice.

Eminent Persons Group

When the WTO was established in 1995, a review of the DSU was mandated to begin in 1998, after three years of operation. That review began on time, but it produced no tangible results before its tenure concluded at the end of 1999. Because of the chaotic circumstances surrounding the Seattle Ministerial meeting, the formal fate of the DSU review remains unclear; some claim it is still in existence, but to all intents and purposes, the review is over.

- *Recommendation: The WTO should create an Eminent Persons Group (as the GATT did with commendable results in the 1980s) to examine the systemic problems and issues surrounding WTO governance and the relations between the WTO and other international regimes, particularly the rapidly growing number of multilateral environmental agreements (MEAs). Three main issues should be at the top of the agenda. The first is to reform the executive functioning of the WTO to accommodate developing countries' complaints that they have been systematically excluded from the inner circle of planning. The second is to devise a less cumbersome system of planning, possibly with the creation of an executive committee.[87] This committee would have to be broadly representative of the interests and regions that compose the WTO today. The third challenge concerns the issues covered in this study: how to reform the legislative and judicial functions to achieve a more viable balance, one that does not overextend and overburden the dispute settlement process.[88]*

The WTO/GATT, unlike other international organizations, has used such an outside group of acknowledged experts and persons of prominence and influence only once. In 1985, the Leutwiler Group completed the task of reporting and making recommendations on a number of systemic GATT issues in preparation for the Uruguay Round. Its widely influential report set the direction for new policy initiatives in the Uruguay Round, including the creation of the Trade Policy Review Mechanism in 1989. This mechanism for evaluating trade policies, which subsequently became part of the agreement establishing the WTO, requires WTO member nations whose policies seem at odds with their WTO/GATT obligations to explain and defend those policies.

Given the events at Seattle and the deep distrust among many developing countries of the WTO's governance system, reform through the regular process of negotiations is unlikely if not impossible. A broadly representative group of "eminent persons" detached from WTO politics, however, could achieve a consensus to recommend practical reforms and the credibility to give those recommendations a chance to pass.

Afterword

The United States has traditionally operated as the central guarantor of the multilateral trading system. To sustain that leadership, U.S. officials will need to show greater imagination in devising policy responses that uphold the fundamental principles of trade liberalization without eroding key elements of national sovereignty on the one hand and domestic democratic accountability on the other hand. As Kal Raustiala has cogently argued, "There is a direct link between state sovereignty . . . and democracy. . . . Democracy protects and legitimizes social choice from challenges within, sovereignty from without. State sovereignty thus acts as a guarantor of democratic control and consent over law."[1] Jeremy Rabkin implicitly built upon this insight in his study, *Why Sovereignty Matters*, and his concluding admonition to U.S. policymakers is directly relevant to the future of U.S.-WTO relations:

> The United States cannot expect to remake the world in its own image, but it does have great influence in the world. If the United States renews its commitment to safeguarding its own sovereignty, it will not be repudiating or turning its back on the world but rather encouraging other countries to return to their own earlier patterns. . . . Where international law rests on well-defined, reciprocal commitments about genuinely international matters, international commitments are far more likely to be honored.[2]

Appendix 1

International Relations Theory, International Legal Theory, and the WTO

For many years, analysis of the GATT/WTO system was dominated by two primary groups: economists, who were interested in the global and national welfare effects of trade liberalization; and international trade lawyers and law professors, who were mainly interested in the narrow, legal aspects of GATT/WTO rules and dispute settlement cases. In recent years, however, an increasing number of scholars have been analyzing the GATT/WTO system in light of evolving international relations theory.[1] The growing collaboration between international legal scholars and international relations theorists is of particular interest to this study, which is deeply concerned with the judicialization of the WTO DSU.[2]

Today, international relations theory and international legal theory provide a rich, although far from integrated, theoretical base for explaining international regimes and institutions. This study does not attempt to integrate international relations and legal theories with its analyses of the WTO dispute settlement system and issues of democratic legitimacy. Rather, in notes and brief commentary on academic research, the study attempts to provide the nonspecialist reader with an understanding of the various schools of contemporary international relations theory and how international legal scholars use these theories. It should be noted that the author is neither an international relations scholar nor a lawyer, but rather a historian who naturally views both disciplines as evolutionary phenomena.

The purpose of this appendix is (1) to describe the major theories of international relations that have emerged during the past four decades and comment on their utility as a means of understanding the history of the GATT/WTO; and (2) to describe and comment upon a variety of normative, idealized models that international legal scholars have advanced for the WTO.

Theories of International Relations

International relations theory is characterized today by a "nondogmatic heterogeneity" whose insights "can be seen as partial theories or theoretical modules of pretended validity." In this study's view, one particular IR theory—liberal theory—provides the most compelling account of domestic and international trade policy, but other theories also contribute to our understanding of the policies, politics, and institutions that govern international commerce and investment. In the words of one IR scholar, a "multicausal synthesis" is appropriate in many situations.[3]

Four main schools of IR theory will be discussed: realism; institutionalism, also known as regime theory; liberalism; and knowledge-based theory, also known as cognitivism or constructivism. The primary challenge to IR theory—namely, public choice theory—will also be explored.

Realism. In international relations, realism became the dominant theory after World War II, and some of its defining tenets remain influential today. The experience of the Second World War, the Cold War that followed, and the purported "unreal" idealism of Wilsonian diplomacy in the interwar years shaped the views of realist scholars. Realists Hans Morganthau and George Kennan held that states were the central actors—the primary "units of analysis," in social science terms—in world affairs and that they acted purely in their own self-interest in a single-minded pursuit of political and military security. The international relations arena was considered anarchic and often compared to a state of war, specifically "a competition of units in the kind of state of nature that knows no restraints other than those which the changing necessities of the game and the shallow conveniences of the players impose."[4]

The "realist challenge" represented a "defiant skepticism" that "international law would ever play more than an epiphenomenal role in the ordering of international life."[5] In the view of realists, systems of international relations, whether conducted through individual nations or international organizations, should aim to ameliorate and facilitate changes in the power structure—but not attempt to impose "legal straitjackets" governing change. As one scholar has noted, "This was the task for diplomacy in the most old-fashioned sense of the term. For this [task], law was too abstract, too inflexible, too hard to adjust to the demands of the unpredictable and the unexpected."[6]

In its early decades, the GATT fit comfortably with the realists' view of state power and international organizations. GATT was (and remains even today) a purely state-to-state operation where the most powerful nations clearly ran (and still run) the show. It was staffed by diplomats, not by lawyers or economists. Disputes were settled through diplomatic negotiations, not through legal proceedings; even after panels were established, their findings had no formal precedential authority. And the prevailing view well into the 1980s was that "GATT dispute resolution should not be particularly formal or adjudicatory."[7]

The most widely accepted realist theory about economic cooperation after the war—hegemony theory—posited that the Bretton Woods system (the IMF, World Bank, and GATT) was possible only so long as a dominant hegemonic power—the United States—both enforced and paid the costs of guaranteeing stability. By the early 1980s, with the United States no longer so dominant but with the Bretton Woods institutions surviving, hegemonic theory came under increasingly hostile scrutiny.[8] In addition, even during the Cold War, a number of international cooperative arrangements and formal multilateral agreements were created and maintained in areas as diverse as energy, crime, aviation, and narcotics. Beginning in the mid-1970s, moreover, both developed *and* developing countries signed onto a whole series of environmental agreements, even though no formal international organization had oversight in this area.[9]

Institutionalism. During the past two decades, and particularly since the collapse of Communism and the end of the Cold War, more broadly based theories have challenged realism's narrow focus on power and military might. The most dominant of these theories is institutionalism, also known as regime theory. (In this study, the terms are used interchangeably.) Although institutionalists share a number of simplifying assumptions with realists, institutionalists often modify them substantially. Like realists, the institutionalists treat states as the primary actors in the international system, but institutionalists acknowledge that internal economic, social, and political pressures buffet governments before they reach a unified national position. Also like realists, they see states as "rational egoists." Thus, in the institutionalists' view, states in international negotiations rationally base their goals solely on their own interests, not just over the short term, but also over the long term:

> Institutionalists hold a broad view of state rationality. . . . In this view, rationality goes beyond the "simple pursuit of immediate self-interest." Rational states can calculate the future benefits and costs of their actions, and they may forgo short-run advantages for greater long-run benefits. They can also choose their actions with reference to the potential responses of other states.[10]

In sharp contrast to the realists, however, institutionalists hold that states strive not only for power, but also for a variety of other goals such as political stability, wealth, cultural independence, and distributive justice. The most salient characteristic of mainstream IR theory for the past two decades has been the study of international regimes that allow states to cooperate in advancing individual national goals: "Regime theory seeks to explain why self-interested states in an anarchic world do, in fact, cooperate with one another."[11] Cooperation is possible only if states accept some constraints on their actions, and international regimes are formed to assure reciprocity of benefits and a reduction in the transaction and information costs of creating and monitoring economic, political, and military agreements.[12]

Two additional points are relevant for this study. First, regime theorists "rediscover[ed] international law" and were instrumental in ending the isolation that was a result of realism's adamant belief that law was a "connection of evanescent maxims."[13] As Anne-Marie Slaughter of the Harvard Law School has argued, the realists refused to recognize international law as a force shaping institutions and states.[14]

Liberalism. In recent years, a restatement of traditional liberalism has emerged to mount a fundamental challenge to the basic assumptions of realism and institutionalism.[15] "Liberal" IR theories were long considered a "grab bag . . . of loosely linked beliefs and approaches."[16] Over the past several years, however, liberal theorists such as Andrew Moravcsik of Harvard University have boldly asserted that liberalism "deserves to be treated as a paradigmatic alternative empirically coequal with and analytically more fundamental than the two dominant theories in contemporary IR scholarship—realism and institutionalism."[17]

In a 1997 reformulation of liberal IR theory, Moravcsik laid out the most comprehensive articulation of its claims for analytic priority. He began by presenting three "core social scientific assumptions." According to the first core assumption, "The fundamental actors in international politics are individual and private groups . . . who organize exchange and collective action to promote differentiated interests under constraints imposed by material scarcity, conflicting values, and variations in societal influence."[18] Thus, liberal IR theory's "bottom-up" view of the political process argues that politics begins with the material and ideological preferences of groups and individuals.

The second core assumption moves up the political ladder and holds that "states . . . represent some subset of domestic society, on the basis of whose interest state officials define state preferences and act purposively in world politics." In this view, the state is not an actor, but merely a "transmission belt . . . subject to capture and recapture, construction and reconstruction by coalitions of social actors."[19] Depending upon the constellation and intensity of domestic interests in foreign diplomatic and economic policy, states can act in a unified manner ("politics stops at the water's edge") or a disaggregated manner. The latter occurs in situations where different groups and government actors continue at the international level their domestic struggle to control a particular policy. During the first years of the Reagan administration, for example, the Commerce Department and the Office of the U.S. Trade Representative vied for mastery of trade policy and, in the process, greatly confused U.S. trading partners.[20]

The third core assumption, which moves to the international level, is as follows: "The configuration of interdependent state preferences determines state behavior." Thus, in liberal IR terms, "what states want is the primary determinant of what they do."[21] Interstate relations are also shaped by the intensity of individual state preferences and by the number of political or economic chits they are willing to expend to achieve their bargaining ends. (Realists argue that power alone determines bargaining outcomes, while institutionalists contend that power conditioned by institutional practices and rules determines such outcomes.)

Examining the dynamics of the entire process, liberals depict IR theory as a two-level game:

> National positions are first formed "liberally" through domestic political processes, often involving conflicts among competing interests. These national positions are then defended by state representatives in bilateral and multilateral "intergovernmental" negotiations. For liberal intergovernmentalists, national positions are not abstract or static, but contingent—shaped by internal pressures from competing stakeholders' interests.[22]

Based upon the three core assumptions of liberal IR theory, Moravcsik argues that it is "essential to treat liberalism as a constant theoretical baseline" against which realist and institutionalist hypotheses are tested. He concedes, however, that there are historical situations where a single "monocausal" theory is inadequate: "If foreign policymaking is a process of constrained choice by purposive states, a view shared by realist, institutionalist, and liberal theory, there may well be cases in which a *combination* of preferences and constraints shapes state behavior." Yet he insists that in such cases of multicausal synthesis, liberal theory enjoys analytic priority. The point, according to Moravcsik, is that unless one knows the nature and intensity of state preferences, it is impossible to assess realist or institutionalist claims linking outcomes to either coercive behavior or game-theoretic actions to reduce transaction costs. Moravcsik concludes, "Variations in state preferences often influence the way in which states make calculations about their strategic environment, whereas the converse—that the strategic situation leads to variation in state preferences—is inconsistent with the rationality assumption shared by all three theories."[23]

In summary, the numerous variations of liberal theory share one common characteristic: an intense focus on politics and pressures inside the state. As a number of analysts have noted, these theories "open the black box" of domestic politics and then expand the horizons of research by viewing "international cooperation not only as the outcome of relations among states, but of the interaction between domestic and international games and coalitions that span national boundaries."[24]

This study views some combination of liberal theory and two-level intergovernmentalism as the most accurate explanation of the dynamics of trade politics and diplomacy (including dispute settlement in the WTO). A fuller explanation of the two-level game theory can be found in the work of Harvard political scientist Robert Putnam, who created the theory, and in the writings of Moravcsik and others who have embellished and extended the basic premises for their own purposes.[25]

Putnam envisions simultaneous and continuous negotiations proceeding at two levels. At the domestic level, the chiefs of governments first engage in bargaining with domestic interests to achieve a consensus for a negotiating position on a particular international agreement. Then, at the second or international level, the COGs bargain with their foreign counterparts to achieve a mutually acceptable compromise. Under Putnam's model, the COGs do retain a monopoly position in international negotiations. Unlike the unitary actors that realists or institutionalists posit, however, the COGs in Putnam's model are constrained because their domestic constituencies must ultimately ratify any agreements the COGs reach. These "win-sets," as Putnam calls them, are "the set of potential agreements that would be ratified by domestic constituencies in a straight up-or-down vote against the status quo."[26]

The breadth and depth of the international agreement depend on two sets of factors: first, the nature of the preferences and the bargaining power of various domestic producer and consumer (or other) groups; and second, the skill and ability of the COGs to deflect opposition from powerful interest groups through political or economic payoffs, along with the manipulation of information about the proposed agreement. (The nature of the ratification process—whether it requires an extended legislative process or a straightforward vote as in U.S. fast-track legislation—may also play a role.)

Contrary to the view of some liberal theorists, the COGs (state actors) are not merely "transmission belts." Their strategic position at both the domestic and international bargaining tables allows them to achieve a fair degree of autonomy to pursue their own political goals by manipulating the process: "It turns out that the strategies and preferences of individual statesmen, or COGs, are central to determining the outcome of any international bargain."[27]

Moravcsik has described three common scenarios for the interrelations between the COGs and their domestic constituencies: statesman-as-agent; statesman-as-hawk; and statesman-as-dove. In the "statesman-as-agent" situation, the COG's preferences are nearly identical to those of the dominant domestic constituencies, and so the negotiation would be targeted to the goals of these groups. For the "statesman-as-hawk," the COG would attempt to manipulate the process and the domestic political situation to build support for a harder line in the negotiations. Conversely, in the "statesman-as-dove" situation, the COG would use such manipulative tactics to build support for additional compromises with other states' preferences to achieve a successful negotiation. It is also possible for two dovish COGs from different countries to achieve their negotiating goals by combining their domestic coalitions to undermine opposition in each other's country. The current New Transatlantic Agenda, organized and promoted by the Clinton administration and top EU officials, has been cited as an example of such COG collusion.[28]

Knowledge-Based (Cognitive or Constructivist) Theories.[29] Cognitivists, who probe even more deeply into the black box, argue that the "explanatory values" are ideas, beliefs, and knowledge: "The core cognitive insight is that cooperation cannot be completely explained without reference to ideology, the values of actors, the beliefs they hold about the interdependence of issues, and the knowledge available to them about how they can realize specific goals."[30]

Cognitive theorists—also known as constructivists—criticize realists and institutionalists for assuming that state identities and interests exist exogenously (independently, outside the process); and they posit that the normative beliefs of decision-makers directly affect regimes and will at times trigger changes in policies and the nature of particular regimes. As one cognitivist has explained, "The knowledge that actors carry in their heads and project in their international encounters significantly shapes their behavior and expectations."[31]

While scholars espousing knowledge-based IR theories disagree about whether states perform as rational actors or are motivated by some deeper sociological commitment to the system itself, they accept state sovereignty as a central unit of analysis. At the same time, cognitive theorists believe that an encompassing moral system underpins that sovereignty:

> Unless embedded within a larger system of values, the principle of sovereignty cannot alone provide the state with a coherent social identity. . . . Sovereignty, like individual liberty, is not a self-referential value capable of independently providing actors with substantive reasons for action. . . . Without reference to some higher-order values, it cannot independently inform plans of action or the strategies to achieve them.[32]

For this study, two other aspects of knowledge-based theories are important: one is the sociological view of regime change through a learning process and the central role of epistemic communities such as NGOs in advancing that process; and the second is the emphasis on norms, legitimacy, and an endogenous "sense of obligation" in inducing compliance with international obligations.

Learning, Regime Change, and Epistemic Communities. Cognitivists view changes in regimes as part of a learning process in a world where international relations are increasingly defined by technological and scientific challenges such as global environmental issues. In contradistinction to realists and institutionalists, cognitivists argue that states seek not only to achieve power and wealth but also to reduce the "veil of uncertainty" caused by technological advances. Political theorist Ernst Haas has explained the connection between learning and regime change as follows:

> By "learning," I mean the process by which consensual knowledge is used to specify causal relationships in new ways so that the results affect the content of public policy. Learning in an international organization implies that the organization's members are induced to question earlier beliefs about the appropriateness of ends of action and to think about the selection of new ones.[33]

The link between learning and regime change has spawned a subset of studies that analyze how scientific and technological knowledge are incorporated into policy. The carriers or translators of new knowledge are specialists who create "epistemic communities," defined as "network(s) of professionals with recognized expertise and competence in a particular domain and an authoritative claim to policy-relevant knowledge within that domain or issue area."[34]

Numerous studies have demonstrated the increasing influence of epistemic communities such as NGOs, particularly in the international politics and policies related to the environment. Members of these communities share not only a common awareness of the problems at hand and a common set of technical solutions, but also a commitment to enter the policy process itself by actively advising decision-makers:

> Acting transnationally, a knowledge-based community can create convergence around its preferred policy solutions. Influence in the epistemic model is thus both cognitive and bureaucratic; while epistemic communities help to shape state preference for cooperation through the knowledge they possess, they also exert influence through the institutionalization of community members into policymaking bureaucracies.[35]

Epistemic communities are often organized across national boundaries and operate through transnational organizations. With the advent of cheap high-speed international communications networks, these communities can mobilize resources and present arguments to influence national and international policymaking at all stages of the political process—from negotiations to create a rule or law, to implementation, to surveillance and compliance monitoring.

Compliance with International Obligations. Another strand of cognitivism or constructivism—the emphasis on norms and the search for legitimacy as causal factors in rules compliance—is also important for the assumptions behind the recommendations in this study. Under this formulation, nations ultimately comply with international rules as a result of a perceived interest in the rule of law itself. English scholar Andrew Harrell explains,

> A good deal of the compliance pull of international rules derives from the relationship between individual rules and the broader pattern of international relations: states follow specific rules, even when inconvenient, because they have a longer-term interest in the maintenance of a law-impregnated international community.[36]

Furthermore, on the international level, "once nations begin to interact, a complex process occurs, whereby international legal norms seep into, are internalized, and become embedded in domestic legal and political processes. . . ."[37]

This strand of constructivism includes what international legal scholars Abram and Antonia Handler Chayes call the "management" model, which is directly related to dispute settlement systems and treaty compliance. Examining why nations obey international law, the Chayeses advance a theory of compliance without coercion or enforcement. They provide "a 'management model,' whereby national actors seek to promote compliance not through coercion but, rather, through a cooperative model of compliance, which seeks to induce compliance through interactive processes of justification, discourse, and persuasion."[38] In their 1996 book, *The New Sovereignty*, the Chayeses argue that an iterative process, jawboning, and rational discourse—not sanctions—are the best means of achieving consensus and obedience to regime norms and rules.[39]

This study uses the research of a number of scholars who espouse elements of constructivist "managerialism" to support its recommendations for changes in the WTO dispute settlement system.

Constructivism and Liberal Theory. In his drive to establish the analytic priority of liberal theory, Moravcsik also reaches out to constructivism. He points out that both theories focus on variations in state preferences, but argues that the ideational feedback process— "that national ideas and identities result from the socializing 'feedback' effects of previous international political interactions"—is untenable without a theory of domestic preference formation. In other words, only those ideas that are espoused by some domestic (or transnational) individual or group will have an impact at either level of the two-stage game. In the end, in keeping with his push for multicausal syntheses, Moravcsik argues for a "constructivist interpretation of liberal theory"—an approach that "backs away from the notion that values result from interstate socialization and argues instead in a liberal vein that ideas and communication matter when they are most congruent with existing domestic values and institutions."[40]

Public Choice Theory: A Challenge to IR Theory. Before turning to IR theories tailored specifically to the WTO, note should be taken of public choice theory in economics and the challenge that it poses for international relations theory—particularly regime theory. Scholars such as Alan Sykes of the University of Chicago and Jonathan Macey of Cornell Law School have written about international trade from this perspective. The challenge to IR theory is illustrated in a 1996 article by Macey and Enrico Colombatto, a professor of economics at the University of Turin.[41]

Macey and Colombatto begin by asking why nations, naturally devoted to the concept of national sovereignty, are increasingly signing agreements and joining institutions that surrender portions of their sovereignty. They argue that political science and economics provide competing answers to this puzzle. First, Macey and Colombatto note that the mainstream political science view of explaining government regulation, known as public interest theory, holds that legal institutions and bureaucrats regulate society to further the common good. Governments seek to achieve this goal by intervening to overcome the failure of the private market to allocate resources properly. One major shortcoming of public interest theory, according to the authors and other public choice proponents, is the "questionable assumption" that government has the "superhuman ability to both identify and correct market failure without cost" and that government is "all-knowing and benevolent."[42]

In contrast to public interest theory, public choice or "interest group" theory assumes that bureaucrats, like all politicians, are rationally self-interested and attempt to maximize their personal power (just as private individuals attempt to maximize their wealth and income), even when these personal goals conflict with public goals. The two authors state that this public choice "assumption of self-interest means that law is traded for political support, money, power, and other things that politicians and bureaucrats demand."[43]

Macey and Colombatto zero in on a deeper comparison of public choice theory with regime theory, which they consider the most important school of IR theory. They note that regime theory adopts some aspects of public choice theory. Both, for example, begin with an assumption of rational self-interest. The main difference between the two theories, however, is that regime theory assumes rational self-interest on the part of states, independent of the interests of individuals, interest groups, politicians, and bureaucrats; public choice theory, in contrast, assumes rational self-interest on the part of individuals and holds that government policy is formulated through a competitive process that also involves interest groups, politicians, and bureaucrats.[44]

Regime theory also assumes that the danger of increased conflict among nations escalates as interdependence in the world economy increases through market competition. Governments, acting independently, attempt to shift the burdens of economic or social adjustment onto other governments, or at least avoid having them shifted onto themselves. These actions create conflict and the need for coordinated actions to facilitate adjustment.

Macey and Colombatto argue that this analysis is flawed on several counts. First, "Institutions in general, and governments in particular do not have preferences, people do. Government policy reflects the preferences of powerful constituencies, not some mystically determined set of preferences that might be described as the 'national interest.'" On the international level, the critical difference between regime and public choice theory stems from the fact that "regime theory posits that interdependence generates conflict, while public choice theory posits that interest groups generate conflict." In addition, public choice theory holds that "interdependence is as likely to guarantee cooperation as conflict. In particular, interdependence will be observed where it is consistent with the interests of bureaucrats and interest groups."[45]

Applying public choice analysis to bureaucracies, the two authors argue that regulatory bodies will attempt to maximize their power and wealth: "They will attempt to maximize the rough value [of their bureaucratic worth], subject to technological, market, statutory, and principal-agent difficulties."[46] Further, all regulatory authorities naturally compete with other regulatory authorities in this power-maximization process.

Empirically, then, Macey, Colombatto, and other public choice theorists demonstrate that on the international level, technological change and more open market competition among states have made it very difficult for national regulatory bodies to control and protect their turf. Thus, rather than accept obsolescence, regulatory authorities have "strong incentives to engage in activities such as international coordination in order to protect their autonomy."[47] Macey illustrates these bureaucratic rent-seeking tactics by analyzing trends and international policy initiatives in two areas: international cooperation on insider trading in the securities markets, an initiative that the SEC and other national securities regulators have promoted; and capital requirements for banks, which national bank regulators advocate.

Several comments about Macey and Colombatto's comparison of IR and public choice theory are in order. First, their description of IR theory is incomplete and does not acknowledge—at least with regard to liberal intergovernmentalism—that there are similarities, although not total congruence, between liberal IR theory and public choice theory. As the two authors note, liberal IR theory also posits that individuals rather than states are the primary actors in the international system. Further, Putnam and Moravcsik's two-level game theory is compatible with at least some of the assumptions and analytic insights of public choice theory.

That said, it is also true that this study has cited important research that clearly could be subject to public choice accounts. For instance, in their paper explaining the difference between transnational and interstate legal systems, Keohane, Moravcsik, and Slaughter describe the characteristics of the transnational system and the obvious rational self-interest of international courts, national courts, and some interest groups to push for greater power in the European Court of Justice.[48] And Kal Raustiala of UCLA argues that in international environmental agreements and regimes, NGOs and national bureaucrats form alliances to elevate regulation to the international level and increase the power of national and international bureaucrats. This is analogous to Macey's description of trends in the financial securities area.[49]

Models for the WTO

In the past several years, international legal scholars have attempted to employ international relations theory to explain the history and evolution of the WTO—often combining theoretical and empirical analysis with normative conclusions and recommendations for changes in the international trading regime. The following sections describe three stylized models that have been put forward to explain and reform the WTO: the Trade Stakeholders Model advanced by Richard Shell, professor of legal studies and management at the University of Pennsylvania's Wharton School; the Global Subsidiarity Model advocated by Robert Howse of the University of Michigan Law School and Kalypso Nicolaides of the Kennedy School at Harvard University; and the Libertarian Model for the WTO, put forward by John O. McGinnis of the Benjamin N. Cardozo School of Law at Yeshiva University.

The Trade Stakeholders Model. Several years ago, Richard Shell put forward a new normative vision for the WTO.[50] Shell's model, the Trade Stakeholders Model, triggered a lively debate with scholars such as Philip Nichols of the University of Pennsylvania's Legal Studies Department, Steven Charnovitz, then at Yale University, and Kenneth Abbott of Northwestern University School of Law.[51]

Shell explains that his constructions are a direct response to two changes wrought by the Uruguay Round: the switch from nonbinding to binding rules; and the switch from a system of arbitration to a legalist framework headed by the Appellate Body. He posits the Regime Management Model as the formulation that most closely resembles the current structure and operation of the WTO. The theoretical underpinning of the Regime Management Model is derived from IR regime theory. Like realism, regime theory holds that states are the primary actors in international relations and "accepts the state as the sole voice for its people."[52] Unlike realism, however, the Regime Management Model holds that states are motivated not simply by the accretion of power, but by a variety of goals such as wealth, prestige, and social justice. Trade treaties are viewed as contracts that help states to resolve conflicts over competing goals; and a binding adjudicatory system provides an enforcement mechanism that allows governments to avoid repeated "prisoner's dilemma" situations.

Shell also suggests a second model that can be used to explain potential future developments within the international trading system: the Efficient Market Model. This explanation of the international trading system combines the IR theory of liberalism with a pure application of neoclassical economic doctrines. Thus, the Efficient Market Model conforms with liberal IR theory in holding that individuals and groups—not states—are the essential actors in international relations: "Under liberalism, nations are not conceived as autonomous, self-maximizing actors, nor as the ultimate subjects of international law. Rather, private actors are the 'essential players' in international society who, in seeking to promote their own interests, influence the national policies of states."[53]

Corporations in particular strongly support this market-based model, which they see as fostering the emergence of a "global business civilization."[54] Under the terms of the Efficient Market Model, moreover, legal rules and the new WTO DSU are seen as the means for business interests and their government allies to overcome domestic resistance to—and barriers to—free trade. "In summary," Shell explains, "the Efficient Market Model of international dispute resolution views international trade laws and tribunals as devices by which governments and businesses that favor free trade may circumvent domestic protectionist groups and increase the world's wealth."[55]

Shell points out that both the Regime Management and the Efficient Market Models give priority to trade over competing domestic or international values or goals.

And finally, he predicts—correctly as it turns out—that following the logic and power structure inherent in the Efficient Market Model, corporations will soon press for standing to participate directly in the dispute settlement process, bypassing governments; he forecasts that, alternatively, corporations will press for international rules that are enforceable within domestic legal systems. Within the WTO, Shell predicts that, without dramatic reform, the Appellate Body will move to become the champion of corporations in the name of free trade and open markets:

> It therefore seems likely that when domestic realities make it difficult or impossible for the leading states in the world trade system to take the risk of championing a particular free trade reform, the WTO Appellate Body may step into the role of an advocate for the free trade agenda. . . . The United States and other nations would then face governance by a group of unelected, multinational judges striking down domestic laws on the basis of economic theory.[56]

Shell's own normative vision of the future of the WTO is embodied in his Trade Stakeholders Model. Like the Efficient Market Model, the Stakeholders Model starts with the liberal assumption that individuals (and groups) should be the primary focus of international law. But the Stakeholders Model goes far beyond the Efficient Market Model in projecting a role in the WTO for many groups (stakeholders) "that are broadly representative of diverse citizen interests."[57] This would include representatives of environmental, labor, consumer, and even human rights and feminist groups:

> The stakeholders model sees trade legalism as an opportunity for domestic and transnational interest groups of all kinds, nonbusiness as well as business, to participate with nations in the activity of constructing common economic and social norms that will make global trade a sustainable aspect of a larger transnational society. . . . [The model] emphasizes direct participation in trade disputes not only by states and businesses, but also by groups that are broadly representative of diverse citizen interests.[58]

Without encompassing broader social justice, environmental, and economic norms, Shell argues, the WTO will lose legitimacy and public support. To avoid this fate, the WTO will have to broaden its purpose and focus to include and enforce "a limited set of globally defined, international trade-related labor, environmental, safety, and consumer norms."[59]

Though abeyance is made to individuals, the most important "actors" in Shell's model are NGOs, which would assume a large role in developing and enforcing international trade law. He makes a direct connection to constructivist theories, favorably quoting scholars such as Peter Haas of the University of Massachusetts, who has argued that NGOs "create networks over, around, and within states that generate the means and incentives for effective cooperation among those states."[60] The vision of government partnering with epistemic communities is at the heart of Shell's model.

Chapter 6 of this study presents a number of arguments against the assumptions and conclusions about the democratic legitimacy of Shell's Stakeholders Model. At this point, several additional comments will suffice. First, in adapting regime theory as the foundation of his Regime Management Model, Shell limits his analysis, because regime theory cannot capture events within the "black box" of domestic politics or the interaction among interests across national boundaries. As a historical fact, these political dynamics have played out ever since the beginning of the GATT itself. Governments have long been at the center of the two-level game in which they first arrive at positions after sorting through and balancing domestic interests and then turn to bargaining with other governments in negotiations at the GATT/WTO. Thus, even as a stylized ideal, the Regime Management Model represents an incomplete and flawed description of past and current workings of the GATT/WTO.

Second, Shell was prescient in predicting that corporations and their legal representatives would press for private rights of action in the WTO. But he was wrong to hold that such a change was likely because there is little or no support for such proposals. Governments appear certain to defend their monopoly on standing in the DSU—particularly governments in developing countries, which are deeply suspicious of the power and influence of NGOs and multinational corporations.

Furthermore, Shell's suggestion that the Appellate Body would increasingly become the champion of corporations and free trade à la his Efficiency Model is not happening. Indeed, as the accounts of the shrimp/turtle decision have pointed out, the AB seems to be bending to the political pressures of NGOs, particularly environmental NGOs. The recommendations put forward in this study point toward a very different future for the WTO—one that, unlike Shell's Trade Stakeholders Model, does not see NGOs becoming the "world court" for a variety of global ills in the areas of the environment, social justice, or the rights of women, children, and indigenous peoples.

The Global Subsidiarity Model. Robert Howse of the University of Michigan Law School and Kalypso Nicolaides of the Kennedy School of Government at Harvard University have advanced an alternate interpretation built around contrasting constitutional models for explaining the GATT/WTO system.[61] They present and critique two potential models for the future of the WTO: the Libertarian Constitutional Model and the European Federal Vision. Both models are discussed in the context of what the authors consider the central tradeoff underpinning the postwar international trading system: the oft-cited "embedded liberalism" bargain first described by IR theorist and UN Assistant Secretary-General John Ruggie. According to Ruggie,

> The task of postwar institutional reconstruction . . . was . . . to devise a framework which would safeguard and even aid the quest for domestic stability without, at the same time, triggering mutually destructive external consequences that had plagued the interwar period. This was the essence of the embedded liberalism compromise: unlike the economic nationalism of the thirties, it would be multilateral in character; unlike the liberalism of the gold standard and free trade, its multilateralism would be predicated upon domestic interventionism. . . . [T]here remained enormous differences between countries over precisely what it meant and what sorts of polities and institutional arrangements, domestic and international, the objective necessitated or was compatible with. This was the stuff of the negotiations on the postwar international economic order.[62]

Proponents of the libertarian view of the WTO see the institution's value in its ability to deter governments from giving in to rent-seeking protectionists. For individual states, therefore, the WTO acts not only to restrain other governments but also to restrain one's own government domestically. According to this view, the libertarian "higher law" norms reinforce the domestic drive for deregulation and the protection of private property. The authors argue that much of the agenda of the Uruguay Round, especially the new rules for services and intellectual property, represents the triumph of a new neoliberal paradigm—Reaganism and Thatcherism—in the international trading system. As a result, according to the authors, "the normative basis for interventionists' adjustment policies was put into question by the moral laissez-faire outlook of the political right, aided and abetted by public choice accounts of interventionism as the payment of rents to concentrated, entrenched constituencies."[63] They also argue that the results of the Uruguay Round had "ambiguous welfare effects, both domestic and global." Howse and Nicolaides criticize the libertarian vision of the WTO as not being democratic (too many "stakeholders," in Shell's terms, are left out); and they charge that it ignores other social and political values that the community may have in areas such as the environment and social justice.

Howse and Nicolaides believe that because pressures on the original terms of postwar embedded liberalism are so great, the results are unpredictable. They cite a number of factors that have contributed to the instability of the postwar bargain: removal of adjustment mechanisms in domestic economies; deregulation and the increasing primacy of property rights; a perception of social dumping and a race to the bottom; and the arrival of the "casino" of free global capital markets. All of these are likely to produce a "disembedded liberalism."[64]

Some observers have both predicted and called for stronger international rules to counter the forces that are undermining the postwar bargain—moves toward a new constitutionalism on the model of the European Union. These observers point to the explosion of WTO dispute settlement case law and hold that, through these judicial mechanisms, the WTO will gradually develop into a fully appointed constitutional order. Howse and Nicolaides doubt that this path can be sustained, however. In the first place, WTO law does not extend to or eclipse domestic laws and regulations, and there is no connection between the WTO and national court systems. Of greater importance is the lack of the institutions and trappings of a democracy internationally, along with the balancing and rebalancing of the rights and obligations of member states. The EU engages in positive integration through policies at the center and has powerful redistributive tools to buy off losers in the integration process.[65]

Howse and Nicolaides then present their own alternative, the Global Subsidiarity Model. It is inspired, they say, by EU experience but does not aim for a formal constitutional structure and rules. Not a comprehensive model, it is presented as a means of providing a transition to whatever form the WTO will take in the distant future. Howse and Nicolaides posit three main principles: the first is institutional sensitivity, under which the WTO dispute settlement bodies would defer to national regulatory decisions and to other international regimes, particularly those in international environmental agreements. (They cite the original tuna/dolphin decision as an example of what *not* to do.) The second principle is that of political inclusiveness at both the national and international levels. The WTO should encourage governments to provide greater public and interest group participation in domestic trade policymaking. The WTO itself should become more open and transparent and allow NGOs to have greater access to WTO institutions and to submit *amicus* briefs to the panels and the AB. The third principle is compliance assistance, under which the WTO would assist global subunits, including states, in fulfilling their international obligations. This could be accomplished through financial assistance and new laws, particularly in extreme cases of "social or environmental dumping."[66]

As with its response to both the Regime Management and Libertarian models discussed in this section, this study's response to the Subsidiarity Model begins by addressing historical accuracy. The idea that the Uruguay Round agenda represented the triumph of Reaganite neoliberalism is far-fetched. Removing barriers to trade in services and investment and establishing rules for intellectual property had widespread support in the United States from both Democrats and Republicans—and the Uruguay Round negotiations were completed under President Clinton, who enthusiastically championed the substantive agenda. Similarly, in the EU, left-of-center parties in England, France, and Germany (Labor, Socialist, and Social Democratic parties, respectively) subsequently endorsed the results of the round.

Furthermore, it is simply not true that Uruguay Round or other recent trade rules inhibit national governments from adopting or modifying the adjustment policies that were a key element of the embedded liberalism bargain; and nothing in the new WTO rules strikes at the programs at the heart of the welfare state. Howse and Nicolaides' statement that the Uruguay Round had "ambiguous" economic results, moreover, is belied by every economic study of the consequences of the negotiations. And economists in general have found little or no evidence of "social dumping" or a "race to the bottom" regarding economic or social regulations in developing countries.[67]

At the same time, however, this study echoes the two authors' warning that the European federal vision cannot be duplicated through WTO rule-making or, more important, through judicial interpretation. As this study argues, the trappings and underpinnings of democratic legitimacy do not exist in the WTO, and Howse and Nicolaides admit that "constitutionalism—if it is to solve rather than exacerbate the legitimacy difficulties of the WTO—would require *constitutional* sources of legitimacy. . . . [T]he rule of law as a source of legitimacy is not self-sufficient or -sustaining outside a framework of public autonomy—institutions of government that are a direct expression of democratic self-determination, in other words outside of democratic federalism."[68]

In response to the authors' Subsidiarity Model and their recommendations relating to deference to other values and bodies of law, as well as more inclusiveness in the WTO rule-making and judicial processes, this study finds areas of both agreement and deep disagreement. One important area of agreement is the approach that Howse and Nicolaides suggest on issues where deeply divergent values preclude an acceptable judicial determination. The beef hormones case is an example. Here, they hold that a political stalemate without resolution may be the only option, but they argue that the United States and the EU should avoid retaliation and use the DSU provisions for compensation:

In a case like this, the outcome of noncompliance can be system-supporting, avoiding inordinate pressure on rules that do not yet have an institutional context that would confer on them the legitimacy needed for supremacy. We would, however, suggest that, in order to forestall risk of escalation, the parties make greater use of the provision for compensation, rather than retaliation. . . . While retaliation is a logical response to non-compliance, compensation is a more optimal approach to deal with unresolvable conflicts. It serves consumers on one side and opens markets for the other side.[69]

This study strongly disagrees, however, with the authors' recommendation that panels and the AB utilize other sources of international law to introduce environmental or social justice values into the WTO. For reasons cited in the text, this study holds that such a tactic of judicial creativity will be unsustainable both substantively and politically. Finally, on the issue of inclusiveness, Howse and Nicolaides urge acceptance of a corporatist vision of the WTO:

It is also important to explore ways of giving greater voice to nongovern-mental actors during political negotiations. This is justified normatively since it may be argued that corporatist notions of democratic legitimacy may be more warranted beyond the nation-state, given the economies of scales of organization, and the fact that groups previously disenfranchised are given access previously denied to them at the national level.[70]

Once again, this study adopts a different view—namely, that corporatist visions of the WTO lack the fundamental attributes of democratic legitimacy and should be strongly resisted in plans for reform and change.

The Libertarian Model. In several articles, Professor John O. McGinnis of Yeshiva University's Benjamin N. Cardozo School of Law has laid out a libertarian vision of the WTO and made recommendations regarding rule-making and dispute settlement changes that would fulfill this libertarian vision.[71] Although this study agrees with certain elements of McGinnis's analysis and conclusions, it views the political economy of the WTO and trade policymaking from a very different perspective.

McGinnis looks at the world through a quite idiosyncratic and personal libertarian/public choice lens. In his view, rent-seeking protectionist interest groups represent a perversion of true democracy because they undermine what economist Mancur Olson labeled the "encompassing interest"—that is, the public interest of a nation. The purpose of multilateral trade agreements is to thwart the ambitions of protectionist special interests by constraining governments and enforcing a "pre-commitment" to free trade. McGinnis states:

> Because of the structure of contemporary democracy, interest groups can often use the political process to obtain policies that increase their income while making the nation as a whole worse off. . . . By constraining the influence of domestic interest groups, the WTO reinforces the democratic power of national majorities. . . . As long as its powers are properly limited, the WTO can promote, rather than diminish, the democratic sovereignty of member states.[72]

McGinnis also puts forward two models for multilateral trade organizations: the GATT/WTO Antidiscrimination Model and the Regulatory Model. Under the Antidiscrimination Model, which McGinnis endorses, the WTO merely enforces the negative rights of nations against discriminatory treatment both at and inside the borders of their trading partners. With the Regulatory Model, the WTO would be structured more like a commission or administrative agency. It would set and enforce global regulatory standards in such areas as environment, labor, and health and safety, and, in the process, threaten national sovereignty through intrusive harmonized standards. To keep the GATT/WTO Antidiscrimination Model viable, McGinnis proposes that the WTO adopt a series of "procedurally oriented" tests to root out covert protectionism in national laws and foreclose a move to the Regulatory Model. This jurisprudence would have four requirements: transparency, performance orientation (for standards), consistency (in the treatment of domestic and foreign companies), and least-restrictive means (for implementing regulations).[73]

There are several problems with McGinnis's political economy, his description of the current jurisdiction of the WTO, and his procedural recommendations. First, while this study shares McGinnis's distaste for rent-seeking protectionist groups, it also believes that "All God's Children" among interest groups should be treated equally and not subject to differential normative judgments. Thus, a robust democracy will include protectionists, exporting free traders, and various other stakeholders who will—like the protectionists—lobby governments to achieve their goals. In this light, protectionist groups are no more "serious obstacles to representative democracy" than are other interest groups. Further, it should be noted that international institutions like the WTO will play only a marginal role in the domestic contests among these stakeholders.

An even greater flaw in McGinnis's models is their historical inaccuracy. He juxtaposes the "nondiscrimination norm" against a projected regulatory institution of the future. The problem is, for better or worse, the future is now. Beginning with the Tokyo Round of GATT negotiations, but emerging fully during the Uruguay Round, GATT/WTO agreements have included dozens of regulatory rules and obligations. They are embedded in the TRIPs Agreement, as Raustiala points out, and even more deeply embedded in the growing number of services agreements and rules regarding health and food safety. As international trade scholar Sylvia Ostry has noted, "The WTO [has] shifted from the GATT model of *negative* regulation—what governments must not do—to *positive* regulation, or what governments must do."[74]

Indeed, a major theme and concern of this study is that the WTO is incapable of reaching and enforcing legally sound decisions on these complex regulatory issues. Consequently, the panels and AB are forced to make judgments far beyond mere questions of discrimination. Finally, McGinnis's procedural tests, while commendable and sensible, do not provide adequate guidance for WTO judicial bodies which, as this study has shown, are already engaged in precisely the kind of regulatory activities he deplores.

Appendix 2

Potential Technical Changes in the DSU Process

A number of technical and even institutional changes have been suggested for the DSU procedures. This appendix examines the most significant of these proposals: eliminating the Interim Report; creating a permanent, professional panel body; abolishing the panels; and empowering the Appellate Body to remand cases.

Eliminating the Interim Report

The Uruguay Round reforms provided for an interim report stage of the DSU process, in which the dispute settlement panel would release drafts of its findings to the contending parties. The object of this interim report was to give the parties an opportunity to provide feedback and register their objections and then allow the panels to correct any unintended errors before going public with decisions. This stage was modeled on the NAFTA experience, although in retrospect, the structure and conduct of the NAFTA and WTO panels have little in common. NAFTA panels are composed of nongovernmental lawyers and academics with no connection to NAFTA institutions and no help from a WTO-like secretariat. In addition, NAFTA panel decisions are final, with no provision for correcting mistakes by appealing to a higher body, as is the case with the WTO. And unlike WTO panels, NAFTA panels have been able to keep interim reports confidential. With WTO panels, interim decisions have almost invariably been leaked to the press of the winning party—a practice that greatly increases pressure and lobbying in the final stage of the panel decision process. As cases become increasingly complex, moreover, producing an interim report reduces the already brief timelines that govern WTO panel decisions. In an effort to address these concerns, some observers have called for either eliminating the interim report and allowing more time for panels to prepare their final reports or adding time to the Appellate Body's portion of the process.[1]

Creating a Permanent, Professional Panel Body

Despite the increased sophistication and clarity of panel decisions in recent years, many observers believe that more legal expertise and intellectual rigor must be introduced into the panel proceedings and decision-making. They also argue that this will not be possible so long as the panelists serve on an ad hoc, part-time basis.

One proposal that has surfaced is to create a permanent, standing panel body of paid professional panelists.[2] Proponents of such a change cite numerous advantages, including a more expeditious panel decision process because battles over panel composition would be eliminated; higher-quality decisions because panelists would be selected for their knowledge of trade law and WTO procedures; and a more effective working relationship among panelists because full-time, professional panelists would already know each other. Opponents of a permanent panel body have pointed out that selection of a cadre of professional panelists would set off major political battles (as happened with the initial selection of the Appellate Body) as nations and regions spar for representation. Though the Appellate Body has developed a reputation for unbiased decisions, national bias—or at least the appearance of national bias—at the panel level might be more difficult to avoid.

While acknowledging the formidable political difficulties of establishing a professional panel body, Robert Hudec concludes: "In [my] view, the need for something like a professional-jurist reform is already at the point where serious consideration is warranted. The more one studies the various other problems with the present panel process, the more they come back to problems centering on the panel members—their professional qualifications and the part-time orientation of their participation. Granting that immediate action may be politically unwise, it is not too early to begin serious discussion of the alternatives."[3]

Abolishing the Panels

A serious discussion of alternatives must also evaluate proposals to do away with the first-tier panels altogether.[4] Logically, the argument goes, there is little need for what has become in many cases a preliminary decision by part-time, nonprofessional panel members with full-time professional judges sitting above them on the Appellate Body. The Uruguay Round negotiators did not set out to establish this anomalous, two-tier approach (anomalous in that no other international system of adjudication is two-tiered). Rather, the Appellate Body was added because the "automaticity" of the system raised great fears among some GATT members that the panel process lacked legal depth and sophistication and might prove incapable of handling complex disputes. Ironically, however, the Appellate Body has become the real power in the new system. All but a handful of adverse decisions have been appealed, and the AB has demonstrated a strong determination to have the final word on all legal issues. Some legal observers believe that, in time, the WTO could add two to five members to the AB and send all disputes to that body for resolution within the twelve- to sixteen-month deadlines established by the new dispute settlement procedures.

Empowering the Appellate Body to Remand Cases

Because confidence in the work of the Appellate Body is high, there is little pressure for major changes in the way it operates. The most frequently mentioned change would be to increase the AB's powers by granting it the ability to remand cases to panels if it finds errors in law that require new analysis of the facts or the legal interpretation of the facts.[5] The major obstacle to empowering the AB to remand cases is the strict time frame built into the dispute settlement system. A remand could add several months to cases and extend the process beyond the sixteen-month completion date. Unless ways could be found to make up time in other parts of the schedule, WTO members are not likely to grant this power to the Appellate Body.

Recommendations

Whatever the merits of these proposals, there seems little likelihood of their acceptance in the near future. Most WTO members are averse to making major changes until the effectiveness of the new system can be evaluated. And the Appellate Body itself, fully absorbed in fulfilling its new and unprecedented role in the multilateral trading system, has not indicated any desire to expand this role. Radical change will occur only if the panel procedures prove unsatisfactory, and reform of the panel decision-making process proves impossible.

Putting aside the timing of these proposals, this study recommends the following three changes in DSU procedures:[6]

1. Whatever larger reforms are contemplated, the case for two smaller proposals seems fairly strong: that is, doing away with the interim report of the panels and allowing the Appellate Body to remand cases to the panels. Having the panels skip preparation of the interim report would undoubtedly save time, and this could offset some of the additional time that would be needed for the panels to respond to remand for errors in law or facts supporting legal interpretations.

2. If first-tier panels are retained, the recommendation here is for a permanent, standing body of professional panelists. This change would increase substantially the quality and the continuity of decision-making at this level. Creating a body of professional panelists would afford the opportunity to add panelists with more diverse backgrounds and expertise, particularly in the area of the environment. The selection process, however, should not be politicized—that is, demands for actual representation by environmental or consumer groups should be denied.

3. With or without a move to a professional body of panelists, the case for abolishing the first-tier panel seems quite strong. The Appellate Body has already established a strong record of judicial competence (despite the reservations set forth in this study regarding constitutional overreach). Removing the first-tier procedure and decision process would allow more time for an

in-depth review of the facts of cases, as well as time for research and construction of the legal foundation of the cases. The reality that most disputes are already appealed reinforces the sense of redundancy in the current two-tier system.

Notes

Chapter 1. Introduction: Issues, Themes, and Recommendations

1. Edward Wong, "A Quiet Forum at Town Opposes the East River Forum," *New York Times,* 6 September 2000, sec. A. For all the controversy it has caused, the WTO is an astonishingly small organization by any standard. The United Nations, whose Secretariat employs 8,700 bureaucrats, had an operating budget of $1.26 billion in 1999. The WTO, in contrast, has 500 employees and a budget of just under $80 million.

2. Elizabeth Olson, "U.S. and Europeans Raising the Stakes in Trade Impasse," *New York Times,* 7 September 2000, sec. C.

3. For details on the June 2001 panel decision and the potential political fall-out, see Edward Alden, "WTO Ruling Raises Trade Tensions," *Financial Times,* 23/24 June 2001; and Guy de Jonquieres, "Simmering Trade Dispute Looks Poised to Boil Over," *Financial Times,* 27 June 2001.

4. The United States and the EU finally settled the bananas dispute in April 2001. See Joe Kirwin, Daniel Pruzin, and Gary G. Yerkey, "U.S. and EU End Decade-Long Dispute over EU's Banana Import Regime," *International Trade Reporter* 8 (12 April 2001): 564–566.

5. For an excellent recent appraisal of the power and demands of NGOs, see Sylvia Ostry, "The WTO after Seattle: Something's Happening Out There, What It Is Ain't Exactly Clear" (paper presented at the annual meeting of the American Economic Association, New Orleans, La., January 2001).

6. Sylvia Ostry, "The WTO: Institutional Design for Better Governance" (paper presented at the Conference on Efficiency, Equity, and Legitimacy: The Multilateral Trading System at the Millennium, Kennedy School of Government, Harvard University, Cambridge, Mass., 1–2 June 2000), 6.

7. J. H. H. Weiler, "The Role of Lawyers and the Ethos of Diplomats: Reflections on the Internal and External Legitimacy of WTO Dispute Settlement," Harvard Jean Monnet Working Paper, Harvard University Law School, September 2000, 9. Professor Weiler very much favors the new "rule of law" in the WTO. The thesis of his essay is that for the new legal

179

paradigm to attain legitimacy, vestiges of the old diplomatic paradigm should be expunged from the dispute settlement rules and procedures. Although his conclusions are very much at odds with those of this study, his description of the two paradigms is dead on.

8. Ibid., 10.

9. Ibid.

10. Ibid.

11. Ibid., 11.

12. Robert Keohane and Joseph Nye, close observers of international organizations in general and the WTO in particular, have recently warned that because these institutions lack strong political ties to domestic political processes and constituencies, "the legitimacy of global institutions will probably remain shaky for many decades." For this reason, the authors also state, "Putting too much weight on international institutions before they are sufficiently legitimate to bear that responsibility is a recipe for deadlock, disruptions, and failure." Although the two political scientists may not agree with the specific proposals in this study, the proposals are advanced with Keohane and Nye's admonitions and warnings very much in mind. See Robert O. Keohane and Joseph S. Nye, Jr., "The Club Model of Multilateral Cooperation and the World Trade Organization: Problems of Democratic Legitimacy" (paper presented at the Conference on Efficiency, Equity, and Legitimacy: The Multilateral Trading System at the Millennium, Kennedy School of Government, Harvard University, Cambridge, Mass., 1–2 June 2000), 22–23.

13. John H. Jackson, "The WTO 'Constitution' and Proposed Reforms" (speech delivered at Graduate Institute of International Studies, Geneva, Switzerland, 15 March 2000), 4–6.

14. Stephen D. Krasner, *Sovereignty: Organized Hypocrisy* (Princeton, N.J.: Princeton University Press, 1999), 9–25. See also the perceptive review of the book by Jack Goldsmith, "Sovereignty, International Relations Theory, and International Law: *Sovereignty: Organized Hypocrisy,*" *Stanford Law Review* 52 (2000): 959. Goldsmith points out that there are two basic perspectives in international relations theory: instrumentalism and constructivism. Krasner writes as an IR realist, within the broad range of instrumentalist theories—that is, he proceeds from the belief that nations, acting rationally to maximize their interests, are the primary units of analysis. And as a pessimistic realist, he is skeptical about the possibilities of international cooperation and holds that most international organizations ultimately reflect distributions of power. Constructivists, in contrast, argue that national interests are shaped by ideas and by international structures. They are concerned with "how preferences are formed and knowledge is generated, prior to the exercise of instrumental rationality." As Goldsmith sees it, Krasner is an "instrumentalist who has taken the constructivist critique to heart." Krasner acknowledges that sovereignty is contingent upon changing historical norms as well as power relationships, but he defends

the primacy of rational power maximization as the key determinant of state action.

For this study, it should be noted that, unlike other realists and in contrast to his own earlier writings, Krasner focuses on the preferences of rulers rather than on an abstract conception of the state. This inevitably leads him back to domestic interest groups and constituencies; it also brings him close to IR "liberal" theories that stress the role of these groups as the final determinants of national preferences. In the end, though neither Krasner nor Goldsmith states the case this way, Krasner's account is an example of a multicausal synthesis of several theoretical approaches. For a more detailed description of IR theories relevant to this study, see appendix 1.

15. Jackson, "The WTO 'Constitution,'" 5.
16. Jeremy Rabkin, *Why Sovereignty Matters* (Washington, D.C.: AEI Press, 1998), 85–89.
17. Barry Eichengreen, "Dental Hygiene and Nuclear War: How International Relations Looks from Economics," *International Organization* 52 (1998): 993–995.
18. For a more detailed description of liberal IR theory, see appendix 1, pp. 153–156; there is also a clear explanation and empirical test of this theory in Gregory Shaffer, "The World Trade Organization under Challenge: Democracy and the Law and Politics of the WTO's Treatment of Trade and Environment Matters," *Harvard Environmental Law Review* 25 (2001): 9–13.
19. Shaffer, "The World Trade Organization under Challenge," 10.
20. See Kal Raustiala, p. 91 in the text.
21. For a more detailed description of constructivist theory, see appendix 1, pp. 156–160. The terms "constructivist" and "cognitivist" have become separate terms of art among IR theorists, but in this study the terms will be used interchangeably. Both quotations in this paragraph are from Kal Raustiala, "Compliance and Effectiveness in International Regulatory Cooperation" (paper presented at the Case Western Reserve *Journal of International Law* Symposium on Compliance, Cleveland, Ohio, February 2000), 22, 52.
22. International Financial Institutions Advisory Commission, *International Financial Institutions Advisory Commission Report* (Washington, D.C.: U.S. Government Printing Office, March 2000).
23. Jackson, "The WTO 'Constitution,'" 3.

Chapter 2. The General Agreement on Tariffs and Trade

1. For details on the events that led to the creation of the GATT, see John H. Jackson, *The World Trading System: Law and Policy of International Economic Relations*, 2d ed., (Cambridge, Mass.: MIT Press, 1997), chap. 2; see also William Diebold, *The End of the ITO* (Princeton, N.J.: Princeton University Press, 1952).
2. Jackson, *World Trading System*, 39–41, 81–83.

3. Ibid., 61–62; see also Robert E. Hudec, "The New WTO Dispute Settlement Procedure: An Overview of the First Three Years," *Minnesota Journal of Global Trade* 8, no. 1 (1999): 1–50.
4. Jackson, *World Trading System*, 111. Additional sources for information on the debate between legalists and pragmatists include Miquel Montana I Mora, "A GATT with Teeth: Law Wins over Politics in the Resolution of Trade Disputes," *Columbia Journal of Transnational Law* 31, no. 1 (1993): 104–179; Kendall W. Stiles, "The New WTO Regime: The Victory of Pragmatism," *Detroit College of Law Journal of International Law and Practice* 4, no. 3 (1995): 1–37; Michael K. Young, "Dispute Resolution in the Uruguay Round: Lawyers Triumph over Diplomats," *The International Lawyer* 29, no. 2 (1995): 389–409; Azar M. Khansari, "Searching for the Perfect Solution: International Dispute Resolution and the New World Trade Organization," *Hastings International and Comparative Law Review* 20 (1996): 183–203; Lisa Sue Klaiman, "Applying GATT Dispute Settlement Procedures to a Trade in Services Agreement: Proceed with Caution," *University of Pennsylvania Journal of International Business Law* 11, no. 3 (1990): 657–689; and Hudec, "The New WTO Dispute Settlement Procedure," 4–16.
5. Young, "Dispute Resolution," 390.
6. R. Phan Van Phi, "A European View of the GATT," *International Business Lawyer* 10 (1986): 150–151. By no means are all Europeans devoted to the diplomatic approach. For strong views espousing legalism in the WTO and even using the WTO as a model for a world constitution, see Ernst-Ulrich Petersmann, *The GATT/WTO Dispute Settlement System: International Law, International Organizations, and Dispute Settlement* (London: Kluwer Law International, 1997).
7. Phan Van Phi, "A European View," 150.
8. The details of these early years are derived from the following sources: Robert E. Hudec, *The GATT Legal System and World Diplomacy* (New York: Praeger, 1975); Hudec, "The New WTO Dispute Settlement Procedure," 4–10; Young, "Dispute Settlement in the Uruguay Round," 391–396; Mora, "A GATT with Teeth," 118–128; and John H. Jackson, "Dispute Settlement in the WTO: Emerging Problems," *Journal of International Economic Law* 1, no. 3 (1998): 330–339. For an exhaustive and authoritative analysis of the development of GATT legal doctrine from the creation of GATT until the establishment of the WTO, see Philip M. Nichols, "GATT Doctrine," *Virginia Journal of International Law* 36 (1996): 379–465.
9. Robert O. Keohane and Joseph S. Nye, Jr., "The Club Model of Multilateral Cooperation and the World Trade Organization: Problems of Democratic Legitimacy" (paper presented at the Conference on Efficiency, Equity, and Legitimacy: The Multilateral Trading System at the Millennium, Kennedy School of Government, Harvard University, Cambridge, Mass., 1–2 June 2000), 4.

10. Scholars disagree about the impact of the Understanding of 1979. Several have argued that the understanding "reveals that . . . there finally prevailed the views of those favoring the preeminence of the diplomatic means of dispute settlement." For this interpretation, see Mora, "A GATT with Teeth," 121–128; and Young, "Dispute Resolution in the Uruguay Round," 194–195. On the other hand, Hudec, in "The New WTO Dispute Settlement Procedure" (7–10), stresses continuity and the growing judicialization of the system after the understanding was concluded. See also Donald E. deKieffer, "GATT Dispute Settlement: A New Beginning in International and U.S. Law," *Northwestern Journal of International Law and Business* 20 (1980): 317.

11. Keohane and Nye, "The Club Model of Multilateral Cooperation." Referring to the two-level-game, liberal theory discussed in the introductory chapter and appendix 1, the Keohane-Nye "club" theory of the GATT is incomplete in that it does not include important elements of the "games"—namely, the interaction among domestic interest groups and national officials that produced shifting in official "state" positions, along with the second game in which national officials negotiated final GATT outcomes (again monitored by various domestic interest groups) in Geneva. To be fair, for a paper of this length and purpose, the two authors clearly did not set out to write a complete account in IR theoretical terms.

12. Ibid., 3. The phrase originated with Herbert Simon.

13. Ibid., 4.

14. Ibid., 9.

15. Ibid., 10. See also J.H.H. Weiler, "The Role of Lawyers and the Ethos of Diplomats: Reflections on the Internal and External Legitimacy of WTO Dispute Settlement," Harvard Jean Monnet Working Paper, Harvard University Law School, September 2000, 3–4. In this paper, Professor Weiler also advances a variation of the "club" theory: "The GATT became a classical network. This phenomenon was a result of several factors, such as the relatively restricted and homogenous membership of GATT . . . the marginalization of trade diplomats with states (considered a second-rate diplomatic career . . .), the supposed 'technical' and 'professional' nature of the subject matter . . . and the consequent media indifference. . . . A trade dispute was an 'internal' affair which had to be resolved as quickly and smoothly as possible within the organization." Weiler also argues that the old GATT had a "communitarian ethos" that is best explained by the IR constructivist theory, in which decisions are reached through a "set of shared normative values [of free trade] and shared institutional [*and personal!*] ambitions. . . ."

Chapter 3. The Uruguay Round: A New Dispute Settlement System

1. The material for the events leading up to and including the Uruguay Round breakthrough is based on Kendall W. Stiles, "The New WTO Regime: The

Victory of Pragmatism," *Detroit College of Law Journal of International Law and Practice* 4, no. 3 (1995): 10–33; Miquel Montana I Mora, "A GATT with Teeth: Law Wins over Politics in the Resolution of Trade Disputes," *Columbia Journal of Transnational Law* 31, no. 1 (1993): 128–136; and Robert E. Hudec, "The New WTO Dispute Settlement Procedure: An Overview of the First Three Years," *Minnesota Journal of Global Trade* 8, no. 1 (1999): 8–16.

2. Hudec, "The New WTO Dispute Settlement Procedure," 8.

3. Ibid., 9.

4. The original Section 301 was adopted in the Trade Act of 1974. John Jackson, describing the meaning of the 1988 amendments, states that "under certain circumstances, the use of Section 301 is to be nearly 'mandatory,' with presidential discretion reduced in certain cases of 'unjustifiable' actions [for example, breach of legal obligations] by foreign governments. Certain exceptions are specified that restore some of the president's discretion, but on the whole, Congress 'tightened' the 301 process and made it at least politically more difficult for the president *not* to retaliate." For a complete description of this history, see John H. Jackson, *The World Trading System: Law and Policy of International Economic Relations,* 2d ed. (Cambridge, Mass.: MIT Press, 1997), 127–132.

5. Hudec, "The New WTO Dispute Settlement Procedure," 14. Hudec describes the specific substantive deal as follows: "In exchange for a U.S. commitment not to employ Section 301-type trade restrictions, the other GATT governments would agree to create a new and procedurally tighter dispute settlement system that would meet U.S. complaints. Although the U.S. was unable to guarantee it would never-ever use 301-type sanctions, it was willing to accept a legal obligation prohibiting such sanctions, and with that caveat accepted the deal."

6. For analyses of the immediate events and causes of the turnaround by leading GATT members, see Hudec, "The New WTO Dispute Settlement Procedure," 13–15; and Kendall W. Stiles, "The New WTO Regime: The Victory of Pragmatism," *Detroit College of Law Journal of International Law and Practice* 4, no. 3 (1995): 23–25. According to Stiles, a less important, but still driving, factor behind the shift in positions by GATT members was the awareness that, for the first time in the postwar years, the United States had signaled its willingness to explore alternatives to multilateralism in trade. The signing of the U.S.–Canadian Free Trade Agreement and subsequent negotiations leading to the North American Free Trade Agreement represented a powerful signal that the United States would pursue other avenues of trade liberalization and dispute settlement if the GATT continued its desultory, inefficient means of operation.

The dramatic change in the rules of the WTO dispute settlement system is a seminal event in the history of the WTO and a richly fascinating "critical juncture" whose theoretical implications have yet to be fully explored by IR and legal scholars. Legal theorist Richard Shell has argued that the transformation of dispute settlement from a diplomatic process to a more legal framework represents a paradigm shift from realism to regime theory. Regime theory, however, cannot explain how and why the transformation took place at the time it did, or the forces that govern the prospects for future change.

Philip Nichols, in a 1998 analysis, suggested that applying insights from the schools of historical institutionalism in political science and sociological institutionalism from sociology into the workings of the WTO and the new dispute settlement system would yield more fruitful results. Two defining characteristics of historical institutionalism are (1) the emphasis on path dependency and (2) the assertion of the importance of "critical junctures or cleavages" that create new paths and opportunities for change. The junctures themselves are constrained by antecedent conditions, and they in turn constrain future organizational or policy options. Historical institutionalism is catholic in its approach to causal forces: institutions themselves are important but so are socioeconomic forces and the diffusion of ideas. Similarly, historical institutionalism accepts both calculus and cultural explanations of how institutions affect the behavior of individuals. Under the calculus approach, institutions provide information to allow individuals to determine their interests rationally and act strategically; under the cultural approach, institutions provide moral and ideational compasses for action. In the case of the new WTO dispute settlement system, an historical institutional approach would examine antecedents that moved toward a more legal approach, such as rules allowing third-party participation and multiple complaints in a single case; the right to a panel; time limits on the issuance of panel reports; and continuing constraints such as support for secrecy in panel proceedings. Neither John Croome's nor Ernest Preeg's detailed histories of the Uruguay Round, cited below in this note, describes in detail the "real" story behind this hugely significant change.

One important insight from sociological institutionalism is important for this study. Philip Nichols points out that sociological institutionalism raises the question of whether there is a truly "global culture" and, if there is not, whether WTO rules can survive. It is the contention of this study that on key issues (labor, environment, national cultural identity, and intellectual property), there is no global culture or consensus and thus, in order to survive, the WTO dispute settlement system must refrain from attempting to force "correct" legal solutions in these areas.

Sources for this note include Richard Shell, "Trade Legalism and International Relations Theory: An Analysis of the World Trade Organization," *Duke Law Journal* 44 (1995): 829–927; Philip M. Nichols, "Forgotten Linkages: Historical Institutionalism and Sociological Institutionalism and Analysis of the World Trade Organization," *University of Pennsylvania Journal of International Economic Law* 19 (1998): 151–183; and Peter A. Hall and Rosemary C. R. Taylor, "Political Science and the

Three New Institutionalisms," *Political Studies* 49 (1996): 396–415. For Uruguay Round negotiations, see John Croome, *Reshaping the World Trading System: A History of the Uruguay Round* (London: Kluwer Law International, 1999); and Ernest H. Preeg, *Trader in a Brave New World: The Uruguay Round and the Future of the International Trading System* (Chicago: University of Chicago Press, 1995).

Just as this study was going to press, a new analysis of the reasons for the WTO's dramatic shift to a more judicial system appeared: James McCall Smith, "Designing Dispute Settlement Systems for International Trade: NAFTA, the WTO, and the Pivotal Role of the United States" (Political Science Department, George Washington University, Washington, D.C., 2001, photocopy). Smith explores the puzzle of why the United States adopted diametrically opposing positions on dispute settlement in the simultaneously negotiated NAFTA and WTO agreements. He finds that no single theoretical framework (realism, liberalism, institutionalism) provides an adequate explanation, but that a combination of domestic political factors and the uneven distribution of economic power among states accounts for the variation in dispute settlement design. In NAFTA, the United States represented a regional hegemony, with little dependence on intrapact trade; hence it pushed for maximum policy discretion with minimum legal bindings. In the WTO, however, the United States faced a situation where its relative power in the world economy had waned during the preceding decades, and it was advancing an ambitious new substantive agenda. Thus, pressed by domestic business coalitions, U.S. negotiators sacrificed unilateral discretion for a more legally binding system that would lock in other WTO member states to the new disciplines in services, investment, and intellectual property. While certainly not the last word on this subject, Smith's account is compelling.

7. Jackson, *The World Trading System,* 124.
8. Ibid., 124.
9. In light of the recommendations for greater reliance on conciliation and consultation presented later in this study, the views of a leading U.S. trade litigator, Alan Wolff, regarding the current status of consultation in the DSU are telling: "In many cases, it has completely disappeared as a meaningful step in the process. To consult openly is to risk your country's case as an advocate, as any admission is going to be used against you in the litigation phase, which will soon be upon you. Only consult seriously if you wish to confess judgment and make amends—that is the lesson of the DSU." E-mail from Alan Wolff to author, 17 December 2000.
10. In the U.S.-EU dispute over bananas, conflicting interpretations emerged over the timing of retaliation after an AB decision that a measure was inconsistent with WTO obligations. The United States argued that it could retaliate against the EU pursuant to DSU Article 22 before a determination was made on whether there had been compliance under Article 21.5. The

EU countered that such a retaliation must be preceded by a ninety-day waiting period under Article 21.5 and that Article 23 forbids a WTO member from making a unilateral determination as to whether a measure had been brought into conformity. The matter remains unresolved. For a description of the legal questions involved, see Hyun Chong Kim, "The WTO Dispute Settlement Process: A Primer," *Journal of Economic International Law* 2 (1999): 475–476; and Gary N. Horlick, "Problems with the Compliance Structure of the WTO Dispute Resolution Process" (paper presented at the University of Minnesota Law School Conference on the Political Economy of International Trade Law, 15–16 September 2000), 4–7.

11. See WTO web site at www.wto.org/english/tratop_e/dispu_e/dispu_e.htm (accessed 21 July 2001).

12. See USTR web site at www.ustr.gov/enforcement/dispute.shtml (accessed 26 January 2001). For a slightly different breakdown of U.S. cases, see Government Accounting Office, *World Trade Organization: Issues of Dispute Settlement* (Washington, D.C.: U.S. Government Printing Office, GAO/NSIAD-00-12, August 2000).

13. The material in this section is from Hudec, "The New WTO Dispute Settlement Procedure," 16–29.

14. Marc L. Busch and Eric Reinhardt, "Testing International Trade Law: Empirical Studies of GATT/WTO Dispute Settlement" (paper presented at the University of Minnesota Law School Conference on the Political Economy of International Trade Law, 15–16 September 2000).

15. Ibid., 8.

16. Ibid., 8–9. See also Henrik Horn, Hakan Nordstrom, and Petros C. Mavroidis, "Is the Use of the WTO Dispute Settlement System Biased?" CEPR Discussion Paper 2340 (London: Centre for Policy Research, 1999); and Eric Reinhardt, "Aggressive Multilateralism: The Determinants of GATT/WTO Dispute Initiation" (Emory University, Atlanta, Ga., 2000, photocopy).

17. Reinhardt, "Aggressive Multilateralism," 19–20.

18. Busch and Reinhardt, "Testing International Trade Law," 11.

19. For a discussion of the Appellate Body's "strategic" behavior, see Geoffrey Garrett and James McCall Smith, "The Politics of WTO Dispute Settlement" (George Washington University and Yale University, Washington, D.C. and New Haven, Conn., September 1999, photocopy).

20. Busch and Reinhardt, "Testing International Law," 12; and Reinhardt, "Aggressive Multilateralism," 19.

21. Busch and Reinhardt, "Testing International Trade Law," 13. For another description of the increased hurdles that developing countries face in the new system, see Bernard M. Hoekman and Petros C. Mavroidis, "WTO Dispute Settlement, Transparency, and Surveillance," *World Economy* 23 (2000): 527–542.

Chapter 4. Emerging Constitutional Problems and Substantive Deficiencies

1. William J. Davey, "Improving the WTO Dispute Settlement," in *The Next Trade Negotiating Round: Examining the Agenda for Seattle,* ed. Jagdish Bhagwati (proceedings of conference at Columbia University, New York, N.Y., 23–24 July 1999), 226. For a review of a number of proposals for dispute settlement reform and change advanced over the past several years, see John H. Jackson, "Dispute Settlement and the WTO" (background note for Conference on Developing Countries and the New Round of Multilateral Trade Negotiations, Harvard University, Cambridge, Mass., 5–6 November 1999, photocopy), 1–13.

2. John H. Jackson, "Dispute Settlement and the WTO: Emerging Problems," *Journal of International Economic Law* 1, no. 3 (1998): 329.

3. Marco C. E. J. Bronckers, "Better Rules for a New Millennium: A Warning Against Undemocratic Developments in the WTO," *Journal of International Economic Law* 2, no. 4 (1999): 550.

4. Judith H. Bello and Alan F. Holmer, "Rewriting the Rule of Law and Trade," *Legal Times,* 20 March 1995, 11; and Alan Wm. Wolff and John A. Ragosta, "Will the WTO Result in International Trade Common Law? The Problem for U.S. Lawyers," in *The World Trade Organization: Multilateral Trade Framework for the 21st Century and U.S. Implementation Legislation,* ed. Terence P. Stewart (Washington, D.C.: American Bar Association, 1996), 695–717.

5. Robert Hudec, *Enforcing International Trade Law: The Evolution of the Modern GATT System* (Salem, N.H.: Butterworth Legal Publishers, 1993), 364; and Robert Hudec, "Transcending the Ostensible: Some Reflections on the Nature of Litigation Between Governments," *Minnesota Law Review* 72 (1987): 114.

6. Bronckers, "Better Rules for a New Millennium," 551–552; Jackson, "Dispute Settlement and the WTO," 345.

7. Jackson, *World Trading System,* 65–73. Also see Bronckers, "Better Rules for the New Millennium," 551–552, 556–564. Bronckers gives several illustrations of the failure since 1995 to fulfill mandates in original negotiations or to mend obvious inconsistencies in the rules, such as unresolved questions regarding subsidies, parallel imports, and competition policy.

8. Early on, Alan Wolff and John Ragosta quite presciently diagnosed the most important flaws in the new DSU and the conditions whereby panels and the AB would be pressed to create law: "Recent history has shown that even GATT 1947 panels are increasingly activist, reticent only in their unwillingness to find that lack of clarity prevents a definitive answer to a complaint. Under WTO dispute settlement, 'non-answers' and indefinite outcomes will be even less likely, especially as a body of decisions develops. There is a danger that extension, rather than interpretation, may become not uncommon. Terms that members used to express ambiguous

concepts and differing interpretations, and applications of those terms, will be defined. Panels may decide, often, what members could not. One can only hope that answers will be developed with the greatest circumspection, and with due respect to members' understanding the continuing paradigm that a country cannot be bound by what it has not agreed to." See Alan Wm. Wolff and John A. Ragosta, "Will the WTO Result in International Common Law?" 703.

9. Raj Bhala, "The Myth about *Stare Decisis* and International Trade Law," *American University International Law Review* 14 (1999): 847. The other two articles are "The Precedent Setters: *De Facto Stare Decisis* in WTO Adjudication," *Journal of Transnational Law and Policy* 9 (1999): 206–297; and "The Power of the Past: Towards *De Jure Stare Decisis* in WTO Adjudication," *George Washington University Journal of International Law* (2001, forthcoming).

10. Bhala, "The Precedent Setters," 264–265; see 208 for a description of the theme of the third piece of the trilogy.

11. Joel P. Trachtman, "The Domain of WTO Dispute Resolution," *Harvard International Law Journal* 40 (1999): 333–336. To be fair and accurate, Trachtman's article is a nuanced, highly sophisticated, and balanced analysis of circumstances when explicit rules are appropriate for normal legislation and when "standards" (more broadly based general guidance) are called for, with a role for dispute settlement bodies. Clearly, however, he contemplates a substantial legislative role for panels and the Appellate Body, and in only one place (335) does he acknowledge potential problems of democratic legitimacy: "From a more critical standpoint, it might be argued that allocation of authority to a transnational dispute resolution body by virtue of standards can be used as a method to integrate *sub rosa*, and outside the visibility of democratic controls."

In another piece analyzing the issues related to the direct effect of international rules on domestic law and the tradeoffs between strong and weak compliance with such rules, however, Trachtman sets forth quite clearly the connection between compliance with rules and democratic legitimacy: "The natural condition of law is rough and imperfect, like our society, and like us. To say that the natural condition of law entails direct effect, or perfect compliance, is surely incorrect. . . . Denial of direct effect and weak mechanisms of compliance may be viewed not necessarily as gaps in compliance, but as mechanisms to reinforce democratic legitimacy, to the extent that the state is the locus of democratic legitimacy. . . . Direct effect without more direct democratic participation in formulation of the directly effective law raises as many issues as it resolves." See Joel Trachtman, "Bananas, Direct Effect, and Compliance," *European Journal of International Law* 10 (1999): 677–678.

12. Jeremy Rabkin, *Why Sovereignty Matters* (Washington, D.C.: AEI Press, 1998), 26–27.

13. Kal Raustiala, "Sovereignty and Multilateralism," *Chicago Journal of International Law* 1 (2000): 401–419.
14. Ibid., 410–411.
15. Ibid., 412.
16. Ibid., 413. Raustiala is not alone in his concerns. In a recent article, Julian G. Ku analyzes the constitutional problems and strains that flow increasingly from international delegations of authority—that is, the "transfer of constitutionally assigned federal powers—treaty-making, legislative, executive, and judicial powers—to an international organization." Ku notes that how one decides the propriety of international delegations is highly dependent on whether a formalist or a functionalist constitutional interpretation is utilized. Formalists evaluate constitutional questions by relying heavily on the Constitution's text, structure, and history, while functionalists take a more expansive view of constitutional interpretation and look beyond text to the broader purposes of the constitutional structure. Formalists will likely take a more skeptical view of international delegation than functionalists do. Ku, however, argues strongly that a formalist approach is necessary in the international arena "because such delegations are meaningfully different from delegations to states and private parties [that is, *domestically*] in at least two important ways. First, international delegations place an unusually heavy strain upon the ideal of political accountability that animates much of the Constitution's structural design. Second, international organizations lack an independent source of political legitimacy. . . . The peculiar characteristics that make the new breed of international organizations so exciting also make them uniquely unaccountable entities within the U.S. constitutional system. The Founders' concern with maintaining lines of political responsibility, and the continued emphasis by courts and commentators on the dangers of political unaccountability, suggests that the delegation of federal power to international organizations creates substantial constitutional stress." Ku argues that U.S. courts must take the lead in defining the bounds of such international delegations. See Julian G. Ku, "The Delegation of Federal Power to International Organizations: New Problems with Old Solutions," *Minnesota Law Review* 85 (November 2000): 72, 76, 125–126.
17. In addition to the three examples given in the text, two other recent illustrations of judicial overreach could have been included: (1) a developing backlash in the United States against the panels and AB for their alleged flouting of WTO rules and overturning of national import-relief measures (antidumping and safeguards actions); and (2) a similar backlash in response to a case relating to an allegation that a WTO member impaired the rights of another WTO nation through one or more of its trade policies, even though those policies did not legally violate an agreement.

The area of import relief is particularly sensitive for the future of the WTO because of the political power of industries that defend the current administration of U.S. laws. (In May 2001, sixty-one U.S. senators sent a letter to President Bush warning against any weakening of U.S. trade remedy laws in the next WTO trade round.) During the Uruguay Round, the United States demanded and largely got language that it thought insulated the administration of antidumping and safeguards decisions from second-guessing by WTO panels and the AB. This was thought to be the case with antidumping in particular because Article 17.6 of the WTO text instructs the panels and AB to defer to national officials in areas where there is more than one permissible interpretation of the WTO text—even though the panels and AB might have chosen another interpretation.

But in a series of at least five decisions (other cases are in the pipeline) relating to antidumping and safeguards actions, panels and the AB have overturned U.S. actions, labeling them "impermissible" under WTO law. These cases include the following: *U.S.–Antidumping Act of 1916; U.S.–Antidumping Measures on Stainless Steel from Korea; U.S.–Antidumping Measures on Hot-Rolled Steel from Japan; U.S.–Safeguards Measures on Wheat Gluten from the EU;* and *U.S.–Safeguards on Lamb Meat from Australia.*

Both antidumping and safeguards actions are fraught with highly technical and intricate rules—designed so purposefully by industries and their legal retainers in an effort to insulate such largely protectionist actions from fundamental economic analysis and scrutiny. And it is true that in each of these cases, lawyers for both sides can spin out quite elaborate attacks and defenses on what the WTO panels and AB have decided. Although I am very much opposed to the current administration of U.S. antidumping and safeguards laws, after plowing through the cases and scholarly interpretations, I believe that the critics have a reasonably strong case that, in the words of one such critic, these decisions are "creating a body of WTO case law that imposes obligations on members that go well beyond those to which they thought they were subscribing when the Uruguay Round Agreements were negotiated."

For arguments against the recent decisions, see Paul C. Rosenthal, "WTO Rulings against U.S. Import Relief Measures" (remarks for a conference on WTO Rulings against U.S. Import Relief Measures, International Trade Committee of the American Bar Association, Washington, D.C., 21 May 2001); Rosenthal's remarks are quoted in the preceding paragraph. See also Paul C. Rosenthal and Robert T.C. Vermylen, "The WTO Antidumping and Subsidies Agreements: Did the United States Achieve Its Objective during the Uruguay Round?" *Law and Policy in International Business* 31 (2000): 871–909; and *United States–Anti-Dumping Measures on Certain Hot-Rolled Steel Products from Japan,* Appellant Submission of the United States before the WTO Appellate Body (AB-2001-2), World Trade Organization, Geneva, Switzerland, 7 May 2001.

For arguments supporting the legal interpretations of the panels and AB, see Lewis Leibowitz, "Impermissible Interpretations of the New WTO Antidumping and Safeguards Rules," Trade Policy Briefing, Cato Institute, Washington, D.C., forthcoming. The aforementioned letter from sixty-one U.S. Senators is reported in Gary G. Yerkey, "Senators Urge President Bush

Not to Weaken U.S. Trade Laws," *International Trade Reporter* 18 (10 May 2001): 755.

In addition, as noted at the outset of this note, questions have been raised concerning the much-discussed film case between the United States and Japan, or more accurately between the Kodak and Fuji companies. The WTO panel ruled against the United States, but interestingly, two U.S. lawyers who represented Fuji, and thus agreed with the results of the case, have recently written a law review article that is severely critical of the legal reasoning of the panel (the panel's findings were not appealed). The most important legal principle in the case involved the concept of "non-violation nullification and impairment (NVNI)," which, stated simply, allows a WTO member to raise claims against another member even if that member has not taken measures that violate a specific GATT/WTO obligation. As a result of their analysis, the two lawyers conclude, "In our view, the panel adopted several legal interpretations that go beyond the language of the treaty text and the original intent of the drafters. . . . In our view, these interpretations are legally flawed. If WTO members are to live with such a broad NVNI remedy, *they should expressly adopt it* [italics added]. It is quite ironic that the country [the United States] that has complained the loudest about preserving its domestic policy autonomy has now triggered the most open-ended legal cause of action in the history of the GATT/WTO." See James P. Durling and Simon N. Lester, "Original Meanings and the *Film Dispute: The Drafting History, Textual Evolution, and Application of the Non-Violation Nullification and Impairment Remedy," George Washington Journal of International Law and Economics* 32 (1999): 215, 269.

18. For a general treatment of Article XX, see Jackson, *The World Trading System,* 232–238.

19. Legal scholars are also vigorously debating the validity of the product/process distinction in relation to GATT/WTO jurisprudence. In an e-mail to the author in response to an early draft of the book, Robert Hudec suggested that I make clear to readers that the product/process doctrine relating to Article III remained very much intact: "The product process doctrine is alive and well. It has been approved by every panel to consider it. . . . What the Appellate Body did [in the shrimp/turtle case] was to indicate that it would approve an Article XX(g) exception to the Article III violation." E-mail from Robert Hudec to author, 27 November 2000. See also Robert E. Hudec, "GATT Legal Restraints on the Use of Trade Measures against Foreign Environmental Practices," in *Fair Trade and Harmonization: Prerequisites for Free Trade?* vol. 2, eds. Jagdish N. Bhagwati and Robert E. Hudec (Cambridge, Mass.: MIT Press, 1996), 95–174.

But see the symposium and debate in the spring 2000 issue of the *European Journal of International Law,* where University of Michigan legal scholars Robert Howse and Donald Regan directly challenged the more traditional interpretations, arguing that "there is no real support in the text and jurisprudence of the GATT for the product/process distinction." In turn, John Jackson rebutted, "The proposition that there is no 'justifiable text' to support the essence of the product/process distinction is questionable. There is 'justifiable text.'" He went on to characterize the Howse/Regan theory as "somewhat remote from reality, and particularly remote from the institutional context of the WTO and its relationship to trade policy." At the moment, Howse and Regan are distinctly in the minority among legal scholars. See Robert Howse and Donald Regan, "The Product/Process Distinction—An Illusory Basis for Disciplining 'Unilateralism' in Trade Policy," and John Jackson, "Comments on Shrimp/Turtle and the Product/Process Distinction," *European Journal of International Law* 11 (2000): 249–289 and 303–307, respectively.

It should be added that Jackson has recently agonized in print over the correctness of the tuna/dolphin versus the shrimp/turtle decision. Writing in 1992, he praised the decision of the tuna/dolphin panel to decline to rule and to call for a legislative mandate, and even today, he supports the distinction between product and process: "In that sense, the tuna/dolphin case was praiseworthy, and in a broader sense should be pursued by the environmentalists who dislike the outcome. It suggests a certain 'judicial restraint.'" See John H. Jackson, "World Trade Rules and Environmental Policies: Congruence or Conflict?" *Washington and Lee Law Review* 49 (1992): 1254. Recently, however, Jackson has revised his views because of the lack of resolution of the issue through negotiation. In the *European Journal of International Law* symposium, Jackson stated: "At the time of the [tuna/dolphin] case, it could be argued (and I have so argued) that the panel took an appropriate approach. But it is my belief, that if after ten years no progress has been made using other procedures, then there is an institutional argument that there should be more accommodation within the 'judicial process.' This may not be the only way, but there is certainly an argument for it." See Jackson, "Comments on Shrimp/Turtle," 305. As noted in the text, however, Jackson also points out that allowing unilateral banning of imports on the basis of production methods is a "slippery slope" that could open the door to widespread protectionist actions. While I am sympathetic to the reasons for Jackson's puzzlement and equivocation, this study contends that use of the DSU to settle divisive policy issues will ultimately undermine, and potentially destroy, the system itself.

20. Jackson, *The World Trading System*, 238. Writing in 1996, Hudec advanced a response to the tuna/dolphin decision that would provide "the most sustainable legal approach to really effective legal disciplines over unilateral trade restrictions." Under this approach, the importing nation would apply for a waiver to allow temporary restrictions for environmental purposes; and as a condition for granting the waiver, the importing nation would agree to enter into longer-term negotiations toward a multilateral solution to the problem. Despite the negative reaction to the tuna/dolphin decision in the United States and from international environmental organizations, Hudec pointed out that all of the other GATT members who spoke out

(thirty-nine members) strongly supported the prohibition against unilateral sanctions in this case. See Hudec, "GATT Legal Restraints," 117, 152–154.

21. Jackson, "Comments on Shrimp/Turtle," 306.

22. For analysis of the problems presented by the AB's decisions in the shrimp/turtle case, see Gary Sampson, *Trade, Environment, and the WTO: The Post-Seattle Agenda,* (Washington, D.C.: Overseas Development Council, 2000), 106–120; and Arthur E. Appleton, "Shrimp/Turtle: Untangling the Nets," *Journal of International Economic Law* 2, no. 3 (September 1999): 476–496. There is also a brief but insightful review of these issues in Gary P. Horlick, "The World Trading System at the Crossroads of Science and Politics," in *The Next Trade Negotiating Round: Examining the Agenda for Seattle,* ed. Jagdish Bhagwati (proceedings of conference at Columbia University, New York, N.Y., 23–24 July 1999).

One legal scholar, Jeffrey L. Dunoff of Temple University School of Law, believes that because of the high political costs involved and major questions regarding the legitimacy of the WTO DSU in matters relating to "trade and" issues (environment and labor, for example), WTO panels and the AB should avoid where possible making decisions in these areas. Citing work by Alexander Bickel, a noted judicial theorist, Dunoff argues that the WTO bodies should adopt "mediating techniques"—raising questions of standing, ripeness of the issue for adjudication, and justifiability—to avoid handing down evaluations of certain contested decisions (or nondecisions) made during trade round negotiations: "It is politically naïve to urge WTO panels to 'struggle openly' with the value conflicts raised by 'trade and' issues. In this context, open struggle will be self-defeating. . . . The fledgling WTO dispute resolution system should not be expected to ignore the political costs that accompany the unsatisfactory resolution of 'trade and' disputes. More importantly, the suggestion that panels abstain from deciding certain issues is not an invitation for the exercise of 'unchanneled, undirected, and uncharted discretion.' Rather, it should be understood as a call for the exercise of prudence in the name of principle." See Jeffrey L. Dunoff, "The Death of the Trade Regime," *European Journal of International Law* 10 (1999): 756, 761.

23. Appellate Body Report, *United States–Import Prohibition of Certain Shrimp and Shrimp Products* (WT/DS58/AB/R), World Trade Organization, Geneva, Switzerland, 1998; Sampson, *Trade, Environment, and the WTO,* 109.

24. Sampson, *Trade, Environment, and the WTO,* 110. Sampson frames the larger issue in the following manner: "Can WTO obligations be breached to ensure that certain standards deemed appropriate by the importing country are applied in the exporting country as a precondition for doing business? Much to the chagrin of many environmentalists, the traditional interpretation has been that trade measures related to environmental standards should be taken only with respect to the fauna and flora and natural resources within the boundaries of the country taking action. The implications are clear. Countries are free to adopt whatever regulations they wish

to reflect standards within their own borders, but they cannot restrict trade on the grounds that other countries do not apply these standards domestically. In practical terms, this means that while a country may adopt whatever fishing practices for tuna or shrimp it wishes to protect dolphins, turtles, or any other sea life, it cannot refuse to import tuna or shrimp from countries that choose not to adopt the same or equivalent standards."

25. Appleton, "Shrimp/Turtle," 481 483, 491–492; John Jackson believes that the "conditional tense" used at crucial points in the decision means that the AB has given no definitive judgment on this issue: "The shrimp-turtle [decision] has a very nuanced statement…which some people have interpreted as recognizing unilateralism, but I think use of the word 'may' in the crucial sentence indicates that the Appellate Board division did not entirely make up its mind yet on this question." E-mail from John Jackson to author, 1 October 2000. There is some language in the AB decision to support Jackson's contention. Thus, the AB stated, "Perhaps the most conspicuous flaw in this measure's application is related to its intended and actual coercive effect on the specific policy decisions made by foreign governments. . . . It is not acceptable in international trade relations for one WTO member to use an economic embargo to require other members to adopt essentially the same comprehensive regulatory program, to achieve a certain policy goal . . . without taking into account different conditions which may occur in the territories of those other members." See Appellate Body Report, *United States–Import Prohibition of Certain Shrimp and Shrimp Products,* paragraphs 161, 164.

26. Sampson, *Trade, Environment, and the WTO,* 110–111.

27. Appleton, "Shrimp/Turtle," 495–496. Appleton (482) also criticized the "evolutionary" approach taken by the AB to Article XX, stating, "Tinkering with the exceptions in Article XX through the application of an 'evolutionary' approach is likely to alter the rights and obligations now viewed as present in the substantive provisions of the GATT 1994."

28. Sampson, *Trade, Environment, and the WTO,* 111. Sampson also criticizes the AB for translating general language in the preamble to the WTO agreement into legal obligations. The preamble speaks of applying WTO principles in light of the necessity for "sustainable development" and the need to "protect and preserve the environment." In challenging the AB's interpretation of the obligations flowing from the language, Sampson (112) writes the following: "Principles as expressed in preambles are general legal commitments rather than specific legal obligations of states. In making a ruling to the contrary, the Appellate Body clearly assigned importance to promoting sustainable development and preserving the environment, something that appears only in the preamble. This objective is certainly recognized and supported by WTO members. The manner in which it is translated into rights and obligations can fundamentally change the character of the exceptions provisions of the WTO."

29. Quoted in Daniel Bodansky, "The Legitimacy of International Governance: A Coming Challenge for International Environmental Law?" *American Journal of International Law* 93 (1999): 606 n. 57. Bodansky also agrees that legislative amendments are needed in this case, as do two other noted legal scholars, Thomas Schoenbaum and John Jackson. See Thomas J. Schoenbaum, "Free International Trade and Protection of the Environment: Irreconcilable Conflict?" *American Journal of International Law* 86 (1992): 717; and John H. Jackson, "World Trade Rules and Environmental Policies: Congruence or Conflict?" *Washington and Lee Law Review* 49 (1992): 1254. In praising the decision of the panel to decline to rule and call for a legislative mandate, Jackson (1254) wrote: "In that sense, the tuna/dolphin case was praiseworthy, and in a broader sense should be praised by the environmentalists who dislike the outcome. It suggests a certain 'judicial restraint.' A contrary approach, with the panel seizing the issue and going forward with it, might in some future case be severely contrary to the interests of environmental policy."

   Finally, it should be noted that the controversy over environmental and health and safety exceptions to Article XX continues unabated. In March 2001, the Appellate Body upheld the French government's ban on the importation of crysotile asbestos against Canada's argument that this action violated Article XX. The AB accepted the argument that the asbestos was a cancer-causing agent and that the French government was allowed to ban it for health and safety reasons. In May 2001, in another wrinkle in the shrimp/turtle case, a WTO panel rejected Malaysia's contention that the United States should be forced to lift its ban on the importation of shrimp from Malaysia. In so doing, the panel, at least by implication, made legal the banning of goods based upon how they are produced so long as the WTO member imposing the ban does not discriminate among WTO members. Neither the panels nor the AB, however, has directly tackled the issue of Article XX environmental exceptions directly. For a description of the two recent decisions, see Daniel Pruzin, "United States Scores WTO Victory in Defense of Its Shrimp-Turtle Ban," *International Trade Reporter* 18 (17 May 2001): 795–796.

30. For analyses of the issues presented by *amicus* briefs, see Sampson, *Trade, Environment, and the WTO,* 112–114 (critical of the AB's reasoning); and Robert Howse, "The Legitimacy of the World Trade Organization" (University of Michigan Law School, Ann Arbor, Mich., 2000, photocopy), 33–37 (favorable to the AB's decision). For more general treatments, see Andrew W. Shoyer and Eric M. Solovy, "The Process and Procedure of Litigating at the World Trade Organization: A Review of the Work of the Appellate Body" (paper prepared for the Georgetown University Law Center Conference on the First Five Years of the WTO, Washington, D.C., 20–21 January 2000), 7–13; and Staff Report, "Review of the Dispute Settlement Understanding: Operation of Panels" (paper prepared for same conference at Georgetown University Law Center), 11–14.

31. Howse, "Legitimacy of the WTO," 36.

32. Ibid., 35–37.

33. Sampson, *Trade, Environment, and the WTO*, 113–114; Shoyer and Solovy, "Process and Procedure of Litigation," 9–10.

34. Daniel Pruzin, "Appellate Body Upholds Panel Ruling against U.S. Steel Duties," *International Trade Reporter* 17, no. 20 (18 May 2000): 788–789. I am grateful to John Ragosta for pointing out the narrow basis of the AB decision. E-mail from John Ragosta to author, 18 December 2000. For a description of the controversy over the Canadian/French case, see Daniel Pruzin, "WTO Appellate Body under Fire for Move to Accept *Amicus Curiae* Briefs from NGOs," *International Trade Reporter* 17, no. 47 (30 November 2000): 1805–1806.

35. Pruzin, "Appellate Body Upholds," 789.

36. These statements were all reported in Daniel Pruzin, "Key WTO Members Score Appellate Body for Decision to Accept *Amicus* Briefs," *WTO Reporter*, 8 June 2000.

37. Pruzin, "WTO Appellate Body under Fire," 1805–1806; see also "WTO: Briefs in a Twist," *The Economist*, 9 December 2000, 85. When their petitions were rejected, the environmental NGOs complained bitterly. A spokesperson for Greenpeace stated, "Once again, the WTO has arbitrarily dismissed the input of civil society, fueling concerns about the secretive way in which it makes decisions that impact on human lives and the environment." (Quoted in Pruzin, 1806.)

38. Pruzin, "WTO Appellate Body under Fire," 1805.

39. Ibid., 1806.

40. India also rejected arguments that WTO members could always file *amicus* briefs as did other organizations that did not formally belong to the WTO. Indian WTO ambassador Srinivasan Narayanan stated, "I do not think that any WTO member would be particularly pleased at the prospect of having to characterize itself as something other than a member just for getting the privileges which nonmembers are being given by the Appellate Body." (Quoted in Pruzin, "WTO Appellate Body under Fire," 1805.)

41. Before this case emerged, Shoyer and Solovy had pointed out that it also appeared that quite specific language in the DSU precluded the AB from accepting *amicus* briefs. See Shoyer and Solovy, "Process and Procedure of Litigation" (9–10): "The relevant DSU provisions seem to make it quite difficult for the Appellate Body to justify the consideration of an independently submitted *amicus* brief. Article 13 of the DSU, under which the AB stated that a panel could consider a free-standing *amicus* brief, addresses only panels, not the AB. Furthermore, Article 17 of the DSU and Rule 24 of the Appellate Working Procedures state only that 'third parties' may make a submission to the AB. In turn, 'third parties' are defined as members of the WTO."

42. Sampson, *Trade, Environment, and the WTO*, 114.

43. The material in this section is taken from Frieder Roessler, "The Institutional Balance between the Judicial and the Political Organs of the WTO" (paper presented at the Conference on Efficiency, Equity, and Legitimacy: The Multilateral Trading System at the Millennium, Kennedy School of Government, Harvard University, Cambridge, Mass., 1–2 June 2000). For a very different view of the facts and legal meaning of these cases, see paper presented at the same conference by William J. Davey, "A Comment on Balancing Judicial and Political Power in the World Trade Organization." Robert Hudec also expressed his disagreement with Roessler's reading of these cases in an e-mail to the author, 27 November 2000.

44. Roessler, "The Institutional Balance," 2–3.

45. Ibid., 10–12.

46. Ibid., 12–16.

47. Ibid., 9, 24.

48. Ibid., 2

49. Ibid., 23.

50. "Are There Better Means for Resolving Trade Disputes?" (panel discussion, Forum on Trade Disputes: The Challenges Ahead, Georgetown University Law Center, Washington, D.C., 26 June 2000).

51. The details of this section are taken largely from Bronckers, "Better Rules for a New Millennium," 559–564. The "Reference Paper" can be found on the WTO website at www.wto.org (accessed 31 July 2001).

52. Ibid., 561.

53. Ibid., 562–563.

54. For descriptions of the SPS agreement and the beef hormones case set forth in this paper, see Donna Roberts, "Preliminary Assessment of the Effects of the WTO Agreement on Sanitary and Phytosanitary Trade Regulations," *Journal of International Economic Law* 1 (1998): 377–405; and Thomas Cottier, "SPS Risk Assessment and Risk Management in WTO Dispute Settlement: Experience and Lessons" (paper presented at the Conference on Risk Analysis and International Agreements, Melbourne, Australia, 10–11 February 1999), 1–22. For broader assessments of the connections between health and safety regulations and WTO rules, see Steve Charnovitz, "The Supervision of Health and Safety Regulation by World Trade Rules," *Tulane Environmental Law Journal* 13 (2000): 271–301; and Joost Pauwelyn, "The WTO Agreement on SPS Measures," *Journal of International Economic Law* 2 (1999): 641–664.

    In addition to the beef hormones case described in the text, there have been two other SPS WTO cases: Australia–Salmon and Japan–Agricultural Products. See Charnovitz, "The Supervision of Health and Safety Regulation."

55. See Cottier, "SPS Risk Assessment." For another analysis of the findings of the panel and the Appellate Body, see James Cameron and Karen Campbell, "Challenging the Boundaries of the DSU through Trade and Environment

Disputes," in *Dispute Resolution in the WTO,* eds. James Cameron and Karen Campbell (London: Cameron May, 1998), chap. 10.

56. Reinhard Quick and Andreas Bluthner, "An Appraisal and Criticism of the Ruling in the WTO *Hormones* Case," *Journal of International Economic Law* 2 (1999): 618, 639; see also Cottier, "SPS Risk Assessment," 13–17, 21.

57. Quick and Bluthner, "Has the Appellate Body Erred?" 639.

58. For these later developments, see Gary G. Yerkey, "Corporate Leaders Say U.S.-EU Disputes Harming Business, Urge Quick Resolution," *International Trade Reporter* 17 (23 November 2000): 1774–1775.

59. For a discussion of the "sound science" and "precautionary principle" as they relate to the SPS agreement, see Gary N. Horlick, "The World Trading System at the Crossroads of Science and Politics," in *The Next Trade Negotiating Round,* ed. Jagdish Bhagwati (proceedings of conference at Columbia University, New York, N.Y., 23–24 July 1999), 257–260.

60. The deep substantive disagreements and the highly emotional responses to the invocation of the precautionary principle were both on display at a conference convened in late September 2000 by the Harvard University Center for International Development. Some experts strongly questioned the validity of the concept, a view typified by the following statement by Gary Marchant, a law professor from Arizona State University: "[The precautionary principle] thrives because it is ambiguous. What you end up with is arbitrariness." Meanwhile, critics of biotechnology charged that behind these criticisms was a plot by industrial interests to undermine the principle for their own purposes (and they charged that the Harvard Center, by merely convening the conference, was playing into the hands of biotech companies). Thus, Philip Bereano of the University of Washington argued, "The precautionary principle is now becoming enshrined in international law, and that is upsetting some powerful interests." Not surprisingly, at the end of the day, Calestous Juma, who convened the meeting for the Harvard Center, concluded, "It is evident that there is no real agreement on what the precautionary principle means and how it should be applied." See Colin MacIlwain, "Experts Question Precautionary Approach," *Nature,* 5 October 2000, 551.

61. T. O'Riordan and J. Cameron, "The History and Contemporary Significance of the Precautionary Principle," in *Interpreting the Precautionary Principle,* eds. T. O'Riordan and J. Cameron (London: Earthscan, 1994).

62. James Cameron and Karen Campbell, "Dispute Settlement in the WTO," chap. 10, 218–219.

63. Hector Rogelio Torres, "Precaution Meets Protectionism at the WTO," *Journal of Commerce,* 13 January 2000, 6.

64. It must be admitted that at times political divisions among negotiators produce contradictory mandates that can hopelessly complicate the resolution of issues. Take, for example, the controversy over the definition and reach of the "precautionary principle" and the jurisdiction of WTO rules versus the rules laid down in environmental treaties and agreements. The issue has

become quite complicated as a result of contradictory language in the 2000 Biosafety Protocol to the Convention on Biodiversity (the Cartagena Protocol). One article of the protocol states that "the Protocol shall not be interpreted as implying a change in the rights and obligations of a Party under any existing international agreements [i.e., the WTO]. . . ." But another article states that ". . . the above recital is not intended to subordinate this Protocol to other international agreements." How a WTO panel or the AB would handle such a dispute is anybody's guess. From the perspective taken in this study, both should adopt the stance of the tuna/dolphin panel and send the dispute right back to the WTO member states for resolution. For a highly critical analysis of the negotiations leading to the Cartagena Protocol, see Hon. Andrew Thomson, Member of Parliament, Australia, "The Dangers of Secret Treaty-Making: The Biosafety Protocol as a Case Study," *Institute of Public Affairs Review* 52 (June 2000): 21–23.

65. Rabkin, *Why Sovereignty Matters*, 32–33. For a description of the evolution of soft law as it relates to the concept of sustainable development and the status of women, see Kenneth W. Abbott, "'Economic' Issues and Political Participation: The Evolving Boundaries of International Federalism," *Cardozo Law Review* 18 (1996): 979–986.

66. Philip R. Trimble, "A Revisionist View of Customary Law," *UCLA Law Review* 33 (1986): 668. International law is governed by two sets of rules: customary law as described above, and treaty law that consists of obligations negotiated freely by nation-states.

67. Rabkin, *Why Sovereignty Matters*, 55. For a critique of techniques used by legal theorists to establish the legitimacy of current customary law, written by an author who is sympathetic to environmental causes, see Daniel Bodansky, "Customary (and Not So Customary) International Environmental Law," *Indiana Journal of Global Legal Studies* 3 (1995): 105–119.

68. Trimble, "A Revisionist View," 718–719, 721. For other powerful critiques of the so-called modern view of customary international law, see Curtis A. Bradley and Jack L. Goldsmith, "Customary International Law as Federal Common Law: A Critique of the Modern Position," *Harvard Law Review* 110 (1997): 800–840; and Jack L. Goldsmith and Eric A. Posner, "A Theory of Customary International Law," *University of Chicago Law Review* 66 (1999): 1113–1177. Goldsmith and Posner employ IR theory to explain the dynamics of customary international law and the behavior of nations with regard to such law. Rather than arising from a heightened sense of legal or moral obligations to common norms, they argue (1113) that nations adopt customary law solely in the pursuit of national self-interest, adopted to different situations in "discrete historically contingent contexts." Using empirical historical tests, they find four different conditions that will lead to adoption of customary international law by individual nations: coincidence of interest with other states; the ability to coerce one or more other states into compliance with a certain principle; cooperation in order to escape a repeated prisoner's dilemma situation; and coordination where the

interests of several states converge. In IR terms (1176), they base their theory on two traditions, realism and institutionalism: "Realism emphasizes that states act rationally to further their perceived national interest, and that the distribution of national power determines international behaviors. Realism is skeptical about international cooperation and international law. By contrast, the second tradition—institutionalism—is more optimistic about international cooperation and international law. It argues that states acting rationally to further their own interests can sometimes overcome conflicts of interest to achieve mutually beneficial cooperative outcomes. But institutionalists put their faith in international organizations. . . . They ignore [customary international law] which, by definition, arises from decentralized and noninstitutional state acts." For more details on realism and institutionalism, see appendix 1, pp. 150–153.

69. Paul B. Stephan, "International Governance and American Democracy," *Chicago Journal of International Law* 1 (2000): 238. For a view challenging the assertions that international customary law threatens U.S. democratic institutions, see Joel Richard Paul, "Is Global Governance Safe for Democracy?" *Chicago Journal of International Law* 1 (2000): 263–271. Paul argues that there are sufficient checks and balances within the U.S. political system to thwart this threat, including, for example, appeals from lower court rulings and the final authority of Congress to determine whether customary law becomes U.S. law.

70. Jackson, *The World Trading System,* 26. The full citation to the *Third Restatement* is *Restatement of the Law (Third): Foreign Relations Law of the United States* (Washington, D.C.: American Law Institute, 1987).

71. "Reform of the WTO's Dispute Settlement Mechanism for Sustainable Development," World Wildlife Fund Discussion Paper (Gland, Switzerland: World Wildlife Fund, July 1999), 6.

72. Ibid. See also Robert Howse, "The Legitimacy of the World Trade Organization," 42.

73. I am grateful to Robert Hudec for suggesting that the precise issues presented here revolve around the status of the Vienna Convention in WTO law. The DSU, as agreed to by all WTO members, explicitly directs the panels and the AB to interpret WTO law in light of existing international law; and the Vienna Convention is acknowledged as the reference source and guide for the treaty interpretation (although, interestingly, the United States has never formally agreed to this convention). Further, the Vienna Convention expressly directs nations to interpret treaty words and phrases in the total "context" of the treaty, including preambles and other introductory or hortatory language. E-mail from Robert Hudec to author, 27 November 2000.

While I agree that the AB must interpret all treaty language in its "context," I would still argue that preambles, hortatory declarations, and other soft law should not be accorded the same binding force as *specific* treaty commitments freely negotiated by national officials and ratified by home legislatures.

74. Sampson, *Trade, Environment, and the WTO,* 111–112.

75. Ibid., 112.

76. World Wildlife Fund *Amicus* Brief, Shrimp/Turtle Dispute (Gland, Switzerland: World Wildlife Fund), 2.

77. Ibid., 13–15.

78. Robert Hudec argues that even though "environmental advocates will claim any good idea to be customary international law," through the use of "sloppy standards, . . . this is not the definition of customary international law employed by the world's leading international law scholars." He points to the strict definitions of the International Law Commission of the UN, which, he asserts, "would not call any of these environmental norms 'customary international law.'" E-mail from Robert Hudec to author, 27 November 2000.

     Other international legal scholars strongly disagree with Hudec's view that the process of incorporating customary international law into international or domestic law is both deliberate and conservative (as to interpretation). See articles cited in this chapter by Trimble; Stephan; and Goldsmith with several coauthors. Rabkin has pointed out that international law journals now speak of "instant customary international law," and he cites authors who argue that, because no nation opposed treaties regarding genocide and the peaceful use of outer space, these treaties became "instant" customary law. See Rabkin, *Why Sovereignty Matters,* 135 n. 22.

79. Howse, "Legitimacy of the WTO," 42.

80. Ibid., 43.

81. Ibid., 44.

82. Rabkin, *Why Sovereignty Matters,* 89–92.

Chapter 5. Critiques from the Right and Left

1. For more detail on Shell's Efficient Market Model, see appendix 1, pp. 164–166.

2. See Alan Wm. Wolff and John A. Ragosta, "Will the WTO Result in International Common Law? The Problem for U.S. Lawyers," in *The World Trade Organization: The Multilateral Trade Framework for the 21st Century,* ed. Terence P. Stewart (Washington, D.C.: American Bar Association, 1996), 697–726; John A. Ragosta, "Unmasking the WTO—Access to the DSB System: Can the DSB Live Up to Its Moniker 'World Trade Court?'" *Law and Policy in International Business* 31 (2000): 739–784; and Alan Wm. Wolff et al. for Dewey Ballantine LLP, Washington, D.C., "Comments on the Four-Year Review of the WTO Dispute Settlement Understanding," presented before the Office of the U.S. Trade Representative, Washington, D.C., 25 June 1998, photocopy.

     During the past several years, the views of the two lawyers have evolved steadily in response to the evolution of the DSU itself. As will be noted in the text, both men now support a return to a more "diplomatic" approach to dispute settlement in the WTO. Pending such changes, however, they both support the procedural reforms discussed in this section. E-mail from Alan Wolff to author, 17 December 2000; e-mail from John Ragosta to author, 18 December 2000.

In January 2001, Wolff announced an important change in his own thinking and position on the DSU: he now believed that because of fatal flaws in the DSU, all WTO panel and AB decisions should be deemed advisory only. Dispute resolution should be reached by means of consultation and mediation (these changes, of course, would require renegotiation of the basic WTO DSU). In explaining his stance, Wolff wrote, "Resolution of differences where matters of national interest are concerned cannot be fobbed off for third-party resolution in the trade arena, just as they cannot in the foreign policy context. . . . [T]he well-meant attempt at achieving breakthroughs in trade liberalization through litigation should be deemed an experiment that shows that litigation often spawns more litigation rather than a positive outcome for the world trading system. It is time to try a different path." See Alan Wm. Wolff, "The Conduct of International Trade Relations: The Corrosive Effect of an Excessive Reliance on Litigation" (paper presented at the New America Foundation, Washington, D.C., January 2001).

3. By no means do all U.S. international trade lawyers favor standing for private parties. For a view opposed to such a revision of WTO rules, see Lewis E. Leibowitz, "The Function of the WTO Dispute Settlement System" (paper prepared for Wilton Park Conference, Wilton House, England, July 2000, photocopy).

4. Ragosta, "Unmasking the WTO," 741.

5. Wolff and Ragosta, "Will the WTO Result in International Common Law?" 701.

6. Ragosta, "Unmasking the WTO," 746.

7. For supporting arguments in favor of more formal procedures for due process, see John P. Gaffney, "Due Process in the World Trade Organization: The Need for Procedural Justice in the Dispute Settlement System," *American Journal of International Law Review* 14 (1999): 1174–1222. For another analysis of the arguments in favor of participation by private counsel in the DSU, see Jessica C. Pearlman, "Note: Participation by Private Counsel in World Trade Organization Settlement Proceedings," *Law and Policy for International Business* 30 (1999): 399–414.

8. Alan Wolff stops short of calling for a private right of action, but he does call for more accountability by governments to private litigants. For instance, the U.S. government should be required to provide a full explanation to Congress and the public of the rationale behind its decisions to either prosecute a WTO complaint advanced by a private party or not prosecute such a case. He also advocates deputizing private lawyers for particular cases to strengthen the legal resources of the USTR. E-mail from Alan Wolff to the author, 17 December 2000.

9. Ragosta, "Unmasking the WTO," 740, 746.

10. Ibid., 747.

11. Ibid.

12. Glen T. Schleyer, "Note: Power to the People: Allowing Private Parties to Raise Claims before the WTO Dispute Resolution System," *Fordham Law Review* 65 (1997): 2293.

13. Martin Lukas, "The Role of Private Parties in the Enforcement of the Uruguay Round Agreements," *Journal of World Trade* 29 (1995): 197. Lukas, however, is skeptical that governments will ever relinquish their power to control DSU actions to private parties (205). See also Ronald A. Brand, "GATT and the Evolution of United States Trade Law," *Brooklyn Journal of International Law* 18 (1992): 102–141. Brand (139) has made the same connection between economic theory (comparative advantage, which assumes the private parties as the principal actors) and the lack of direct access to the WTO: "This theory [comparative advantage] is based upon the assumption that those who control scarce resources will move those resources to the production of goods in which their national economy holds a comparative advantage. In market economic systems (those systems consistent with GATT concepts), those who control the scarce resources are private parties. Thus, an intellectually honest consideration of comparative advantage theory in today's world would require the participation of private parties in the application of the rules designed to implement the theory."

14. Ragosta, "Unmasking the WTO," 747.

15. Gregory Shaffer, "The Law-in-Action of International Trade Litigation in the United States and Europe: The Melding of the Public and the Private" (University of Wisconsin Law School, June 2000, photocopy), 5. Shaffer (37–85) finds that the EU public-private interaction, while quite different, is becoming more like the U.S. system as time goes by. The major contrasts he identifies include the following: EU trade officials have a much greater role in fostering public-private relationships; traditionally, EU companies have not been so active in openly lobbying EU government officials; the EU Parliament is not so active in pushing the EU Executive to defend corporate interests; EU public officials traditionally have been aloof from the private sector, and there is little of the "revolving door" between public and private life that characterizes the American scene; convoluted EU decision processes hamper public-private collaboration; and, finally, in great contrast with U.S. corporations, EU companies make much less use of lawyers and litigation, preferring to depend upon civil servants.

16. Ibid., 18.

17. Ibid., 17.

18. Ibid., 21–22.

19. Ibid., 29, 35.

20. Ibid., 31.

21. Ibid., 33.

22. Ibid., 13, 32, 95. The assertion of the national interest against a variety of private or claimed "public" interests is a crucial element for governments in this process, in the opinion of the author. Jeffrey L. Dunoff of the Temple University School of Law and other legal commentators have argued that the debate over the participation of corporations or NGOs in the WTO DSU is "misguided" because in many cases the real conflict is between private actors and, as Shaffer's paper chronicles, private parties are already in close partnership with governments. Dunoff cites the Kodak/Fuji film case as a typical example. But Dunoff's arguments, although not themselves misguided, miss the more important issue: namely, whatever the shifting alliance between governments and corporations, it is the public officials who retain the final say. While this study will argue for deeper and more frequent contacts among governments, corporations, and NGOs, it will also argue that the WTO has the best chance to retain legitimacy by adopting a long, arms-length relationship with both NGOs and corporations. See, however, Jeffrey L. Dunoff, "The Misguided Debate over NGO Participation at the WTO," *Journal of International Economic Law* 1 (1998): 433–456.

23. See appendix 1, pp. 154–155, for a more detailed description of two-level liberal intergovernmental theory.

24. Shaffer, "The Law-in-Action of International Trade Litigation," 11–12. For a more detailed discussion of public choice theory, see appendix 1, pp. 160–163. It should be noted that as environmental NGOs gain influence and power within domestic politics, trade officials will also begin to calculate how to use them to maximize their own power over other government agencies and within the WTO. The advent of Green Parties in European national politics has clearly had such an impact on the EU national bureaucracies and Brussels' EU bureaucracies.

25. The phrase originated with UN Secretary-General Kofi Annan, as quoted in Marguerite A. Peeters, "Hijacking Democracy: Global Consensus on Global Governance" (American Enterprise Institute, Washington, D.C., 2001, photocopy), Preface, 1. Citations to Peeters are from a working draft and may not match paging in subsequent drafts of this lengthy study.

26. For two detailed introductions to the new roles of NGOs, which use environmental regimes as the model, see Oran R. Young, ed., *Global Governance: Drawing Insights from the Environmental Experience* (Cambridge, Mass.: MIT Press, 1997), chaps. 1–3, 9, 10; and Thomas Princen and Matthias Finger, *Environmental NGOs in World Politics: Linking the Local and the Global* (New York: Routledge, 1994), chaps. 1–3, 7, 8. In addition, for role of NGOs in global politics, see Gareth Porter and Janet Welsh Brown, *Global World Politics* (Boulder, Col.: Westview Press, 1996), 50–66; and a highly critical analysis by Henry Lamb, "Global Governance: Why? How? When?" Clint W. Murchison, Sr., Chair of Free Enterprise publication, College of Engineering, University of Texas, 1997. See www.wtowatch.org/library/admin/up...files/Global_Governance_Why_How _When.htm (accessed 31 July 2001).

27. Peeters, "Hijacking Democracy," chap. 1, p. 23. For another description and analysis of the growing role of NGOs in international organizations, see Riva Krut et al., "Globalization and Civil Society: NGO Influence in International Decisionmaking," Discussion Paper No. 83, United Nations Research Institute for Social Development, Geneva, Switzerland, 1997. For an insightful theoretical paper that traces the role of NGOs in UN world conferences on the environment, human rights, and women, see Ann Marie Clark, Elisabeth J. Friedman, and Kathryn Hochstetler, "The Sovereign Limits of Global Civil Society: A Comparison of NGO Participation in UN World Conferences on the Environment, Human Rights, and Women," *World Politics* 51 (1998): 1–35.

28. Peeters, "Hijacking Democracy," chap. 1, pp. 24–25, 30; Clark, Friedman, and Hochstetler, "The Sovereign Limits of Global Civil Society," 8–9.

29. Peeters, chap. 1, p. 26.

30. Ibid., chap. 1, pp. 26–27. For two highly critical views of NGO activities in the UN and in the creation of international environmental agreements, see James M. Sheehan, *Global Greens: Inside the Environmental Establishment* (Washington, D.C.: Capital Research Center, 1998), chap. 1; and Jeremy Rabkin and James M. Sheehan, "Global Greens, Global Governance," Environment Working Paper No. 4 (London: Institute of Economic Affairs, 1999).

31. Diane Otto, "Nongovernmental Organizations in the United Nations System: The Emerging Role of the International Civil Society," *Human Rights Quarterly* 18 (1996): 110.

32. For a lucid description of the roles assumed over time by NGOs (with particular emphasis on environmental NGOs), see Kal Raustiala, "The 'Participatory Revolution' in International Environmental Law," *Harvard Environmental Law Review* 21 (1997): 537–586.

33. Peeters, "Hijacking Democracy," chap. 1, pp. 9–13. See also Clark, Friedman, and Hochstetler, "The Sovereign Limits of Global Civil Society." The three authors demonstrate that in most key decision-making meetings and on issues that directly relate to national sovereignty, governments excluded NGO participation and jealously guarded their national rights and prerogatives.

34. Peeters, 34. For another sympathetic account of the rising influence of NGOs in UN affairs, see Kenneth W. Abbott, "'Economic' Issues and Political Participation: The Evolving Boundaries of International Federalism," *Cardozo Law Review* 18 (1996): 996–1005. Abbott evinces broad sympathy with the "new model of governance," in which NGOs play a prominent role along with elected governments. But at the end of his article, in warnings similar to those raised in this study, Abbott cautions, "It is not at all clear that participation by a set—even a large set—of self-selected organizations will provide anything like a representative or balanced view of complex issues. . . . Indeed . . . it can be questioned whether particular

NGOs are representative of larger constituencies or simply vehicles for the political activity of a few organizations' leaders."

35. Peeters, "Hijacking Democracy," chap. 1, p. 9. Without providing detailed numbers, Clark, Friedman, and Hochstetler, "The Sovereign Limits of Global Civil Society" (5–6, 33–34), confirm the overwhelming predominance of northern NGOs in the programs they analyze.

36. Otto, "Nongovernmental Organizations in the UN System," 112.

37. Peeters, "Hijacking Democracy," chap. 1, p. 2. Kenneth Anderson, another critic, has similarly written, "Proponents of civil society . . . actually mean, not civil society in all its plural glory, but instead new social movements, and in fact a narrow range of them. For them, civil society is a term interchangeable with the feminist movement, the environmental movement, the peace movement, the international human rights movement, and many of the smaller movements that have fractured away from those movements. . . ." In large part, Anderson's study is a warning of the dangerous analytic consequences of "normatively 'loading' the term civil society by conflating it with the idea of new social movements that, by their theorists' own preference, denotes a particular brand of politics. . . ." See Kenneth Anderson, "After Seattle: Public International Organizations, Nongovernmental Organizations, and Democratic Sovereignty in an Era of Globalization: An Essay on Contested Legitimacy" (Washington College of Law, American University, Washington, D.C., August 2000, photocopy), 26–27.

38. Peeters, "Hijacking Democracy," chap. 1, pp. 3, 8.

39. Ibid., chap. 1, p. 9.

40. Gregory Shaffer, "The World Trade Organization under Challenge: Democracy and the Law and Politics of the WTO's Treatment of Trade and Environment Matters," *Harvard Environmental Law Review* 25 (2001): 38.

41. For a more complete description of liberal IR theory, see appendix 1, pp. 153–156.

42. Otto, "Nongovernmental Organizations in the UN System," 131.

43. Ibid., 131.

44. Ibid., 134.

45. Ibid., 135.

46. David Henderson, "False Perspective: The UNDP View of the World," *World Economics* 1 (2000): 16–19. Henderson's piece contains a hard-hitting attack on what he perceives as the economic fallacies in the UNDP report. Also see Peeters, "Hijacking Democracy," chap. 1, pp. 45–51.

47. Peeters, "Hijacking Democracy," chap. 1, p. 49.

48. For parallel views regarding the necessity of a "people-centered transnational legal order," see Claudio Grossman and Daniel D. Bradlow, "Are We Being Propelled towards a People-Centered Transnational Legal Order?" *American University Journal of International Law and Policy* 9 (1993): 178–194. Grossman and Bradlow (185–186) conclude,

> The deficiencies of the present international legal order based on the *de jure* sovereignty of the nation-state and a relatively clear distinction between

international and domestic legal issues are obvious. The nation-state is no longer functionally "the master of its own territory." Some private actors and international organizations have at least as much power as the sovereign state. . . .

These developments pose two challenges for international law. First, it needs to recognize and incorporate into its jurisdiction all international actors. The states, international organizations, and private actors such as transnational corporations; trade unions; consumer, environmental, development and human rights NGOs; and private individuals are now engaged in the ongoing process of formulating and implementing international legal standards. An international legal process that fails to allow nonstate actors to participate fully in the process cannot develop legal norms that are fully responsive to the needs of the international community....

Two . . . principles that should shape the new legal process can be identified [*participation and accountability*]. . . . The fact that sovereignty is irrelevant to these two principles means that they will help shape an international legal order that is people-centered, rather than state-centered. This focus creates the possibility for a much more cooperative and rights based legal order than exists under the present state-centered international order.

49. James M. Sheehan, *Global Greens,* chap. 1.

50. For a description of the organization and operation of the UNEP through 1990, including its role in negotiating numerous multilateral environmental agreements, see Carol Annette Petsonk, "The Role of the United Nations Environment Programme (UNEP) in the Development of International Environmental Law," *American University Journal of International Law and Policy* 5 (1990): 351–391. Ms. Petsonk (390) describes the overall strategy as follows: "[UNEP's] approach has been first to formulate scientific positions, then develop legal strategies, and in the process carefully build political support. An important component of this approach has been UNEP's negotiation of 'soft law' guidelines or principles as a prelude to the development of binding international law." For later developments, see Sheehan and Rabkin, "Global Greens, Global Governance," 49–57.

51. Sheehan and Rabkin, "Global Greens, Global Governance," 15–16; see also Matthias Finger, "Environmental NGOs in the UNCED Process," in *Environmental NGOs in World Politics,* eds. Thomas Princen and Matthias Finger (New York: Routledge, 1994), 187–213. For broader theoretical perspectives on the role of environmental NGOs, see also Thomas Princen, "NGOs: Creating a Niche in Environmental Diplomacy," 29–47; and Matthias Finger, "NGOs and Transformation: Beyond Social Movement Theory," 48–65, in aforementioned volume.

52. Sheehan and Rabkin, "Global Greens, Global Governance," 16.

53. For a review of the UNCED process from an environmental perspective, see chapter 4, "Global Economic Development and Environmental Politics" in Gareth Porter and Janet Welsh Brown, *Global Environmental Politics* (Boulder, Col.: Westview Press, 1996).

54. See Sheehan and Rabkin, "Global Greens, Global Governance," 69; and Finger, "Environmental NGOs."

55. Finger, "Environmental NGOs," 199.

56. Ibid., 186.

57. Ibid., 11. Finger is one of several IR theorists who contend that NGOs are an independent element in global governance See Paul Wapner, "Governance in Global Society," in Young, *Global Governance,* 65–84. Wapner argues that NGOs participate directly with governments in the "governance" of global society by forcing changes in norms, pressuring multinational corporations to change policies even without a change in laws, and leading an end-run around national governments to empower local activities to bring about change even without state authority. But see also the skeptical critique of these assertions by Mark Pollock and Gregory Shaffer, who note that "Wapner's definition of governance . . . stretches an already elastic term to the point where almost any action that affects the behavior of individuals constitutes 'governance.'" See Mark A. Pollock and Gregory C. Shaffer, eds. *Transatlantic Governance in the Global Economy* (Lanham, Md.: Rowman and Littlefield, 2001), 32.

58. For another description of the role played by environmental NGOs in these conventions and treaties, see Kal Raustiala, "States, NGOs, and Environmental Institutions," *International Studies Quarterly* 20 (1997): 719–740.

59. Ibid., 723.

60. Ibid.

61. Sheehan, *Global Greens,* 2; see also Princen and Finger, *Environmental NGOs,* "Introduction," 2–6.

62. Sheehan, *Global Greens,* 2–3.

63. Rabkin and Sheehan, "Global Greens, Global Governance," 37. The World Bank distributed over $36 million in support funds to NGOs in 1996; see Rabkin and Sheehan, "Global Greens, Global Governance," 91–94.

64. Sheehan, *Global Greens,* 165–174. The data are for 1996 unless otherwise noted in the text. Data on Greenpeace and WWF income for 1998 are from Shaffer, "The World Trade Organization under Challenge," 64 n. 242.

65. Raustiala, "The Participatory Revolution"; Raustiala, "States, NGOs, and Environmental Institutions"; and Shaffer, "The World Trade Organization under Challenge."

66. Shaffer, "The World Trade Organization under Challenge," 8.

67. Raustiala, "States, NGOs, and Environmental Institutions," 720.

68. Ibid., 727; for another description of environmental NGO technical competence, see William M. Reichert, "Resolving the Trade and Environment Conflict: The WTO and NGO Consultative Relations," *Minnesota Journal of Global Trade* 5 (1996): 219–246.

69. Raustiala, "States, NGOs, and Environmental Institutions," 728.

70. Ibid., 730–731; see also Raustiala, "The Participatory Revolution," 556–564, for somewhat more detailed descriptions of these NGO functions.
71. Raustiala, "The Participatory Revolution," 564–565.
72. Ibid., 538.
73. Ibid., 574, 579.
74. Ibid., 584.
75. Raustiala, "States, NGOs, and Environmental Institutions" 726. IR theorists have labeled NGOs who provide scientific input to environmental and other policymakers as "epistemic communities"—defined specifically as "networks of professionals with recognized expertise and competence in a particular domain and an authoritative claim to policy-relevant knowledge within that domain or issue area." According to these constructivist theorists, epistemic communities become agents of change in environmental and other international regimes by creating new paradigms that change the views of national and international regime leaders. As Raustiala's comments emphasize, however, it is also true that many of the leading NGOs have highly developed and passionately held political, economic, and social beliefs and agendas. They do not represent merely the disinterested, detached approach of "philosopher kings (or queens)." For more detail on IR theory and "epistemic communities," see appendix 1, pp. 157–158.
76. Raustiala, "The Participatory Revolution," 586; see also Raustiala, "States, NGOs, and Environmental Institutions," 737.
77. Enrico Colombatto and Jonathan R. Macey, "The Decline of the Nation-State and Its Effect on Constitutional International Economic Law: A Public Choice Model of International Economic Cooperation and the Decline of the Nation-State," *Cardozo Law Review* 18 (1996): 925. See appendix 1, pp. 160–163 for more detail on public choice theory.
78. Ibid., 925–935.
79. Ibid., 954, 927.
80. Shaffer, "The World Trade Organization under Challenge," 6.
81. Ibid., 12.
82. Wapner, "Governance in Global Society"; see also Paul Wapner, "Politics Beyond the State: Environmental Activism and World Civic Politics," *World Politics* 47 (1995): 311–340.
83. Shaffer, "The World Trade Organization under Challenge," 47–52, 55–61.
84. Ibid., 11.
85. Ibid., 11, 52.
86. Ibid., 66–67.
87. Ibid., 6–7.
88. Ibid., 81–82.
89. Ibid., 6. With a group of collaborators, Shaffer and coeditor Mark Pollack have extended and deepened the analysis of the role and relationship of major actors—elected officials and bureaucrats, private corporations, and NGOs—with a 2001 volume of papers on aspects of the New Transatlantic Agenda, established by the United States and the European Commission in

1995. This agenda has resulted in the establishment of new relationships between lower-level government officials in such areas as food safety, competition policy, and standard setting; in a series of dialogues between government officials, corporate officials, and labor officials from Europe and the United States; and in new opportunities for NGOs to interact with both government and private sector officials. Using concepts from IR theory similar to those Shaffer employed in his study of the WTO trade and environment committee, the studies describe the history of the new transatlantic economic relationship from three levels: an intergovernmental level, where high-level elected or appointed national officials negotiate on behalf of the United States and the European Union; a transgovernmental level, where lower-level bureaucrats have established new relationships with their transatlantic counterparts; and a transnational level, where private actors—corporations and civil society—coordinate efforts to advance their particular goals. The central questions posed by the experience relate to whether governments and intergovernmental networks are being replaced by either transgovernmental or transnational networks as the most important determiners of transatlantic economic policies. Pollack and Shaffer find that no single model or type of network completely describes what has taken place, and they posit the "primacy of *mixed* networks of COGs, lower-level government officials, and private groups" to explain transatlantic economic policymaking.

Still, Pollack and Shaffer believe that, in the end, intergovernmental networks of high-level EU and U.S. officials made the key decisions: "Put simply, we argue that *intergovernmental networks,* consisting of high-level U.S. government and European Commission officials, were the architects of the New Transatlantic Agenda and remain central to it; *transgovernmental networks* have emerged in certain areas . . . but remain immature or unimportant in many others; and *transnational networks* have played an important role in transatlantic governance but nevertheless fall far short of the ideal type predicted by the literature on global civil society." Pollack and Shaffer, *Transatlantic Governance in the Global Economy,* 293, 301.

Chapter 6. Whose WTO Is It? Democratic Governments versus Stakeholders

1. Richard Shell, "The Trade Stakeholders Model and Participation by Nonstate Parties in the World Trade Organization," *University of Pennsylvania Law Journal* 17 (1996): 370.

2. Richard Shell, "Trade Legalism and International Relations Theory: An Analysis of the World Trade Organization," *Duke Law Journal* 44 (1995): 915. Similarly, in a recent paper, Francesca Bignani and Steve Charnovitz state, "The traditional model of legitimacy in international lawmaking is . . . oblivious to the realities of contemporary politics. NGOs have begun to demand direct input into intergovernmental organizations. International NGOs and their networks aspire to act on a global level and will not be

content to participate solely in national governments. . . . [A]s a matter of political fact, NGO participation cannot be cabined at the national level." See Francesca Bignani and Steve Charnovitz, "Transnational Civil Society Dialogues" (paper presented at the Conference on the New Transatlantic Dialogue: Intergovernmental, Transgovernmental and Transnational Perspectives, University of Wisconsin at Madison, 1–2 June 1999), 11. A somewhat different version of this paper appeared in Mark A. Pollock and Gregory C. Shaffer, eds., *Transatlantic Governance in the Global Economy* (Lanham, Md.: Rowman and Littlefield, 2001), 255–284.

3. Daniel C. Esty, "Why the World Trade Organization Needs Environmental NGOs" (London: International Centre for Trade and Sustainable Development, 1998), 135, 137. A plethora of academic articles describe and/or support calls for more "participatory democracy" and a larger role for NGOs in the WTO and other international institutions. See, for instance, the following: Kenneth W. Abbott, "'Economic' Issues and Political Participation: The Evolving Boundaries of International Federalism," *Cardozo Law Review* 18 (1996): 971–1010; Robert F. Housman, "Democratizing International Trade Decision-Making," *Cornell International Law Journal* 27 (1994): 699–747; David Scott Rubinton, "Toward a Recognition of the Rights of Non-States in International Environmental Law," *Pace Environmental Law Review* 9 (1992): 475–494; Daniel Bodansky, "The Legitimacy of International Governance: A Coming Challenge for International Environmental Law," *American Journal of International Law* 93 (1999): 596–623; David A. Wirth, "Reexamining Decision-Making Processes in International Environmental Law," *Iowa Law Review* 79 (1994): 769–802; William M. Reichert, "Resolving the Trade and Environment Conflict: The WTO and NGO Consultative Relations," *Minnesota Journal of Global Trade* 5 (1996): 219–246; Robert Howse, "The Legitimacy of the World Trade Organization" (University of Michigan Law School, Ann Arbor, Mich., 2000, photocopy); and Robert Howse and Kalypso Nicolaides, "Legitimacy and Global Governance: Why Constitutionalizing the WTO Is a Step Too Far" (paper presented at the Conference on Efficiency, Equity, and Legitimacy: The Multilateral System at the Millennium, Kennedy School of Government, Harvard University, Cambridge, Mass., 1–2 June 2000).

4. Claudio Grossman and Daniel B. Bradlow, "Are We Being Propelled towards a People-Centered Transnational Legal Order?" *American University Journal of International Law and Policy* 1 (1993): 185.

5. Robert O. Keohane and Joseph S. Nye, Jr., "The Club Model of Multilateral Cooperation and the World Trade Organization: Problems of Democratic Legitimacy" (paper presented at the Conference on Efficiency, Equity, and Legitimacy: The Multilateral Trading System at the Millennium, Kennedy School of Government, Harvard University, Cambridge, Mass., 1–2 June 2000), 8.

6. Ibid., 9.

7. Ibid., 16. The complex issues surrounding the question of the "democratic legitimacy" of international organizations have been explored in *Democracy's Edges,* eds. Ian Shapiro and Casiano Hacker-Cordon (New York and Cambridge: Cambridge University Press, 1999). In the lead paper in this collection, Robert Dahl of Yale University, the distinguished political authority on democratic institutions, expressed great skepticism that any international organizations could ever be regarded as democratic. He wrote (32, 34), "[I]t is difficult enough for ordinary citizens to exercise much influence over decisions about foreign affairs in their own countries, should we not conclude that the obstacles will be far greater in international organizations? . . . I see no reason to clothe international organizations in the mantle of democracy simply to provide them with greater legitimacy." Conversely, on the issue of national sovereignty, Dahl went on to argue, "Supporters of democracy should resist the argument that a great decline in the capacity of national and subnational units to govern themselves is inevitable because globalization is inevitable. . . . The last three centuries are a graveyard packed with corpses of 'inevitable' developments."

Ultimately, there is also the problem of whether there is emerging a "cosmopolitan" worldview that prefigures a world *demos* that broadens identities beyond national boundaries. There is little evidence that the emergence of such a political community is at hand—even among European states where the existence of common transnational goals has been present for several decades. See Pippa Norris, "Global Governance and Cosmopolitan Citizens," in *Governance in a Globalizing World,* eds. Joseph S. Nye and John D. Donahue (Washington, D.C.: Brookings Institution, 2000), 155–177.

8. Kal Raustiala, "Democracy, Sovereignty, and the Slow Pace of International Negotiations," *International Environmental Affairs* 8 (1996): 7, 11.

9. Steve Charnovitz, "Participation of Nongovernmental Organizations in the World Trade Organization," *University of Pennsylvania Journal of International Economic Law* 17 (1996): 339

10. Philip M. Nichols, "Extension of Standing in the World Trade Organization," *University of Pennsylvania Journal of International Economic Law* 17 (1996): 319.

11. Philip M. Nichols, "Realism, Liberalism, Values, and the World Trade Organization," *University of Pennsylvania Journal of International Economic Law* 17 (1996): 859–860.

12. Charnovitz, "Participation of Nongovernmental Organizations," 342.

13. Esty, "Why the World Trade Organization Needs Environmental NGOs," 10.

14. There is, however, a more difficult problem: the dominance of the executive branch in trade policymaking and implementation. Acknowledging that the U.S. Congress should be more involved in foreign economic policy, this study recommends a greater oversight role for the legislative branch of government (see pp. 143–146 in text). For discussions of the issues raised by the executive-legislative imbalance, see Joel Richard Paul, "Is Global

Governance Safe for Democracy?" and Kal Raustiala, "Sovereignty and Multilateralism," in *Chicago Journal of International Law* 1 (2000): 263–271, and 401–419, respectively.

15. See, for instance, the assessments in Gerald P. O'Driscoll, Jr., Kim R. Holmes, and Melanie Kirkpatrick, *2001 Index of Economic Freedom* (Washington, D.C.: Heritage Foundation and Dow, Jones & Company, 2001). This survey tracks both economic *and* political freedom, including the existence of democratic institutions and practices in individual countries.

16. Daniel Verdier, *Democracy and International Trade: Britain, France, and the United States, 1860–1990* (Princeton, N.J.: Princeton University Press, 1994), 290.

17. Daniel C. Esty, "Nongovernmental Organizations in the World Trade Organization," *Journal of International Economic Law* 1 (1998): 131, 137.

18. *Financial Times*, 1 September 1999, 12.

19. Esty, "Nongovernmental Organizations," 132.

20. Sylvia Ostry, "WTO: Institutional Design for Better Governance" (paper presented at the Conference on Efficiency, Equity, and Legitimacy: The Multilateral Trading System at the Millennium, Kennedy School of Government, Harvard University, Cambridge, Mass., 1–2 June 2000), 19.

21. Kenneth Anderson, "After Seattle: Public International Organizations, Nongovernmental Organizations, and Democratic Sovereignty in an Era of Globalization: An Essay on Contested Legitimacy" (Washington College of Law, American University, Washington, D.C., August 2000, photocopy), 108.

22. *Financial Times*, 1 September 1999, 12.

23. Nichols, "Extension of Standing," 318.

24. In a March 2001 article, a WTO Secretariat staff member and an environmental lawyer, Gabrielle Marceau and Matthew Stillwell, put forward substantive and procedural criteria for accepting *amicus* briefs: "Practical Suggestions for Accepting *Amicus Curiae* Briefs before WTO Adjudicating Bodies," *Journal of International Economic Law* 4 (2001): 155–187. I remain skeptical that such a system could be managed in a way that would not adversely affect developing-country WTO members.

25. Ostry, "WTO: Institutional Design," 18.

26. Gregory Shaffer, "The World Trade Organization under Challenge: Democracy and the Law and Politics of the WTO's Treatment of Trade and Environment Matters," *Harvard Environmental Law Review* 25 (2001): 99.

27. Esty, "Nongovernmental Organizations," 131–132.

28. Peter J. Spiro, "New Global Potentates: Nongovernmental Organizations and the 'Unregulated' Marketplace," *Cardozo Law Review* 18 (1996): 962–963; see also Peter J. Spiro, "New Players on the International Stage," in *Hofstra Law and Policy Symposium*, vol. 2 (Hempstead, N.Y.: Proceedings of Hofstra Law and Policy Symposium, 1997), 19–36; Nichols, "Realism, Liberalism," 871–872. To be fair, supporters of NGO participation in the

international political process are calling for increased accountability and minimum standards of conduct; see A. Dan Turlock, "The Role of Non-Governmental Organizations in the Development of International Environmental Law," *Chicago-Kent Law Review* 68 (1992): 61–76.

29. Spiro, "New Global Potentates," 963.

30. Nichols, "Extension of Standing," 327.

31. Robert O. Keohane, Andrew Moravcsik, and Anne-Marie Slaughter, "Legalized Dispute Resolution," *International Organization* 54 (2000): 457–488.

32. Ibid., 483.

33. For more detail on Macey's analysis, see appendix 1, pp. 160–162. In later commentary on the Keohane-Moravcsik-Slaughter analysis, Keohane and Nye argued that it demonstrated that "opening up WTO dispute settlement proceedings could well have far-reaching consequences. . . . The major apparent consequences of differential access is that transnational dispute resolution is much more expansive than international dispute resolution." The reason (in terms that Macey could well have written) is that "this dynamic expansion is fueled by a *de facto* alliance between plaintiffs and their lawyers, on the one hand, and the [European Court of Justice] on the other. . . . Ready access to a tribunal creates cases. . . . " See Keohane and Nye, "The Club Model of Multilateral Cooperation," 13.

34. Keohane, Moravcsik, and Slaughter, "Legalized Dispute Resolution," 488.

35. Gregory Shaffer, "The Law-in-Action of International Trade Litigation in the United States and Europe: The Melding of the Public and the Private" (University of Wisconsin Law School, June 2000, photocopy), 91–92.

36. Ibid., 92–93.

37. Ibid., 93–94.

38. Ibid., 94.

Chapter 7. Proposals for Reform and Reasons for Retaining the Status Quo

1. As described in chapter 1, John Jackson has decried the use of certain "mantras" by trade specialists and has argued that these "phrases are used to *avoid thinking* certain issues through." One of the phrases he lists is "government-to-government," which, he says, "implies that NGOs have no role" at the WTO. As will be seen, this study treats NGOs as an important phenomenon to be reckoned with and utilized, although not in all the ways they prefer or demand. See John H. Jackson, "The WTO 'Constitution' and Proposed Reforms" (speech delivered at Graduate Institute of International Studies, Geneva, Switzerland, 15 March 2000), 4–6.

2. The texts of the Uruguay Round agreement are reproduced in *The Results of the Uruguay Round Agreement: The Legal Texts* (Geneva, Switzerland: GATT Secretariat, 1994).

3. For an early critique of a judicialized approach to the new WTO services disciplines, see Lisa Sue Klaiman, "Applying GATT Dispute Settlement

Procedures to a Trade in Services Agreement: Proceed with Caution,"
University of Pennsylvania Journal of International Business Law 11 (1990):
657–685. Klaiman (677) wrote, "The flexibility and pragmatism offered by
an anti-legalistic approach . . . are more crucial for the services code
because it is unlikely that the agreement will enjoy the full support of its
signatories. Rigorous procedures which force legal rulings where there is no
consensus backing the substantive rules will lead trade disputes into unpro-
ductive channels and could ultimately weaken the legal structure itself
through a loss of confidence in the system." For another perspective, which
argues that in big cases the most powerful members of the WTO will force
"diplomatic" solutions if they lose, see Azar M. Khansari, "Searching for the
Perfect Solution: International Dispute Resolution and the New World
Trade Organization," *Hastings International and Comparative Law Journal* 20
(1996): 183–203.

4. As this study was going to press, it looked as if the United States and the
   EU might be moving toward a separate system of mediation and "pre-
   clearance" for their individual disputes over WTO rights and obligations. In
   early June 2001, U.S. Trade Representative Robert B. Zoellick proposed
   that the United States and the European Union establish an "early warning"
   system that would result in an "enhanced dispute management procedure."
   As reported in several press accounts, under this proposal, the United
   States and the EU would make a formal commitment to enter into extended
   bilateral negotiations for a "diplomatic" settlement before proceeding to the
   WTO dispute settlement process. EU reaction was mixed: Initially, a
   spokesman for the EU warned that the procedure might merely introduce
   "another quasi-legal institutional hurdle" to delay resolution of disputes.
   Subsequently, EU trade commissioner Pascal Lamy expressed cautious support for some kind of early warning dispute management system between
   the two WTO members. One substantial problem with this approach, however, is that unless handled carefully, bilateral negotiations between the two
   largest trading nations in the WTO could evoke strong resentment among
   other WTO members who could well see this move as a means of establishing a separate dispute settlement system for the "big boys," outside of
   the purview of the new judicial system. For details on these discussions, see
   Gary G. Yerkey, "U.S. Proposes New Mechanism for Settling Trade
   Disputes with EU Involving Early Talks," *International Trade Reporter* 18
   (2001): 889; and Gary G. Yerkey, "EU Welcomes U.S. Plan for Resolving
   Trade Disputes, but Expresses Some Concern," *International Trade Reporter*
   18 (2001): 928.

5. Thomas J. Schoenbaum, "WTO Dispute Settlement: Praise and Suggestions
   for Reform," *International and Comparative Law Journal* 47 (1998): 647–659.
   Although the thrust of their recommendations runs counter to the proposals in this study, two other legal scholars with strong sympathies for environmentalists' recommendations for reform of the DSU also suggest that
   "consideration should be given to the potential for a comprehensive

mediation system, to operate alongside panel procedure." They believe that the system should be administered by the DSB *and that* (like Schoenbaum) it should be left to the panels to decide when to recommend mediation as the preferred solution. Along with major environmental groups, they believe that the shrimp/turtle case should have been resolved through mediation. See James Cameron and Karen Campbell, "Challenging the Boundaries of the DSU through Trade and Environmental Disputes," in *Dispute Resolution in the World Trade Organization,* eds. James Cameron and Karen Campbell (London: Cameron May, 1998), chap. 10.

6. The proposal for creating a procedure for shifting highly political cases to mediation has received support from a distinguished legal theorist and practitioner, Professor Mitsuo Matsushita, now at Seikei University. A member of the WTO Appellate Body from 1995 to 2000, Professor Matsushita observed first-hand many of the legal and political issues that have been raised by the new system. In an e-mail to the author, he wrote, "It seems to make sense to construct some mechanism whereby the WTO selects 'wrong cases' from among cases at the consultation stage or at the initial period of the panel process, removes them from the dispute settlement mechanism, and puts them in a different dispute settlement process. . . . Your idea is a very important one. I believe that some of the cases, especially the banana case and the hormones case, imposed too great a burden on the DS process." Professor Matsushita also believes that giving authority to a committee of the DSB is the better alternative because "intervention by the DG would not work" due to "strong political opposition from some of the members, especially from the United States." E-mail from Mitsuo Matsushita to author, 15 August 2000.

7. Robert O. Keohane and Joseph S. Nye, Jr., "The Club Model of Multilateral Cooperation and the World Trade Organization: Problems of Democratic Legitimacy" (paper presented at the Conference on Efficiency, Equity, and Legitimacy: The Multilateral Trading System at the Millennium, Kennedy School of Government, Harvard University, Cambridge, Mass., 1–2 June 2000), 14–15.

8. Ibid. Additional support for increasing the power and clout of the Director-General comes from former (1985–89) U.S. Trade Representative Clayton Yeutter, who states: "Your study debates whether these alternatives should be produced through actions of a DSB committee or the Director-General, and I too would opt for the latter. For this and other unrelated reasons, the WTO needs to add strength and authority to the DG position. Let's give the DG the muscle to respond to the challenge and see what happens. . . . The WTO member nations need to make a considered decision on the matter of DG authority and responsibility, and support the DG in moving forward as outlined above." Fax from Clayton Yeutter to author, 31 December 2000.

9. John A. Ragosta, "Unmasking the WTO—Access to the DSB System: Can the DSB Live Up to Its Moniker 'World Trade Court?'" *Law and Policy in International Business* 31 (2000): 747.

10. Steve Charnovitz, "Participation of Nongovernmental Organizations in the World Trade Organization," *University of Pennsylvania Journal of International Economic Law* 17 (1996): 353.

11. Alan Wm. Wolff and John A. Ragosta, "Will the WTO Result in International Trade Common Law? The Problem for U.S. Lawyers," in *The World Trade Organization: Multilateral Trade Framework for the 21st Century and U.S. Implementation Legislation,* ed. Terence Stewart (Washington, D.C.: American Bar Association, 1996), 708. As noted in the text, both Wolff and Ragosta now believe that the WTO dispute settlement system should move back to a more diplomatic model. In explaining their current position, Ragosta notes the demands that corporations and NGOs be granted greater direct participation is legitimate "if we allow the WTO DSB to continue to operate (and be understood to operate) as a 'court.' Under the current "judicialized" system, he states, "We believe . . . that the system of adversarial dispute settlement [with disputants represented by their own counsel: author] ensures that the best arguments are made and the best result achieved. When the U.S.G. [U.S. government] is representing you in Geneva, it is highly likely that they will pull their punches based on interests in other cases." E-mail from John Ragosta to author, 18 December 2000.

12. It is certainly true that with regard to unfair trade laws and trade remedy actions, Congress has allowed "individuals" to intervene in the process, though in the end government officials retain a great deal of leeway in determining the final disposition of particular claims. It is also true that in the NAFTA dispute settlement agreement, NGOs or corporations may indirectly influence environmental decisions through direct petitioning of the tripartite Commission on Environmental Cooperation. But the point being made here is that the "individuals" in these disputes usually are organizations or corporations and not individual private citizens. On NAFTA environmental dispute settlement, see Richard H. Steinberg, "Trade-Environment Negotiations in the EU, NAFTA and WTO: Regional Trajectories of Rule Development," *American Journal of International Law* 91 (1997): 248–253; on U.S. trade remedy laws, see John H. Jackson, *The World Trading System: Law and Policy of International Economic Relations,* 2d ed. (Cambridge, Mass.: MIT Press, 1997), 127–133.

13. Philip M. Nichols, "Extension of Standing in the World Trade Organization," *University of Pennsylvania Journal of International Economic Law* 17 (1996): 320.

14. Matthew Stillwell, "Applying the EPTSD Framework to Reconcile Trade, Development, and Environmental Policy Conflicts," Center for International Environmental Law and Worldwide Fund for Nature, EPTSD Working Paper, Gland, Switzerland, October 1999; and "Reform of the WTO's

Dispute Settlement Mechanism for Sustainable Development," discussion paper (Gland, Switzerland: World Wildlife Fund, 1999). See also two earlier World Wildlife Fund discussion papers, "Dispute Settlement in the WTO: A Crisis for Sustainable Development" (July 1998), and "Trade Measures and Multilateral Environmental Agreements: Resolving Uncertainty and Removing the WTO Chill Factor" (November 1999).

15. Stillwell, "Applying the EPTSD," 6.

16. Ibid., p. 5. It should be noted that there are elements in the CIEL/WWF proposals that differ substantially from what is being proposed here: for instance, though they don't spell out how it would be accomplished, they foresee much greater participation in the process by "stakeholders" and NGOs. Also while stressing the preventive goals of mediation/arbitration, they do hold out a threat of sanctions if all else fails.

17. Ibid., 6.

18. Ibid., 13.

19. Ibid. In commenting on the shrimp/turtle outcome, Stillwell (13–14) writes that "because of its adversarial nature, the WTO dispute settlement process was unable to offer an effective solution to the *Shrimp-Turtle* dispute. Instead, it created a legal compromise. . . . For this dispute to be resolved properly, the parties will need to go beyond the adversarial approach adopted at the WTO."

20. "Cincinnati Recommendations," Trans-Atlantic Business Dialogue, Cincinnati, Ohio, 16–18 November 2000. An unanswered question, obviously, is whether the corporate community would also bite the bullet and allow the Director-General or a committee of the DSB to mandate mediation or arbitration in certain circumstances.

    Another interesting suggestion has been advanced by an Italian professor of law and a member of the EU trade directorate (speaking only for himself). They recommend the use of international commercial arbitration mechanisms for future cases involving competition policy—although by extension their rationale could be utilized in a number of the so-called new areas of WTO law, such as services regulations and intellectual property. As they describe their approach, "[It] proposes an alternative bottoms-up approach on how to settle these competition-related disputes which points to a middle ground between the top-down negotiation of a fully-fledged international antitrust code, and the long-run (and uncertain), mainly endogenous, process of convergence of competition laws. The main tenets of this approach are the negotiation of minimum substantive standards and the use of arbitration between the private parties involved in the dispute resolution mechanism." Andrea Giardina and Americo Beviglia Zampetti, "Settling Competition-Related Disputes: The Arbitration Alternative in the WTO Framework," *Journal of World Trade* 331 (1997): 5–27.

21. Alan Wm. Wolff, "The Conduct of International Trade Relations: The Corrosive Effects of Excessive Reliance on Litigation" (paper presented to the New America Foundation, Washington, D.C., January 2001).

22. Kenneth W. Abbott and Duncan Snidal, "Hard and Soft Law in International Governance," *International Organization* 54 (2000): 421–456; Judith Goldstein and Lisa L. Martin, "Legalization, Trade Liberalization, and Domestic Politics: A Cautionary Note," *International Organization* 54 (2000): 603–632.

23. Kal Raustiala, "Compliance and Effectiveness in International Regulatory Cooperation" (paper presented at Case Western Reserve *Journal of International Law* Symposium on Compliance, February 2000, photocopy). A third major strand of IR theory—liberalism—does not figure prominently in Raustiala's account, though he affirms its importance in any final assessment of major causal factors that explain the domestic and international dynamics of WTO decision-making. Thus, he points out (25) that in IR theory, "[T]he locus of attention is on domestic actors, the institutions that aggregate and shape the interests of such actors, and the variation among states in these internal attributes." And he concludes (27) that "one factor explaining compliance with international trade law is the shifting interests of firms and the balance between firms aided and firms injured by extensive economic interdependence."

24. Abram and Antonia H. Chayes, *The New Sovereignty: Compliance with International Regulatory Agreements* (Cambridge, Mass.: Harvard University Press, 1996).

25. Raustiala, "Compliance and Effectiveness," 23.

26. Ibid., 52. In addition to the work of the Chayes, Raustiala acknowledges that his article builds upon a decade of research by both international legal theorists and international relations scholars. As examples, see David G. Victor, Kal Raustiala, and Eugene Skolnikoff, eds., *The Implementation and Effectiveness of International Environmental Commitments: Theory and Practice* (Cambridge, Mass.: MIT Press, 1998); Oran Young, ed., *The Effectiveness of International Regimes* (Cambridge, Mass.: MIT Press, 1999); Harold H. Koh, "Why Nations Obey International Law," *Yale Law Journal* 106 (1997): 2599; George W. Downs, David M. Rocke, and Peter N. Barsoom, "Is the Good News about Compliance Goods about Cooperation?" *International Organization* 50 (2000): 2; and James Cameron, Jacob Werksman, and Peter Roderick, eds., *Improving Compliance with Environmental Law* (London: Earthscan, 1996). For additional evaluations of the effectiveness of particular environmental regimes, see note 3 in Raustiala, "Compliance and Effectiveness."

27. Raustiala posits a distinction between compliance and effectiveness. In his usage, compliance with international agreements and treaties refers to the formal conformity to a legal rule or standard, whereas effectiveness is a measure of how much a legal rule or standard induces changes in behavior. One can, for instance, have a high level of compliance but a low level of effectiveness, as demonstrated by international whaling rules; or a low level of formal compliance with relatively high effectiveness, as demonstrated by American cities and the U.S. Clean Air Act.

28. Raustalia, "Compliance and Effectiveness," 31–37.

29. Ibid., 42.

30. Ibid., 45.

31. Ibid. For TRIPs discussion, see 45–58; for quotes, see 57. Raustiala has strong support from other legal academics that specialize in environmental law. Jeffrey L. Dunoff, in an article calling for a new international environmental organization to handle trade/environmental disputes, writes, "Trade-environment conflicts should be considered . . . in a nonbinding forum, using a consultation, negotiation, and consensus-building approach. . . . Addressing trade-environment conflicts in a diplomatic forum offers the promise of multilateral resolution of what are fundamentally issues involving the entire international community. . . . Moreover, in contrast to the rules-oriented approach, the negotiation-centered approach outlined above offers the flexibility to respond to new information and changing circumstances. . . . In the international environmental area, the development of the law rarely results from binding adjudication or declarations of rules. . . . Thus the appropriate approach should be for a nonbinding forum and process that is most likely to be effective, rather than for an institution empowered to coerce compliance with binding determinations." See Jeffrey L. Dunoff, "Institutional Misfits: The GATT, the ICJ, and Trade-Environment Disputes," *Michigan Journal of International Law* 15 (1994): 1110, 1122, 1124.

32. Judith Goldstein, Miles Kahler, Robert O. Keohane, and Anne-Marie Slaughter, "Introduction: Legalization and World Politics," *International Organization* 54 (2000): 394.

33. Abbott and Snidal, "Hard and Soft Law," 422.

34. Ibid., 430–431. The authors note the common distinction made between "contracts" and "covenants" by IR theorists—a distinction they find misplaced in studying international legalization. As Abbott and Snidal explain (424–425), in IR scholarship, "covenants and contracts correspond to the rationalist and constructivist perspectives, respectively. In the stereotypical view, rationalists (1) see the relevant actors (usually states) as motivated largely by material interests; (2) view international agreements as 'contracts' created to resolve problems of coordination, collaboration, or domestic politics; and (3) understand contracts as operating by changing incentives or other material features of interaction. . . . Constructivists or normative scholars, on the other hand, (1) focus on nonstate and intergovernmental actors, often motivated by moral or social concerns, as the source of international norms; (2) view international agreements as 'covenants,' embodying shared norms and understandings; and (3) understand covenants as operating through persuasion, imitation, and internalization to modify intersubjective understandings of appropriate behavior, interests, and even identities. In studying international legalization, this sharp bifurcation is clearly misplaced. . . . States and other actors look to law to achieve their ends, whether they are pursuing interests or values. . . . Legal rules and

institutions operate both by changing material incentives and by modifying understandings, standards of behavior, and identities."

35. Ibid., 433–434.
36. Ibid., 438–439.
37. Ibid., 455–456.
38. Ibid., 455.
39. Goldstein and Martin, "Legalization, Trade Liberalization, and Domestic Politics," 619.
40. Ibid., pp. 622–632. For a more detailed account of the theory of "optimal imperfection," see George W. Downs and David M. Rocke, *Optimal Imperfection: Domestic Uncertainty and Institutions in International Relations* (Princeton, N.J.: Princeton University Press, 1995).
41. Goldstein and Martin, 621.
42. Ibid., 626.
43. Ibid., 631–632.
44. Robert E. Hudec, "The Judicialization of GATT Dispute Settlement," in *In Whose Interest: Due Process and Transparency in International Trade,* eds. Michael M. Hart and Debra P. Steger (Ottawa: University of Ottawa Press, 1992), 23.
45. Wolff and Ragosta, "Will the WTO Result in International Common Law?" 701.
46. John H. Jackson, "Dispute Settlement in the WTO: Emerging Problems," *Journal of International Economic Law* 1, no. 3 (1998): 345, 347.
47. Hudec, "The Judicialization of GATT Dispute Settlement," 23–24. Writing at about the same time, Kenneth Abbott also expressed concern about the imbalance between the judicial and legislative functions and suggested the possible need for a "political filter": "In national systems, based on the separation of powers, however, the political branches have procedures for responding to judicial decisions that they see as inappropriate or socially harmful. . . . In light of these considerations, it might be wise to consider retaining some kind of 'political filter' within the procedure for approving panel and appellate reports—where issues like this have traditionally been dealt with—for situations that could damage the institution. Such a procedure should be based on written and fairly narrow standards, and should have a fairly high procedural threshold." Kenneth W. Abbott, "The Uruguay Round and Dispute Resolution: Building a Private-Interests System of Justice," *Columbia Business Law Review* 17 (1992): 111–148.
48. Hudec, "The Judicialization of GATT Dispute Settlement," 30.
49. I am prepared to be flexible on the question of the exact percentage of WTO members that should constitute a blocking minority. Some have argued for a smaller percentage (10–20 percent): e-mail from John Ragosta to author, 18 December 2000. Others believe that the threshold should be higher and would push for at least a majority to produce a blocking action: interview with James Durling, partner, law firm of Willkie, Farr, and Gallagher, Washington, D.C., 24 October 2000; and fax from Clayton

Yeutter to the author, 31 December 2000. My personal judgment is that there should be a significant showing of opposition, although not necessarily an outright majority of those nations present and voting in the DSB: thus, the range between 30 and 40 percent of WTO members seems about right.

50. Daniel Pruzin, "Special Report: WTO Members Make Unfriendly Noises on Friends of the Court Decision," *International Trade Reporter* 17 (17 August 2000): 1283–1286.

51. Robert Howse, "The Legitimacy of the World Trade Organization" (University of Michigan Law School, Ann Arbor, Mich., 2000, photocopy), 44. Even so acute a scholar as Philip Nichols has suggested a role for the DSU in "interpreting" WTO rules on the environment and labor to give "empirical legitimacy" to the WTO: that is, legitimacy "refers to popular acceptance of a legal regime." See Nichols, "GATT Doctrine," 458–463.

52. In comments on the recommendations in this study, Robert Keohane has suggested that an alternative means of redressing the constitutional imbalance would be to strengthen and facilitate the legislative (rule-making) process in the WTO. Keohane explained, "The institutions are a mess: too much judicialization, too little legislation. . . . If this is the problem, why not strengthen the legislative elements of the WTO? . . . [T]his change should correct the overweening influence of the Appellate Body, as Qualified Majority Voting in the EU has limited the ability of the European Court of Justice to make new law. The legislative body of the WTO would be intergovernmental, but it would be continuous rather than sporadic. Firms and NGOs could observe what is going on, and lobby; but they would have to lobby their national governments. Some weighted voting system would have to be instituted. . . ." E-mail from Robert Keohane to the author, 11 June 2001.

Keohane raises a fair point, but there are several important reasons— both political and substantive—why I chose to leave the consensus rule-making process in place and instead to introduce "diplomatic" mediation and/or conciliation and a blocking mechanism. First, politically the idea of extensive voting in the GATT/WTO has always been—and, I think, continues to be—a nonstarter for the United States. Major constituencies and interest groups, as well as Congress, would strongly oppose tying U.S. hands with such a system—even if it were possible to introduce some system of weighted voting. (Some old GATT hands in Washington have reacted negatively to the much more limited shift proposed in this study for a blocking mechanism, effected by the expressed opposition of one-third of the members of the DSB.) Further, it is the judgment here that other WTO members are not ready to accept new WTO rules, or important amendments to existing rules, that are not part of a package of trade round proposals, with all of the reciprocal tradeoffs that necessitates. Nor would a system of weighted voting be easy to fashion without great political fractiousness among WTO members. (In the current attempt to create some sort of executive committee in the WTO, larger developing countries have suggested substituting population for trade volumes as a means of calculating representation, and others have argued that regional interests must also be considered in the calculation.)

Second, in my view, a continuous legislative body in the WTO would raise important substantive issues of democratic legitimacy. One of the recommendations advanced below (in the text) is for national legislatures and parliaments to become more deeply involved in the WTO—at least to assume greater oversight regarding rules and obligations that affect national laws and values. Easing the process by which new international trade and regulatory rules are made—without much stronger checks at the national level—has major implications for the balance between national sovereignty on the one hand and the governing authority of international organizations on the other. This is particularly true with the WTO, given its unique power to institute sanctions when its rules are violated.

Finally, in the post-Seattle paranoid atmosphere, a move to make the WTO a "continuous" legislative body would galvanize and energize once again the unholy alliance of Patrick Buchanan and Ross Perot on the right and Ralph Nader and Lori Wallach on the left—and although this spectacle is always amusing, it would not advance the fortunes of the WTO.

53. See Jackson, *The World Trading System*, 126; see also Ronald Brand, "Direct Effect of International Economic Law in the United States and the European Union," *Northwestern Journal of International Law and Business* 17 (1997): 550–596.

54. Judith Hippler Bello, "The WTO Dispute Settlement Understanding: Less is More," *American Journal of International Law* 90 (1996): 416–417. Joel Trachtman has stated that "both are right," explaining, "As a matter of law, it appears, as Jackson argues, that the slightly better interpretation of the DSU is that it intends states to have an obligation to reform non-compliance measures. . . . As a matter of practice, as Bello argues, states may fail to comply with this obligation and would be obligated under the DSU to continue to provide compensation. There are no penalties for obstinacy." See Joel Trachtman, "Bananas, Direct Effect, and Compliance," *European Journal of International Law* 10 (1999): 677–678.

55. In a well-crafted discussion of the pros and cons of sanctions in the WTO, Steve Charnovitz finds that the arguments against sanctions are more compelling. See Steve Charnovitz, "Should the Teeth Be Pulled? A Preliminary Assessment of WTO Sanctions" (paper presented at University of Minnesota Law School Conference on the Political Economy of International Trade Law, 14–16 September 2000).

56. For additional analyses of the adverse effects of sanctions and details of proposed reforms that would shift from sanctions to compensation, see Brink Lindsey, Daniel T. Griswold, Mark A. Groombridge, and Aaron Lukas, "Seattle and Beyond: A WTO Agenda for the New Millennium," Trade

Policy Analysis, no. 8 (Washington, D.C.: Cato Institute, 1999), 28–31; and Jagdish Bhagwati, "An Economic Perspective on the Dispute Settlement Mechanism," in *The Next Trade Negotiating Round: Examining the Agenda for Seattle,* ed. Jagdish Bhagwati (proceedings of a conference at Columbia University, New York, N.Y., 23–24 July 1999), 277–278.

57. A member of the WTO Secretariat (writing independently) has also suggested this change. See Joost Pauwelyn, "Enforcement and Countermeasures in the WTO: Rules Are Rules—Toward a More Collective Approach," *American Journal of International Law* 94 (2000): 343–344.

58. Bhagwati, "An Economic Perspective," has suggested an approach that would impose public fines; Lindsey et al., "Seattle and Beyond," put forward the equivalent liberalization alternative. Charnovitz, in his recent paper on WTO and sanctions, also endorses the fine approach as superior to two other possible alternatives he explores: loss of vote in WTO proceedings and removal of eligibility for technical assistance (an alternative that would primarily affect developing countries). See Charnovitz, "Should the Teeth Be Pulled?" 27–28.

Finally, it should be noted that the well-known Meltzer Commission on international financial institutions (which included in its mandate the WTO) endorsed both the fine approach and the liberalization approach as superior alternatives to sanctions. See International Financial Advisory Commission, *International Financial Institutions Advisory Commission Report,* (Washington, D.C.: U.S. Government Printing Office, March 2000), 57.

59. Charnovitz, in ""Should the Teeth Be Pulled?" (33–35), has suggested that in cases where new legislation is needed to implement a decision, a DSU Optional Protocol should be established under which WTO members would agree to (1) establish a Domestic Body that would come up with proposed new legislative language bringing the country into compliance with the WTO ruling; and (2) hold a vote on the proposed remedy within three months and come into full compliance within a "reasonable period of time."

60. See "Cincinnati Recommendations." Gregory Shaffer has suggested another alternative to suspension of trade concessions in the case of developing countries. Pointing out that in many instances, small developing country economies would suffer great harm from suspension of concessions to one or more larger developed economies (higher tariffs leading to higher consumer prices), Shaffer recommends a system that would allow developing countries to obtain monetary damages in lieu of suspension of concessions. See Shaffer, "The Law-in-Action of International Litigation," 97–98. This option is worthy of consideration.

61. Kal Raustiala made this point in an e-mail to the author, 13 November 2000. It must be noted, however, that sanctions—or even the threat of sanctions—also have major distributional consequences for both exporters in the offending country and importers in the aggrieved country, as

witnessed in the bitter wrangles among interests groups over which goods would be part of U.S. sanctions in the beef hormones and bananas cases.

62. For an analysis of the issues presented by direct effect, see Thomas Cottier and Krista Schefer," The Relationship between World Trade Organization Law, National and Regional Law," *Journal of International Economic Law* 1 (1998): 83–122; and John H. Jackson, "Status of Treaties in Domestic Legal Systems: A Policy Analysis," *American Journal of International Law* 68 (1992): 310–340.

63. Quoted in Cottier and Schefer, "The Relationship between WTO Law," 94.

64. See John H. Jackson, "Status of Treaties in Domestic Legal Systems," 310–340.

65. Trachtman, "Bananas, Direct Effect, and Compliance," 659. Shaffer, "Law-in-Action of International Trade Litigation," 90–95, also argues against direct effect on grounds of democratic legitimacy: "Because of the WTO's frail legitimacy, governments should retain the sole authority to determine when—and when not—to initiate WTO lawsuits."

66. Trachtman, "Bananas, Direct Effect, and Compliance," 677. For another view strongly supporting the "non-self-execution" of treaties and agreements because of the impact on domestic democratic institutions, see John C. Yoo, "Rejoinder: Treaties and Public Lawmaking: A Textual and Structural Defense of Non-Self-Execution," *Columbia Law Review* 90 (1999): 2218–2258. Yoo argues (2218) that "requiring congressional implementation of treaties that regulate matters within Congress's Article I, Section 8 powers respects the Constitution's basic separation of the legislative and executive powers. This approach also ensures that treaties, which are asserted to be free from the Constitution's federalism and the separation of powers limitations, will not assume an unbounded legislative power, and it promotes the Constitution's principle that domestic legislation be made by democratic processes."

67. Trachtman, "Bananas, Direct Effect, and Compliance," 678.

68. For details of the U.S. proposals, see *International Trade Reporter* 15 (20 May 1998): 889.

69. For details regarding the arguments on transparency, pro and con, see William J. Davey, "Improving the WTO Dispute Settlement" in *The Next Trade Negotiating Round: Examining the Agenda for Seattle,* ed. Jagdish Bhagwati (proceedings of conference at Columbia University, New York, N.Y., 23–24 July 1999), 229–230; Robert E. Hudec, "The Agenda for Reform of the Dispute Settlement Procedure," also in *The Next Trade Negotiating Round,* 241–243; and Gary Sampson, *Trade, Environment, and the WTO: The Post-Seattle Agenda* (Washington, D.C.: Overseas Development Council, 2000), 116–117.

70. Hudec, "The Agenda for Reform," 243.

71. Thus far, the USTR has refused to "deputize" private lawyers as part of its litigating teams, but from the perspective and recommendations of this study, nothing would preclude them from doing so—so long as the private

lawyers agreed to abide by the overall legal strategy adopted by the government's lawyers.

72. Daniel Pruzin, "Special Report: WTO Members Make Unfriendly Noises on Friends of the Court Briefs," *International Trade Reporter* 17 (17 August 2000): 1283–1286.

73. Ibid., 1285.

74. Nichols, "Expansion of Standing," 318–319.

75. Ibid., p. 317. For another analysis of the issues related to *amicus* briefs, see Sampson, *Trade, Environment, and the WTO,* 112–114.

76. Quote from WTO member in Sampson, *Trade, Environment, and the WTO,* 114.

77. Daniel C. Esty, "Nongovernmental Organizations at the World Trade Organization: Cooperation, Competition, or Exclusion," *Journal of International Economic Law* 1 (1998): 135–137.

78. Shaffer, The World Trade Organization under Challenge," 52–53, 55–56.

79. Philip Nichols, "Extension of Standing" (328), has advanced a similar proposal.

80. Sampson, *Trade, Environment, and the WTO,* 138. The only aspect of Sampson's proposal that causes concern, or at least needs clarification, is the idea of having the moderator propose a solution. In order to be effective, this would have to be done privately; otherwise, the disputants would not risk being handicapped later if the proceeding went to formal dispute settlement. Gregory Shaffer has also suggested the creation of a joint standing committee between the WTO and either the UNEP or UNCTAD to handle environmental disputes. See Shaffer, "The World Trade Organization under Challenge," 115–118.

81. Shaffer, "The World Trade Organization under Challenge," 107–111.

82. Ibid.

83. Raustiala, "Compliance and Effectiveness," 50–57.

84. Keohane and Nye, "The Club Model," 17.

85. Lisa L. Martin, *Democratic Commitments: Legislatures and International Cooperation* (Princeton, N.J.: Princeton University Press, 2000), 13, 202.

86. For a description and critical analysis of the Dole proposal, see Andrew D. Herman, "The WTO Dispute Settlement Commission: An Unwise Extension of Extrajudicial Roles," *Hastings Law Journal* 47 (1996): 1635–1667.

87. This proposal is similar to the recommendations of Jeffrey J. Schott and Jayashree Watal of the Institute for International Economics, who in a recent paper suggested the establishment of an informal steering committee (with about twenty members) that would be delegated responsibility for developing consensus on trade issues among WTO members. See Jeffrey J. Schott and Jayashree Watal, "Decision-Making in the WTO," in *The WTO after Seattle,* ed. Jeffrey J. Schott (Washington, D.C.: Institute for International Economics, 2000), 283–292.

88. Sampson has similar proposals, though the substantive assignments are somewhat different. See Sampson, *Trade, Environment, and the WTO*, 139–141.

Afterword

1. Kal Raustiala, "Democracy, Sovereignty, and the Slow Pace of International Negotiations," *International Environmental Affairs* 8 (1996): 6.
2. Jeremy Rabkin, *Why Sovereignty Matters* (Washington, D.C.: AEI Press, 1998), 100–101.

Appendix 1. International Relations Theory, International Legal Theory, and the WTO

1. For a recent survey and analysis of IR theory, see Andreas Hasenclever, Peter Mayer, and Volker Rittberger, eds., *Theories of International Regimes* (Cambridge: Cambridge University Press, 1997). There is also a good overview of various theories in Oran R. Young, ed., *Global Governance: Drawing Insight from the Environmental Experience* (Cambridge, Mass.: MIT Press, 1997); and Charles W. Kegley, Jr., ed., *Controversies in International Relations Theory* (New York: St. Martins Press, 1995).
2. A groundbreaking article exhorting international lawyers to master IR theory was written by Kenneth W. Abbott, "Modern International Relations Theory: A Prospectus for International Lawyers," *Yale Journal of International Law* 14 (1989): 335–411. For more recent treatments, see the following: Anne-Marie Burley (now Slaughter), "International Law and International Relations Theory: A Dual Agenda," *American Journal of International Law* 87, (1993): 205–295; Anne-Marie Slaughter, Andrew S. Tulumello, Stepan Wood, "International Law and International Relations Theory: A New Generation of Interdisciplinary Scholarship," *American Journal of International Law* 92 (1998): 1–18; Stephan Haggard and Beth A. Simmons, "Theories of International Regimes," *International Organization* 41 (1987): 492–517; and William J. Aceves, "Institutionalist Theory and International Legal Scholarship," *American University Journal of International Law and Policy* 12 (1997): 227–245.
3. Andrew Moravcsik, "Taking Preferences Seriously: A Liberal Theory of International Politics," *International Organization* 51 (1997): 513–553. It should also be noted that the description of the various schools of IR theory is highly selective and will not attempt to capture the myriad of quite nuanced subtexts and subschools that now abound in the field.
4. Robert O. Keohane, *After Hegemony: Cooperation and Discord in the World Political Economy* (Princeton, N.J.: Princeton University Press, 1984), 7; and Stanley Hoffman, *The State of War* (New York: Praeger, 1965), vii. For a discussion of realist theories, see Hasenclever et al., *Theories of International Regimes*, chap. 4; Keohane, *After Hegemony*, chaps. 1–3; Robert O. Keohane, ed., *Neorealism and Its Critics,* (New York: Columbia University Press, 1986); and an earlier discussion in Ray Maghroori and Bennett Ramberg,

eds., *Globalism versus Realism: International Relations' Third Debate,* (Boulder, Col.: Westview Press, 1982).

5. Burley, "International Law . . . A Dual Agenda," 208–218. Burley chronicles the shift in realist theory, particularly the powerful redefinition and refinement of realism by Kenneth Waltz, who became the leading theorist of neorealism, also known as structural realism. Burley (217) explains, "Unlike the structure of domestic political systems, Waltz argued, the structure of the international political system contains only two of the three potential components: anarchy (the ordering principle) and the number of great powers within the system (the distribution of capabilities across units). From this 'positional picture' could the basic laws of international politics be deduced. . . . In a discipline hungry for theoretical apparatus that accompanies self-definition, [Waltz] systematized the international system." For Waltz's own defense of his neorealism and the challenges of his critics, see Keohane, ed., *Neorealism and Its Critics.*

6. Burley, "International Law . . . A Dual Agenda," 207–209.

7. Richard Shell has identified the right of GATT members to veto decisions by a dispute resolution panel as the talisman of the GATT's "essentially realist character." See Richard Shell, "Trade Legalism and International Relations Theory: An Analysis of the World Trade Organization," *Duke Law Journal* 44 (1995): 856–857.

8. Note should be taken, however, of a 1997 article that argues persuasively that in good neorealist fashion, the United States and the EU have been able to use regional negotiations to "force" smaller powers to adopt some of their environmental goals in trade—goals they are unable to achieve in the more diffused power of the WTO. See Richard H. Steinberg, "Trade Environment Negotiations in the EU, NAFTA and WTO: Regional Trajectories of Rule Development," *American Journal of International Law* 91 (1997): 231–267.

9. Keohane, *After Hegemony.* For discussion and analysis of environmental treaties and regimes, see Oran R. Young, ed., *Global Governance: Drawing Insights from the Environmental Experience* (Cambridge, Mass.: MIT Press, 1997).

10. Abbott, "Modern International Relations Theory," 351; also see Abbott for a general discussion of modern international relations theory. For other treatments of institutionalism, see Hasenclever et al., *Theories of International Relations,* chap. 3; Haggard and Simmons, "Theories of International Relations"; and Keohane, *After Hegemony.* .

11. Shell, "Trade Legalism and International Relations Theory," 858–859.

12. The most commonly accepted (though still widely debated) definition of regimes, advanced by Stephen Krasner, states that regimes are sets of "implicit or explicit principles, norms, rules, and decision-making procedures around which actors' expectations converge in a given area of international relations." A more explicit definition, one that may be more relevant for this study, has been advanced by the leading theorist of institutionalism, Robert Keohane, who writes, "Regimes are institutions with

explicit rules, agreed upon by governments, that pertain to particular sets of issues in international relations." See Stephen D. Krasner, ed., *International Regimes* (Ithaca, N.Y.: Cornell University Press, 1983), 2; and Robert Keohane, *International Institutions and State Power: Essays in International Relations Theory* (Boulder, Col.: Westview Press, 1989), 4.

The emphasis placed on international rules, institutions, and the goal of reciprocity has led theorists such as Keohane and others to borrow tools of analysis from economists' game theory and institutional economics. Game theory models illustrate the result of different combinations of actions in relation to the actors' stated preferences. In a simple two-players "prisoner's dilemma" game, for instance, each player will be worse off from cheating unless both players cheat, in which case both are worse off. Subsequent iterations of the game would give both players the knowledge and incentive not to cheat. In addition, institutional economics provide political theorists with insight into the role of institutions in reducing transactions costs as conduits of information. For a description of IR use of game theory, see Abbott, "Modern International Relations Theory," 354–411; and Keohane, *After Hegemony,* chaps. 5 and 6.

13. Burley, "International Law . . . A Dual Agenda," 210, 219.
14. Ibid., 51; she is speaking specifically about Keohane here.
15. To confuse the matter, the term "neoliberal" is used in some circumstances to describe a free market alliance between government and business in which government "deregulates" markets in order to advance corporate goals of profit maximization. For samples of critiques of the current international trading system from this perspective, see David C. Korten, *When Corporations Rule the World,* (Bloomfield, Conn.: Kumarian Press, 1996). For another discussion of the corporate model of liberalism, see Shaffer, "The World Trade Organization under Challenge," 5 n. 8. This definition of neoliberalism corresponds in part to Shell's Efficient Market Model.
16. Burley, "International Law . . . A Dual Agenda," 227.
17. Moravcsik has emerged as the most articulate advocate of a liberal IR theory that is "nonideological and nonutopian" and that most rigorously meets both theoretical and empirical tests of relations among states. To follow the development of his views, see Andrew Moravcsik, "Liberalism and International Relations Theory," Working Paper, Center for International Affairs, Harvard University, Cambridge, Mass., 1992; "Preferences and Power in the European Community: A Liberal Intergovernmental Approach," *International Organization* 31 (1993): 473–523; and "Taking Preferences Seriously: A Liberal Theory of International Politics," *International Organization* 51 (1997): 513–553. Slaughter uses Moravcsik's Harvard Working Paper as the base for her discussion of IR theory, though she adds a broader perspective by placing liberal theory in the context of the intellectual history of IR during the past half-century.
18. Moravcsik, "Taking Preferences Seriously," 516–517.

19. Ibid., 518. As will be noted below in the text, Moravcsik's views on the role of the state—or at least the terminology he uses—lead to some confusion. In "Preferences and Power" (480), he states that one core element of liberal intergovernmentalism is the "assumption of rational state behavior." Yet in the first assumption given above in the text, he describes the state as a "transmission belt . . . subject to capture and recapture, construction and reconstruction," an image that hardly bespeaks rational or "purposive" behavior in all situations. For reasons laid out below, I would argue that in trade policy, there is empirical evidence that state policy officials and bureaucrats can and do manipulate the interest groups that are pressuring them; these officials and bureaucrats are more than "transmission belts." Thus, Moravcsik's oft-quoted phrase, "Groups articulate preferences; governments aggregate them," from "Preferences and Power" (483), presents an incomplete picture of the second stage of the "two-stage game." Depending on the particular circumstances, states can both manipulate the process and be forced to act irrationally (at least from an economic or political perspective).

20. I. M. Deshler, *American Trade Politics: System under Stress* (Washington, D.C. and New York: Institute of International Economics and Twentieth Century Fund, 1986), 100–104.

21. Moravcsik, "Taking Preferences Seriously," 520; and Burley, "International Law . . . A Dual Agenda," 228.

22. Gregory Shaffer, "The World Trade Organization under Challenge: Democracy and the Law and Politics of the WTO's Treatment of Trade and Environment Matters," *Harvard Environmental Law Review* 25 (2001): 12; the original formulation of the two-stage game came from Robert Putnam, "Diplomacy and Domestic Politics: The Logic of the Two-level Game," *International Organization* 42 (1988): 427–460.

23. Moravcsik, "Taking Preferences Seriously," 542. Moravcsik (515) also identifies three strains of liberal theory, each of which produces a causal link between social preferences and state behavior: "Ideational liberalism stresses the impact on state behavior of conflict and compatibility among collective social values or identities concerning the scope and nature of public goods provision. Commercial liberalism stresses the impact on state behavior of gains and losses to individuals and groups in society from transnational economic interchange. Republican liberalism stresses the impact on state behavior of varying forms of domestic representation and the resulting incentives for social groups to engage in rent-seeking."

24. Haggard and Simmons, "Theories of International Regimes," 513.

25. An excellent discussion of the use of two-level theory can be found in the introduction of Mark A. Pollock and Gregory C. Shaffer, eds., *Transatlantic Governance in the Global Economy* (Lanham, Md.: Rowman and Littlefield, 2001). See also Andrew Moravcsik, "Introduction: Integrating International and Domestic Theories of International Bargaining," in *Double-Edged Diplomacy: International Bargaining and Domestic Politics,* eds. Peter B. Evans,

Harold K. Jacobson, and Robert D. Putnam (Berkeley: University of California Press, 1993).

26. Quoted in Moravcsik, "Introduction," 23.

27. Pollack and Shaffer, *Transatlantic Governance,* 22.

28. Ibid., 31; see also Moravcsik, "Introduction," 31.

29. Although "cognitivist" and "constructivist" are now terms of art with somewhat different IR theory subtexts, for the purposes of this study they are used interchangeably.

30. Hasenclever et al., *Theories of International Regimes,* 136; Moravcsik, "Taking Preferences Seriously," 539; and Haggard and Simmons, "Theories of International Regimes," 509–510. Among the strains of knowledge-based theories, so-called constructivists (labeled "strong cognitivists" by some scholars) have mounted the strongest attack on the rationalist mode of analysts in IR theory: "Strong cognitivists . . . advocate a sociological turn in the study of international regimes (and of international relations more generally) to reflect their basic insight that knowledge not only affects states' interests but is constitutive of their identities. . . ." (Quote from Hasenclever et al., *Theories of International Regimes,* 138). For representative analyses by constructivists, see Alexander Wendt, "Collective Identity Formation and the International State," *American Political Science Review* 88 (1994): 384–396; Friedrich Kratochwil, *Rules, Norms, and Decisions: On the Conditions of Practical and Legal Reasoning in International Relations and Domestic Affairs* (Cambridge: Cambridge University Press, 1989); and Peter Katzenstein, ed., *The Culture of National Security: Norms and Identity in World Politics* (New York: Columbia University Press, 1996).

31. Ernst B. Haas, *When Knowledge Is Power* (Berkeley: University of California Press, 1990), 9.

32. Hasenclever et al., *Theories of International Regimes,* 138; the longer quote is from Christian Reus-Smit, "The Constitutional Structure of International Society and the Nature of Fundamental Institutions," *International Organization* 51 (1997): 251.

33. Hasenclever et al., *Theories of International Regimes,* 146; Haas, *When Knowledge Is Power,* 23–24, 34–35.

34. Peter M. Haas, "Introduction: Epistemic Communities and International Policy Coordination," *International Organization* 46 (1992): 3.

35. Kal Raustiala, "Domestic Institutions and International Regulatory Cooperation: Comparative Responses to the Convention on Biological Diversity," *World Politics* 49 (1997): 487.

36. Andrew Harrell, as quoted in Harold Hongju Koh, "Review Essay: Why Do Nations Obey International Law?" *Yale Law Journal* 106 (1997): 2634.

37. As quoted in Kal Raustiala, "Compliance and Effectiveness," 22.

38. Koh, "Review Essay," 2636.

39. Abram and Antonia Handler Chayes, *The New Sovereignty: Compliance with International Regulatory Agreements* (Cambridge, Mass.: Harvard University Press, 1996).

40. Moravcsik, "Taking Preferences Seriously," 539–540.

41. Enrico Colombatto and Jonathan R. Macey, "The Decline of the Nation-State and Its Effect on Constitutional International Economic Law: A Public Choice Model of International Economic Cooperation and the Decline of the Nation State," *Cardozo Law Review* 18 (1996): 924–955; see also Alan O. Sykes, "Regulatory Protection and the Law of International Trade," *University of Chicago Law Review* 66 (1999): 3–46. Sykes' analysis draws on a blend of public choice theory and the theory of optimal contracts. It posits that trade agreements may be understood as sophisticated contracts among the self-interested political officials representing each member nation. These actors are not concerned with 'welfare maximization'. . . but with the maximization of their own political fortunes as measured by votes, campaign contributions, and the like." Sykes suggests that two types of insights follow from this analysis of regulatory versus other forms of protection: (1) the reason why, even though regulatory protectionism is an inferior form of protection, nations may employ it because there are constraints on their ability to use other forms of protection; and (2) "regulations that are nondiscriminatory and necessary to the attainment of legitimate, nonprotectionist regulatory objectives will not be prohibited by politically savvy trade agreements. . . . The political economy explanation for this claim rests on the disjunction between economic efficiency and political efficacy, and the extreme difficulty of fashioning legal rules to identify measures that are politically undesirable from the perspective of trade negotiators even though essential to domestic regulatory goals." Thus, he argues, trade officials will prefer to negotiate directly over the use of such measures rather than leave them to the uncertainty of court or administrative decisions. See Sykes, "Regulatory Protection," 5–6.

42. Colombatto and Macey, "The Decline of the Nation-State," 928.

43. Ibid., 929.

44. Robert Keohane takes strong exception to this characterization of regime versus public choice theory: "What Macey doesn't understand is that in the IR context, the 'rational state actor' assumption is just that: a simplifying assumption. What lies behind the state actor is precisely what political scientists generally (and not just public choice theorists) see: self-interested firms and groups seeking advantages, and self-interested politicians trying to broker such pressures for their advantage. . . . I agree 90 percent with the rational-choice political scientist's assumption that pluralist self-interest drives the world. . . . I deny that it drives everyone's behavior all the time . . . but believe . . . that it is an indispensable first-cut. And I certainly have never espoused the 'public interest' view of action." E-mail from Robert Keohane to author, 11 June 2001. For an earlier use of the theory of "rational egoism" to explain political interactions, see Keohane, *After Hegemony* (1984), chap. 5.

45. Colombatto and Macey, 931–932.

46. Ibid., 933.

47. Ibid., 935.

48. See p. 109 of this study.

49. See pp. 90 and 109 of this study.

50. For Shell's theories, see Richard Shell, "Trade Legalism and International Relations Theory: An Analysis of the World Trade Organization," *Duke Law Journal* 44 (1995): 829–927; and "The Trade Stakeholders Model, and Participation by Nonstate Parties in the World Trade Organization," *University of Pennsylvania Journal of International Economic Law* 17 (1996): 24–38.

51. For the contending arguments made by Nichols, Charnovitz, and Abbott, see Philip M. Nichols, "Trade Without Values, *Northwestern University Law Review* 90 (1996): 658–718; Philip M. Nichols, "Extension of Standing in the World Trade Organization," *University of Pennsylvania Journal of International Economic Law* 17 (1996): 295–329; Philip M. Nichols, "Realism, Liberalism, Values, and the World Trade Organization," *University of Pennsylvania Journal of International Economic Law* 17 (1996): 851–881; Steve Charnovitz, "Participation of Nongovernmental Organizations in the World Trade Organization," *University of Pennsylvania Journal of International Economic Law* 17 (1996): 331–345; Kenneth W. Abbott, "Economic Issues and Political Participation: The Evolving Boundaries of International Federalism," *Cardozo Law Review* 18 (1996): 971–1010. For an environmentalist view of NGO participation, see also Daniel C. Esty, "Nongovernmental Organizations at the World Trade Organization: Cooperation, Competition, or Exclusion," *Journal of International Economic Law* 1 (1998): 123–147.

52. Shell, "The Stakeholders Model," 360; also see 359–370 for a description of the Regime Management Model. A more complete description of this model can be found in Shell, "Trade Legalism," 835, 858–877.

53. Shell, "Trade Legalism," 836; also see 877–901 for a more complete description of the Efficient Market Model. Regarding the historical place of each of the three models, Shell writes, "(1) The Regime Management Model best describes the present overall structure of the WTO; (2) the Efficient Market Model helps explain the most striking innovations in the WTO system, suggesting that globally oriented businesses will soon pressure states for more direct access to the WTO machinery in future rounds of WTO reforms; and (3) the Trade Stakeholders Model articulates an alternative to the Efficient Market Model as a blueprint for future reforms that is both normatively superior and more likely to result in long-run trade government stability." See Shell, "The Trade Stakeholders Model," 370.

54. Shell, "Trade Legalism," 836. The phrase is from Susan Strange, whom Shell (and others) often quotes as the leading authority on (and critic of) the control of the political process by multinational corporations. The full quote from Strange is: "By the end of the 1980s, a metamorphosis of the international political economy had begun: the old, close relationship between state, civil society, and the economy was in the process of being replaced by a new relationship between authority and economy, and between authority and society. A global business civilization had emerged. . . ." (Shell, "Trade Legalism," 836 n. 30).

55. Shell, "Trade Legalism," 885.

56. Ibid., 906.

57. Ibid., 910; for a complete description of the Trade Stakeholders Model, see 907–927.

58. Ibid., 837, 913.

59. Ibid., 913.

60. Ibid., 912 n. 64.

61. Robert Howse and Kalypso Nicolaides,"Legitimacy and Global Governance: Why Constitutionalizing the WTO Is a Step Too Far" (paper presented at the Conference on Efficiency, Equity and Legitimacy: The Multilateral Trading System at the Millennium, Kennedy School of Government, Harvard University, Cambridge, Mass., 1–2 June 2000).

62. John G. Ruggie, "International Regimes, Transactions, and Change: Embedded Liberalism and the Post-War Economic Regimes," *International Organization* 36 (1982): 379.

63. Howse and Nicolaides, "Legitimacy and Global Governance," 8.

64. Ibid., 7–13.

65. Ibid., 20–26.

66. Ibid., 26–38.

67. For studies reviewing various economic assessments of the Uruguay Round, see Jeffrey J. Schott, *The Uruguay Round: An Assessment* (Washington, D.C.: Institute for International Economics, 1994); and Council of Economic Advisers, *America's Interest in the World Trade Organization: An Economic Assessment* (Washington, D.C.: U.S. Government Printing Office, 16 November 1999).

68. Howse and Nicolaides, "Legitimacy and Global Governance," 25.

69. Ibid., 31.

70. Ibid., 33.

71. John O. McGinnis, "The Political Economy of Global Multilateralism," *Chicago Journal of International Law* 1 (2000): 381–399; for a more detailed account of the issues McGinnis laid out in this paper, see John O. McGinnis and Mark L. Movsessian, "The World Trade Constitution: Reinforcing Democracy through Trade" (Hofstra University School of Law, Hempstead, New York, forthcoming 2001, photocopy).

72. McGinnis and Movsessian, "The World Trade Constitution," 2–4.

73. McGinnis, "The Political Economy of Global Multilateralism, 392–396.

74. Sylvia Ostry, "The WTO: Institutional Design for Better Governance" (paper presented at the Conference on Efficiency, Equity, and Legitimacy: The Multilateral Trading System at the Millennium, Kennedy School of Government, Harvard University, Cambridge, Mass., 1–2 June 2000), 6.

Appendix 2. Potential Technical Changes in the DSU Process

1. For a discussion of these proposals, see Robert E. Hudec, "The Agenda for Reform of the Dispute Settlement Procedure," in *The Next Trade Negotiating Round: Examining the Agenda for Seattle,* ed. Jagdish Bhagwati (proceedings

of conference at Columbia University, New York, N.Y., 23–24 July 1999), 239–240.

2. Ibid., 234–235. See also William J. Davey, "Improving the WTO Dispute Settlement," in *The Next Trade Negotiating Round,* ed. Bhagwati, 229; Yugi Iwasawa, "Improving the Dispute Settlement Mechanism, also in *The Next Trade Negotiating Round,* 246.

3. Hudec, "The Agenda for Reform of the Dispute Settlement Procedure," 238.

4. Ibid., 234; and Iwasawa, "Improving the Dispute Settlement Mechanism," 248.

5. Iwasawa, "Improving the Dispute Settlement Mechanism," 249–250; and Constantin J. Joergens, "True Appellate Procedure or Only a Two-Stage Process? A Comparative View of the Appellate Body under the WTO Dispute Settlement Understanding," *Law and Policy in International Business* 30 (1999): 224–229.

6. I have omitted one highly technical set of questions regarding the timing and sequence of events leading to retaliation. The gaps and lack of consistency between the language in DSU Articles 21 and 22—which came to public attention in the imbroglio between the United States and the EU in the bananas case—will necessitate amendments to the compliance and retaliation procedures in future negotiations. For a discussion of the problems these discrepancies present, see Davey, "Improving the WTO Dispute Settlement," and Hudec, "The Agenda for Reform of the Dispute Settlement Procedure."

Index

About the Author

Claude E. Barfield is a resident scholar at the American Enterprise Institute, where he is director of trade policy studies, as well as science and technology policy studies. Mr. Barfield has written extensively and directed numerous research projects on international trade policy. He served as a consultant with Office of the U.S. Trade Representative during the Reagan administration. He has taught at Yale University, George Washington University, and the University of Munich.

Mr. Barfield's most recent books on international trade policy are *The New World of Services: Implications for the United States,* with Cordula Thum (Florida International University Press, 2001), and *Tiger by the Tail: China and the World Trade Organization,* with Mark A. Groombridge (AEI Press, 1999). He is editor of *Expanding U.S.–Asian Trade and Investment: New Challenges and Policy Options* (AEI Press, 1997) and *International Financial Markets: Harmonization versus Competition* (AEI Press, 1996). Mr. Barfield's articles on international trade and U.S. competitiveness have appeared in the *Wall Street Journal,* the *New York Times,* and the *Washington Post.*

A Note on the Book

Juyne Linger of the AEI Press edited this book.

*Kenneth Krattenmaker designed the book
and set it in the typeface ITC Berkeley Oldstyle.*

Nancy Rosenberg prepared the index.

*Edwards Brothers, Inc., of Lillington, N.C.,
printed the book on permanent acid-free paper.*

The AEI Press is the publisher for the American Enterprise Institute for Public
Policy Research, 1150 Seventeenth Street, N.W., Washington, D.C. 20036;
Christopher DeMuth, publisher; *Montgomery Brown,* director; *Juyne Linger,* editor;
Ann Petty, editor; *Leigh Tripoli,* editor; *Kenneth Krattenmaker,* art director; *Jennifer
Morretta,* production editor; and *Amber Wilhelm,* production assistant. The AEI
web site is located at *www.aei.org.*

DATE DUE

Mok DUE NOV 1 8 2003		
MCK RTD NOV 1 8 2003		